Scared Poopless

The Straight Scoop on Dog Care

Chiclet T. Dog

Jan Rasmusen

dogs4dogs
Rancho Santa Fe, California

Scared Poopless: The Straight Scoop on Dog Care

DISCLAIMER: Readers are strongly cautioned to consult with a qualified veterinarian or pet health care provider knowledgeable in alternative/complimentary/preventive medicine before using any information contained in this book. No book can substitute for professional care or advice. Extreme caution is urged when using the information and therapeutic programs contained in this book. If your pet is taking medication, or if it is pregnant or nursing, you must consult your veterinarian to see if anything suggested in this material is contraindicated. The author, contributors and publisher are not engaging in rendering veterinary services. If medical problems appear or persist, the reader should consult with a qualified veterinarian or other animal healthcare professional. Accordingly, the author, contributors and publisher expressly disclaim any liability, loss, damage or injury caused by the contents of this book.

No dogs or children were stressed, endangered or harmed in any way in the production of this book, although they did occasionally report being bored.

ATTENTION ANIMAL WELFARE ORGANIZATIONS, DOG CLUBS, SCHOOLS AND OTHER SELECTED GROUPS: Discounts are available on bulk purchases for reselling, fund raising, incentives or educational purposes. Booklets may be prepared to meet special needs. Learn more at www.dogs4dogs.com.

PUBLISHER'S CATALOGING-IN-PUBLICATION DATA

Rasmusen, Jan.

Scared poopless : the straight scoop on dog care / Chiclet T. Dog, Jan Rasmusen -- 1st ed. -- Rancho Santa Fe, Calif. : dogs4dogs, c2006

p. ; cm.

Includes bibliographical references and index
ISBN: 0-9771265-0-1
ISBN-13: 978-9771265-0-7

1. Holistic veterinary medicine. 2. Alternative veterinary medicine. 3. Dogs--Diseases--Alternative treatment. 4. Care of sick animals. 5. Dogs--Food 6. Animal welfare. I. Title

SF745.5 .R37 2006
636.089/55--dc22   0510

Printed in Hong Kong

Contents

Acknowledgments

So many people gave generously of their time and expertise to help us help dogs. We thank all of them wholeheartedly for their invaluable assistance and many suggestions. This book could never have been written without them. (Find contact information for many of our experts at *www.dogs4dogs.com*.)

Veteri-narians **Richard Pitcairn, DVM, Ph.D.**; author, *Dr. Pitcairn's New Complete Book of Natural Care for Dogs and Cats;* founding member, The Academy of Veterinary Homeopathy; member, the American Holistic Veterinary Medical Association, National Center for Homeopathy, and National Vaccine Information Center.

Allen M. Schoen, DVM, MS; author, *Kindred Spirits: How the Remarkable Bond Between Humans and Animals Can Change the Way We Live; Love, Miracles and Animal Healing;* and co-author of *Complementary and Alternative Veterinary Medicine: Principles and Practice;* internationally recognized authority on natural integrative animal health care; editor of *Veterinary Acupuncture: Ancient Art to Modern Medicine.*

Greg Ogilvie, DVM, Diplomate, American College of Veterinary Internal Medicine, Oncology; AVMA 1995 Veterinarian of the Year; AAHA 1996 Veterinarian of the Year; Colorado Veterinary Medical Association 1996 Outstanding Faculty Award; 1999 SHARE Human-Animal Bond Companion Animal Award; and the 2001 World Small Animal Veterinary Association Hills Award for Excellence in Veterinary Healthcare.

W. Jean Dodds, DVM; internationally recognized authority on immune system and blood disorders, thyroid disease, and nutrition; President of Hemopet, the nation's first nonprofit animal blood bank; The American Holistic Veterinary Medical Association's 1994 Holistic Veterinarian of the Year.

Ronald D. Schultz, DVM, Ph.D., Diplomate American Academy of Veterinary Medicine; Department Chairperson and Professor, School of Veterinary Medicine, Pathobiological Sciences, University of Wisconsin-Madison, member, AAHA Canine Vaccine Task Force.

Martin Goldstein, DVM; holistic practitioner; author, *The Nature of Animal Healing;* lecturer; columnist for *Animal Wellness Magazine;* certified in veterinary acupuncture.

Stephen Blake, DVM; author, *The Pet Whisperer,* certified Homeopathic Veterinarian and veterinary acupuncturist.

Brook Niemiec, DVM, Diplomate, American Veterinary Dental College and Fellow, Academy of Veterinary Dentistry; internationally-recognized authority on veterinary dentistry.

Jean Hofve, DVM; Editor-in-Chief, *Journal of the American Holistic Veterinary Medical Association;* internationally known pet food expert; for two years, official liaison to the Association of American Feed Control Officials (AAFCO); special interest in flower essences and energy therapies such as E.F.T.

Michael Paul, DVM; former president of the American Animal Hospital Association; chair of the AAHA Canine Vaccine Task Forces; member, Companion Animal Parasite Council.

Sarit Dhupa, DVM, B.V.Sc, Diplomate, American College of Veterinary Surgeons; expertise in neurosurgery, surgical oncology, orthopedics and advanced diagnostic imaging.

Peter J. Pascoe, DVM, Diplomate, American College of Veterinary Anesthesiologists and European College of Veterinary Anesthesia; Professor of Anesthesiology, University of California-Davis School of Veterinary Medicine.

Myrna Milani, DVM; consultant, teacher and holistic vet; author of seven books including *DogSmart* and *Preparing for the Loss of Your Pet.*

Claire Sosna, DVM; certified veterinary acupuncturist, special interest in physical rehabilitation and Chinese medicine.

William K. Kruesi, DVM, MS; Veterinary Pathology Award and the Amelia Peabody Award from Tufts University; continuing education in acupuncture, homeopathy, bioenergetic evaluation, clinical nutrition, ultrasound imaging, gastroenterology, neurology and cardiology; certified veterinary acupuncturist.

    Nancy Scanlon, DVM; special interest in holistic approaches to cancer, arthritis and skin problems, Chinese herbs and homotoxicology; certified acupuncturist.

    Robert L. Rogers, DVM; lecturer and activist in the campaign to change laws regulating vaccination.

SPECIAL THANKS TO: **Tamara Hebbler, DVM** for her many tutoring sessions, countless hours spent "vetting" this manuscript and especially for starting us on our journey to holistic healing.

Photo Credits **Scott Miner** *(www.scottminerphotography.com),* working at a reduced rate to contribute to a book helping dogs, took most of the wonderful photos (including the cover photo) of Chiclet, Jiggy and Jan. His skill, wit and patience were greatly appreciated. See his photos on pages 3, 6, 9, 19, 33, 45, 51, 64, 67 (with Jim Johnston), 72, 81, 87, 88, 92, 94, 97, 104, 114, 116, 118, 122, 127, 133, 153, 160, 167, 169, 172, 174, 177, 183 (with John Casler), 189-90, 201, 203, 205, 209, 215, 220, 223, 227, 228, 257, and 258. (Additional photos of Chiclet and Jiggy were taken by Jan Rasmusen.)

    Jon Casler *(www.envision-studios.com)* specializes in fine portraiture of dogs. Based in Pennsylvania, he travels to selected dog shows. We asked Jon if he'd allow some of his terrific photos to be included in this project; he most generously said yes! Find his photos on pages 26, 38, 40, 75, 99, 100, 107, 151, 183 (dog in photo), 186, 192, 196-97, 233, 238, and 250.

    Clay Myers *(clay@bestfriends.org)* is a professional nature photographer and is photo manager and lead photographer at Best Friends Animal Society. Find his photos on pages 17, 243, and 253.

    Jim Johnston *(www.imageblast.com),* founder of ImageBlast Inc., donated the wonderful graphic "mosquito" for Scott Miner's photo on page 67.

Thanks to Karyn Stoffels for all her suggestions and for allow-ing her beautiful children Sophia and Kai to appear in this book. Martin Abelar DDS very generously, and patiently, posed with Chiclet in his dental office.

Thanks also for photos from Beth McCarthy-Flores (p. 54), Shannen Roy (pages 173 and 246), Doug and Missy Taylor for "Matchless" (p. 250) and to Gladys Collins of the Dinosaur Gal-lery for her terrific props. Our thanks, too, to Mulberry Square Productions for their photo of Benji on page 231. (Benji is a regis-tered trademark of Mulberry Square Productions, Inc.)

Other Experts and Organizations Maureen Hall *(www.animalcoaching.com)*, an animal trainer with fifty years experience, helped us immensely. Her animals have appeared in movies, television shows and commercials; she also consults and offers seminars on training.

Many thanks, too, to Amy Shever, founder of PetGuardian and 2nd Chance 4 Pets, for her very generous help with pet trusts; and to Gayle Martz, founder of Sherpa's Pet Trading Company, and to Sherpa consultant and former airline industry executive Bea Lutz, for their assistance with travel matters.

Others Who Helped So Much We are deeply honored by the wonderful early endorsements we have received from Dr. Richard Pitcairn, Dr. Allen Schoen, Mike Arms, Joe Camp and Benji, Betty White, Wendie Malick, Jenny Garth, and Ken Howard. Special thanks to Linda Howard for her amazing efforts on our behalf.

Heartfelt thanks to Brett Jaffee, publicist Antoinette Kuritz, and author Greg Godek for all their help, to Robert Goodman for his design expertise, and to novelist Alan Russell for his brilliant editing and endless good humor.

Our love and eternal gratefulness goes to Dr. Anna Ryan and her son Gabriel for their many wonderful suggestions and guidance in the writing of this book. And last, but certainly not least, our love and endless thanks for his patience, sacrifice and good humor to Jan's husband (and Chiclet's and Jiggy's "Dad") Roger.

WELCOME!

All right, you're not going to believe this. Really, you're not.

Oops, I'm getting ahead of myself. Mom sometimes warns me about that when she takes me on walks. Introductions first: my name is Chiclet and I'm four pounds of canine perfection, otherwise known as a Maltese. Anyway, I'm writing to tell you how scared I am, and how scared you should be, too.

That I'm writing to you is not the unbelievable part. I am a writer—some think a doggone good one. I can't see why that would surprise you. We dogs "see" for you Humans; we hear for you; we fetch for you; we herd for you; we do A LOT of therapy for you. Now, out of desperation, one of us is *writing* to you. You need the straight scoop on dog care and you need it from a source you can trust. So here it is.

Almost everything you've been told about dog care is WRONG! We're supposed to be your best friends, but without even realizing it, you're treating us like your worst enemy. We know you're doing your best, and we haven't wanted to offend you by being confrontational, but the news just can't wait any longer.

You need information straight from the dog's mouth (far more accurate than from the horse's mouth) about what you're doing wrong. They say you can't teach an old Human new tricks, but I don't believe that. Like the writer Corey Ford said, "Properly trained, a man can be dog's best friend." (Women, too.)

Take a look at the front cover and you'll see a picture of my true love, Jiggy. If it appears that he's freaking out, it's because he is. The best of Human intentions almost killed him, just like they're hurting and killing so many of our friends.

Jiggy has autoimmune hepatitis. How we think he got it you're not going to believe. Our pal Sophie, only two years old, is dying of cancer, typically an old dog's disease. What's up with that? Other buddies of ours are scratching themselves raw, living on steroids and eating diets that taste like straw. And poor little Buster, he lost an eye to untreated gum infection. What happened to him shouldn't happen to a dog.

Preventable accidents are taking a lot of our friends. Harley, running loose, lost a fight with a truck. Sam ran away. Max broke his neck smashing into a dashboard when his Dad's S.U.V. was rear-ended. Saddest of all, a coyote ate my best friend, Courtney. (Mom says I mustn't hate, but I hate coyotes all the same.)

I ask you: when was the last time you heard of a dog dying peacefully of old age? Do you even know what *old* is? For most breeds, it's not eight or nine. We should be living to fifteen or twenty or even longer. And we would if you hadn't been brainwashed into thinking that it's normal for us to be sick and itchy and have the trots all the time. What a bunch of dogwash that is!

You're being manipulated for your money and misled by people who refuse to read the new writing on the wall. The more well-versed you are in what passes for conventional dog wisdom, the more likely it is that you're hurting us. Surprised? Don't be. I mean, it wasn't long ago that the epitome of Human medicine was leeching, bleeding and magical elixirs.

Hey, give me a leech any old day over some of the crazy things Humans are doing to us now!

Anyway, lend me an ear (no, make that two ears; Humans don't hear well) and you'll be happy you did. You'll save a ton of money on vet bills, and your dog will likely lead a longer, healthier life. That's what your species calls a win-win situation. It's also a payoff that will earn you thousands of dog kisses you wouldn't have otherwise had. And guess what? You'll even eliminate the doggy breath that formerly came with those kisses (well, at least to a certain extent, but more on that later).

I know what you're thinking. I'm some sort of fanatic, a dog on a mission. You're right. Jiggy's illness really changed me. I went from being a carefree lapdog (and loving every minute of it) to an intrepid reporter. Mom says I'm a digger. Sometimes she sounds annoyed when she calls me that, but I'm proud of myself. I went digging for the truth. I went digging for Jiggy and you and your dog. And after learning what I learned, nothing will keep me from getting my message out. Okay, sometimes a fire hydrant will slow me down, but that's just a moment's distraction.

I guess you could call me dogged. I've worked my paws to the bone researching and writing this book. And I just didn't rely on the bark on the street. Mom and I interviewed the top experts in dozens of fields, read the latest reports and books, and surfed the far reaches of the Web. Eighteen veterinarian friends—most of them activists like us—taught us how to use our health care dollar to actually improve health, not just for patching us up until next time. We're going to tell you what we learned.

For controversial matters, like dental care and diet and vaccination, we'll give you all relevant points of view, supplying the facts you need to make intelligent, informed decisions—decisions based on studies and reason rather than habits, emotions or fear.

With all the facts in paw, I am armed and dangerous. I want you to listen to me as carefully as you would the warning growls of a junkyard dog.

Grrrrrrrrrrrrr. You listening? You better.

You may think this is a case of my biting the hand that feeds me, but it's not. It's a case of licking it long and lovingly. I have no agenda other than keeping dogs healthy and safe and leaving you solvent in the process. Even Mom is in this for love, not money. Author royalties from my book will go to help dogs (though she's promised to throw me and Jiggy a treat or two if we're good).

I know you're worried about all the work ahead, but don't be. Retraining you will be a walk in the park. And don't you just love walks in the park?

Join me this minute, won't you? Your dog's very life could be at stake. Tomorrow may be too late.

Love and licks,
Chiclet

P.S. ONE FAVOR, PLEASE . . .

Before we start our journey together I want you to do one thing for me. I'll even do a trick for you first.

There. Pretty good, huh? Okay, now how about a little quid pro quo? Since I did my trick, please go and do yours. Sit at your computer and, under your *Favorites*, bookmark *www.dogs4dogs.com*. There are many good reasons for doing this, not the least of which is that the site features all sorts of photos of your favorite pint-sized wordsmith and her mucho macho companion Jiggy. Those of you not into cute won't be disappointed either. You'll find numerous links (alas, not the yummy sausage type) to dog care articles, research documents, famous veterinarians, plus fascinating health and safety quizzes. Dog stuff of all sorts.

Within the pages of this book, I'm going to give you lots and lots of information, but my editor (a Human I call *The Gator* because he bites off chunks of my sentences) told me I had to keep all my explanations "short and sweet." He says it has something to do with Human attention spans. Anyway, I've had to sneak information onto my website before he gobbles it all up. (I humor The Gator, but just between the two of us, he's really not all that bright. I mean, what do you say about someone who arbitrarily pulled most of my photos from my own book?)

Okay. Let's move on. Bookmarking done? That's a good Human. Here's a treat.

Chiclet's Trivia Treat: *Do you ever notice your dog really boogying to music? You definitely weren't imagining things if you saw her react to the Beatles's song "A Day in the Life." To say "hi" to his Shetland sheepdog at the end of the song, dog-lover Paul McCartney added a sound audible only to dogs. And that wasn't the only time Mr. McCartney's muse had canine inspiration. He immortalized his sheepdog Martha in his song "Martha My Dear."*

Hey, Mr. McCartney? How does "Chiclet My Dear" grab you?

WHAT I KNOW THAT YOU DON'T

Bet you think you already know an awful lot about caring for your dog. Our Human Mom sure thought she did when we agreed to move in with her. Perhaps, like her, you've lived with dogs your entire life. Maybe you've read a lot about us, or have spent a lot of time at your vet's (which could be a clue that you may still have more to learn).

To see if your knowledge is up-to-date, and not polluted by advertising "messages," I invite you to take my *Dog Quotient* test. Most people fail it miserably, but I'd like you to take it anyway. If you do well, you can lord your superiority over all your fellow homo sapiens, and your dog can relax in the knowledge that her Human is a genius. If, on the other paw, you have trouble with the test, maybe it'll tempt you to read—really read—the greatest book ever written by a dog! No guessing at the answers, please. If you don't know something for certain, the answer is wrong. Life and death stuff is best not faked.

What's Your Dog Quotient?

1) A **titer** test shows if your dog:
   a) Has kidney stones
   b) Is immune to a virus
   c) Will be able to properly her nurse puppies
   d) Has elevated liver enzymes
   e) Needs many, many more very, very expensive tests

2) You just received a notice that it's time for your dog's annual booster shots for parvovirus and distemper virus. You should:
   a) Go get the shots right away. Your dog's health is at stake
   b) Procrastinate until guilt overwhelms you
   c) Presume your dog's immune for life but test her just to make sure
   d) Vaccinate against distemper only; parvo is really just necessary for pups
   e) Vaccinate against parvovirus only; distemper is only a problem for pups

3) Which of these vaccines is **most** likely to produce an adverse reaction 10 to 45 days after the shot?
   a) Rabies
   b) Kennel cough
   c) Swine flu
   d) Parvovirus
   e) Leptospirosis

4) Which of these statements is **false**?
   a) Vaccinations can be dangerous for dogs with ear infections
   b) Vaccines protecting against multiple viruses at once are linked to immune system problems
   c) Dogs are safest if they receive yearly "booster" shots for the important viruses
   d) Chiclet is the cutest dog author on earth
   e) Dogs can delay getting rabies vaccination with a letter from their vet

5) Regarding kibble, which statement is **false**? Kibble is:
   a) Better for your dog's teeth than canned food
   b) Must be no more than 50% meat because of how it's made
   c) Can lead to dehydration
   d) Contains more preservatives than canned food
   e) Rhymes with dribble

6) You want something for your dog to chew on. Your safest choice could be:
   a) A raw chicken neck
   b) The steak bone leftover from dinner
   c) Dad's Gucci loafers
   d) A rawhide chew
   e) A large bovine leg bone

7) Which statement is **true**? Heartworms:
   a) Are easy to contract and are almost always deadly
   b) Are difficult to contract but are almost always deadly
   c) Are killed, not prevented, by heartworm medication
   d) Are best prevented with a product that also protects against fleas and other worms
   e) Party on Valentine's Day

8) The **most important** thing you can do to keep your dog's teeth and gums healthy is to:
    a) Feed hard biscuits
    b) Use a special dental rinse
    c) Offer nylon chews or pig's hooves
    d) Brush your dog's teeth monthly
    e) Teach your dog to floss between meals

9) Commercial dog food *may not* legally contain:
    a) Roadkill or zoo animals
    b) Preservatives banned in Human food
    c) Dying or diseased animals
    d) All of the above are legal
    e) None of the above is legal

10) Which of the following can be poisonous to your dog?
    a) Onions
    b) Grapes and raisins
    c) Acetaminophen pain relievers
    d) All of the above can be poisonous
    e) None of the above is poisonous

11) Regarding calcium, a ten-pound dog has:
    a) Half the requirements of the average Human female
    b) The same requirements as the average Human female
    c) Twice the requirements of the average Human female
    d) A great need only during puppyhood
    e) A definite preference for vanilla ice cream

12) If **optimum health** is the only consideration, a female dog should:
    a) Be spayed after her first "heat" or "season"
    b) Be spayed before her first "heat" or "season"
    c) Be spayed after her first litter
    d) Have the less invasive procedure of tubal ligation
    e) Keep her uterus intact and her knees together

13) Which statement is **false**? Male dogs that have been neutered:
  a) Are less likely to run away
  b) Are protected against testicular cancer
  c) Are protected against prostate cancer
  d) Can be fitted with prosthetics so they don't look strange
  e) Never forgive their Humans

14) The claim that a food is *complete and balanced* guarantees that:
  a) It contains all the nutrients dogs need in a form they can assimilate
  b) It has been tested on at least 30 dogs for at least one year
  c) Only that it meets certain theoretical standards
  d) Both a and b
  e) The food was made from animals who practiced yoga

15) Which statement is *true?*
  a) Because dogs pant as well as sweat, they're highly resistant to heat
  b) As long as a dog is panting, it's fine
  c) A dog may voluntarily exercise more than it should
  d) A flat-faced dog is more tolerant of heat than a long-nosed dog
  e) The best way to warm up a cold dog is with a hot dog—hold the mustard

Answers

1) b…A titer test assesses antibodies to a virus. Aside from you, it's your dog's best friend.

2) c…Your dog may already be immune for life from distemper and parvovirus. A titer test can prove immunity.

3) d…Though any vaccine can cause a long- or short-term reaction, vaccines containing modified-live viruses, like the parvovirus vaccine, are more likely to cause reactions 10-45 days after the shot. Viruses containing killed viruses or bacteria are more likely to cause reactions within a few days.

4) c…Vaccinating a dog even ten times for one disease does not guarantee protection from that disease.

5) a…It's unlikely kibble will improve dental health. A more healthful diet will.

6) a…Fresh raw (not cooked!) chicken necks provide a healthy dog with calcium, meat and a good chewing experience. The other listed items may break teeth, cause intestinal blockage or contain harmful chemicals.

7) c…Heartworm medication kills immature heartworms already in the bloodstream.

8) b…A 0.12% chlorhexidine gluconate rinse or gel can help your dog fight gum disease. Hard chews can break teeth.

9) d…All these ingredients, and more you won't like either, are within Association of American Feed Control Officials' guidelines.

10) d…All of these items are potentially toxic to dogs.

11) b…Dogs have a huge need for calcium, the same as an adult Human female. Getting your dog sufficient calcium can be problematic.

12) b…If you spay a dog before her first "heat," you reduce her risk of breast cancer to almost nothing. Mammary tumors are relatively common and often malignant.

13) c…Neutering a male dog will not keep him from getting prostate cancer; he should be checked at least annually.

14) c…To be designated "complete and balanced," a dog food needs only meet certain theoretical standards. It need not be tested on dogs.

15) c…Dogs are *not* self-limiting in their exercise and must work up to hard exercise gradually. During hot weather especially, watch for signs of heat exhaustion (like panting that won't stop).

Results

- **15 correct:** Congratulations. You're an Honorary Dog.
- **11 to 14**: You cheated. Clearly, your dog helped.
- **7 to 10**: You're way smarter than the average Human. What species are you?
- **4 to 6**: Do not handle sharp objects or dogs.
- **3 or less:** Quick! Give your dog CPR.

So are you puffed up with pride? Or wallowing in the depths of despair? If you're gloating, good work! You're one in a million! But also know that many of the top vets in the country helped us write this book. Surely they can teach you a few things you don't already know, something that may someday save your dog's life. Or maybe *you* can teach *us* something. Go to *www.dogs4dogs.com* and send us an e-mail. Give us a gem of wisdom and we'll post it on-line and make you famous. Well, semi-famous. Okay, not totally obscure if you tell your mother you posted it there.

If you're despairing, stop it. Consider this quiz a reality check. If Jiggy hadn't gotten sick, and Mom and I hadn't spent over 2,000 hours doing research and interviewing everyone we could think of, we wouldn't have known the answers either.

A bigger concern is *why* you don't know the answers to these very important questions. I'd guess it's because you learned most of your health and safety knowledge from people trying to sell you something. Think about it. Mom was initially "educated" this way, too. It has something to do with washing brains.

Another possibility is that you, unlike us, may actually have a life. You have things to do other than spending every minute of every day learning this stuff. At least, I hope you do.

So, here we go. Before we get started with the laugh-a-minute vaccination chapter—yes, it's almost fun—I'd just like to offer you a few several life-and-death tips. I also need to tell you a little more about Jiggy's illness and what it taught us. Please don't worry that I've written a whole book on The Saga of Jiggy (which would be boring), or even The Saga of Chiclet (which might be unduly exciting). Jiggy's story is the story of all dogs, of your mother's dog, of yours.

The first thing I need to tell you is that your dog could be really ill and you might not know it. That's partly because Humans, compared to dogs, aren't very observant. (Though we have only 20/75 vision, we notice absolutely *everything*. Our very lives depend on it.) Even if you *were* as observant as we are, most of you have never been told what you're supposed to observe. Oh, you're pretty good at detecting tumors and broken bones and gushing blood, but pretty much everything else you're likely to miss. Not to worry. When you've finished reading this book, I promise you'll do better. In the meantime, you might check out the "21 Symptoms You Should Never Ignore in Your Dog" from *www.petplace.com*. (Or link to it from *dogs4dogs*.) It'll give you a running start.

Another problem with diagnosing our illnesses is that dogs lie. Really. We're huge fibbers. For as long as we can manage it, we'll pretend we're healthy and sound, even if we're in pain. That may sound bizarre, but it's in the Official Canine Rule Book. (I checked it to ensure accuracy.)

Whereas two-leggers like to complain long and loud about the smallest ailments, to dogs that's suicidal. Looking healthy is Number One on the survival-of-the-fittest Top Ten list. You see, when our ancestors were evolving, a dog who couldn't keep up with the pack was left behind, thereby buying himself a ticket to the Happy Hunting Ground in the sky. You know what Humans say: it's a dog-eat-dog world. (We don't think much of that expression, by the way, but as you now know, we're not much for complaining.)

This is where Jiggy's story comes in. When he went in for his first annual physical four years ago, he did his macho posing and flashed his gorgeous tail (I call him Hot Tail), acting like his bod deserved the Good Housekeeping Seal of Approval. Our vet said he looked terrific except that his pearly whites were dark beige with tartar and plaque buildup. Fortunately, Mom insisted on a pre-anesthesia blood test prior to proceeding with teeth cleaning. If she hadn't, I fear I'd be a lonely widow today.

I have to tell you, Jiggy's test results completely floored us. His ALT liver enzymes, which should have hovered between 12 and 118, had skyrocketed to 1,600! Practically every other marker was "out of range" as well. While he ran around looking like his usual athletic, exuberant self, his immune system was attacking his liver.

Please, let this be a warning to you. That innocent looking dog smiling at you right now may be hiding a deadly secret. He may be afraid that if he lets on about feeling crummy or being in pain,

you'll throw him out of your pack. Are you so sure he's not hiding something? When was the last time he had a thorough check-up with a urinalysis and a complete blood test? Has he ever had one? There's an old doggy proverb: *good* actors get Oscars; *great* actors get Canines. Sadly, most Canines are awarded posthumously.

Well, you've been a good sport so far, taking my quiz and all. I hope you're not mad at me for you giving you such a hard test. If you forgive me, I'll give you a treat. Even if you don't forgive me, you still get a treat. We dogs, as you know, are big on unconditional love.

Chiclet's Trivia Treat: *Dogs come in more sizes, shapes and colors than any other mammal on the planet. Ever wondered why? Bet you never thought that a Russian geneticist's experiments with foxes would hold the answer.*

Asked by Siberian fox farmers to breed a less nasty animal, Dr. Dmitry K. Belyaev started disregarding other traits and breeding for tameness alone. Just ten generations into the study, the foxes not only became nicer, but also started sounding and looking more like dogs (ears flopped, tails curled up and coat colors changed). The foxes even started barking. Arf! As decades passed, changes became even more striking. Blood tests showed a drop in adrenaline levels, a rise in serotonin, plus changes in breeding habits, litter sizes and skull shapes. All this and more stemmed from breeding for tameness. Think what this practice could do for Humans!

Rethinking Vaccination

Whenever my personal photographer (The Snapper) queries, "You know what would be really cool?" I dive under a bed. An impatient fellow, he usually answers his own questions, like when he said: "What if we throw hypodermic needles at Chiclet, like in those old knife-throwing acts in the circus?" When Mom, my great protector, responded, "I love it!" I nearly passed out. My first thought was, *Have you lost your minds, people?* I am *so* not into pain. Besides, what's funny about needles? More important, what point does the shot make? Shots protect us, don't they? They don't hurt us, do they? Artistically, intellectually and physically, I gave the needle idea two big paws down.

That was before I knew the facts. The Snapper explained that I'd never be endangered or stressed or even inconvenienced. (In fact, I slept through the whole thing.) We'd do the entire thing with trick photography, he said. I liked that; I'm good at tricks. Then Mom explained we had to do something wild, something really dramatic, to bring people's attention to this very important subject. After she showed me her research on vaccines, I jumped on board. When canine health is at stake, I'm one gung ho doggy. Maybe I can motivate you, too. Here goes.

Know what Dr. Jean Dodds, a veterinarian world-renowned for her work in immunology, endocrinology and hematology, calls the vaccines Humans inject into dog's bodies? *Toxic tissue-culture soups!* All these years our Humans thought they were protecting us; who knew they were turning our bodies into toxic soup dumps? I've learned vaccines can contain multiple live viruses, foreign animal tissue, formaldehyde, mercury, aluminum hydroxide, antibiotics, and other scary-sounding things I wouldn't want in my body. They even contain dyes so the vaccine will look pretty while it's going in. (Pink toxins are my favorite.)

Throughout our short lifetimes, many of us get fifty or more shots of this toxic soup. Some shots protect us, but a lot of them we get needlessly. We get shots for diseases we've probably been immune to since we were pups, shots for diseases we'd never get in a million years, and even shots for diseases that don't exist outside laboratories. And, though it can be really harmful to us, we even get shots for multiple diseases and bacteria at once.

Does that mean you should never vaccinate your dog? No, that could be dangerous, too (although some famous holistic vets believe otherwise; more about this later). I bet you're confused. Who can blame you? A lot has changed in the past few years. Why is it that dogs and their Humans are always the last ones to know?

Here's something else I bet you don't know. Pretty much since the beginning, vaccine manufacturers (who coincidentally profit from vaccine sales) have dictated which vaccines to give and how often to give them. (Silly me. I'd always assumed some group representing *dogs* made these decisions.) As more and more vaccines popped up for more and more diseases, some heroic vets started worrying that we might be getting vaccinated too often. They began investigating the problem, having symposiums and making recommendations. The latest and perhaps most widely publicized group is the 2003 Canine Vaccine Task Force of the American Animal Hospital Association. This fourteen-vet group of experts announced that vaccines should be given according to whether the disease was a problem for all dogs, or only for dogs with special needs. For reasons this dog doesn't understand, I hear a lot of vets considered this revolutionary thinking! (Link to the AAHA report, and read the expected 2006 update, at *www.dogs4dogs.com*.)

Anyway, the Task Force report states, "... no vaccine is always safe, no vaccine is always protective, and no vaccine is always indicated." Great. Clear as mud, right? So, who gets what?

The American College of Veterinary Internal Medicine endorsed these guidelines and most, if not all, American vet schools have moved to a core/non-core approach. Many vets, like Dr. Dodds, take these recommendations even further. They believe that adenovirus-2 belongs in the non-core group because it protects against diseases that are either mild or rare in North America. Others, like Dr. Ronald D. Schultz, Task Force member and head of Pathobiology at the University of Wisconsin-Madison, worry that canine hepatitis will come back; he recommends just one adenovirus-2 shot after a dog reaches 12 weeks of age.

AAHA Recommendations

Distemper, parvovirus and adenovirus-2, called the **"core vaccines," are highly recommended**. The **rabies vaccines** should be given as required by law.

Non-core vaccines, which protect against short-lived or easily treated diseases, *should be given only when specifically indicated by lifestyle and geography.* These include Bordetella (kennel cough), parainfluenza, leptospirosis, Lyme disease and distemper-measles (for at-risk puppies only). **"Generally not recommended"** vaccines include coronavirus, Giardia lamblia, and adenovirus-1.

Annual Boosters Many of you probably get reminders from your vet that it's time for your dog's annual boosters yet, according to the AAHA, ". . . there is strong and growing consensus among immunology and infectious disease experts that **annual vaccination is neither necessary or advisable**." Dr. Martin Goldstein, author of *The Nature of Animal Healing,* told us that he thought "succumbing to annual vaccines for multiple diseases" was the worst mistake people make in caring for their dogs. (Read Chapter 4: "The Dubious Legacy of Vaccines" in this terrific book.)

You hear that, people? You could be killing us with kindness giving us vaccines we may not even need! As a dog, I think that stinks. As a journalist, I want the kind of banner headline they run in the tabloids: VACCINE CONSPIRACY KILLING MAN'S BEST FRIEND! Generally, I don't think of myself as a sensationalist, but this is mighty important stuff.

So why isn't an annual booster necessary? The simple answer is *immunity*, and we're not talking the kind the FBI gives one mobster for testifying against another. We're talking about the immunity from a virus a dog can get from as little as one shot.

What does the Task Force recommend we do? Taking a cautiously radical position, they say to revaccinate with the core vaccines every three years and only as absolutely necessary for other vaccines. Many vets, even Task Force members like Dr. Schultz, say even that's too often.

Highly-respected vet and author Dr. Richard Pitcairn (*Dr. Pitcairn's New Complete Guide to Natural Health for Dogs and Cats*) believes that revaccination is rarely necessary after a dog's immunity has been proven. The inestimable Dr. Dodds agrees. She told Mom, "Immunity is like pregnancy. Once you're pregnant, being more pregnant isn't useful." I'm no expert, but I'm pretty sure it's not even possible. And guess what? If your dog's immune to a disease, she's also immune to the virus in the "booster" vaccine. Bet you didn't know that.

Pay attention. This gets better. According to Dr. Schultz, "Once immunity to a virus exists, it persists for years or for the life of an animal." Studies show that vaccines containing "modified-live viruses" provide immunity for at least seven years for the core viruses: parvovirus, distemper and adenovirus-2. *At least seven years!* That's 49 years in Human terms. (Link to a chart showing typical immunity to a particular vaccination at *dogs4dogs*.)

I bet some of you are still feeling nervous about the prospect of forgoing your dog's annual ladlefuls of toxic soup, and would feel safer going ahead and giving that annual booster just in case. Actually, it doesn't work that way. Dr. Michael Paul, Vaccine Task Force chair and a veteran of three others, told Mom that vaccinating a dog even ten times doesn't guarantee protection. Some immune systems will never respond properly. Others may be blocked for a while. Did you know puppies get multiple shots because immunity given by their moms may temporarily block the shot? Being immune from immunity. Who would have thunk it?

Titer Testing There's only one way to know if your dog has immunity to distemper and parvovirus, the two diseases everyone hates, and that's testing your dog's titers (pronounced like tighter). Titer testing means checking blood antibodies to see if she's immune to a disease. Would you allow your doctor to poke *your* backside every year for measles and whooping cough when you're already immune and could prove it? I think not. So why do you let your vet poke *ours*?

Titer testing costs more than a shot, but you don't have to repeat it for years (if ever) once immunity is proved. Pretty much everyone agrees that strong titers prove immunity, although some vets worry that low titers mean it's time to revaccinate. Dr. Dodds and many others disagree, believing that once we have immunity our bodies will probably always "remember" how to attack the disease (just like dogs always remember *exactly* how to chase cats). In fact, Dr. Schultz says at least 80% of dogs vaccinated with a "modified-live" core vaccine *just once* after their 12-week birthdays are likely to be immune to these diseases for life. For life!

I hate to keep harping at the tabloids, but why isn't the *National Enquirer* working on this story? It's so much more interesting than *which dysfunctional star has a secret two-headed baby fathered by an alien?* Don't any of their reporters have dogs?

Still nervous about going cold turkey? I haven't had parvovirus or distemper "boosters" for more than three years. Jiggy, because of his bad liver, hasn't had boosters for almost five years. A recent titer test shows he still has strong immunity. Mom has promised us that we'll never get a "booster" again.

Making Vaccinating Safer One of my favorite expressions is, "There's more than one way to skin a cat." Jiggy says I overuse it. Nevertheless, there's more than one way to make vaccinations safer. Any dog can react badly to any vaccine, but you can improve your dog's odds with knowledge. Dogs particularly at high risk for bad reactions include those who:

- Have had an extreme allergic reaction to a previous vaccine, or have a close relative who did.
- Have ear, skin or gum infections, arthritis, autoimmune dysfunction or any other illness.
- Are emotionally or environmentally stressed out.
- Are under anesthesia, facing surgery or recovering from surgery.
- Are old.

- Are already immune. (Draw titers instead.)
- Are using antibiotics or other drugs, including insecticides and antiparasitics.
- Are pregnant, in heat or lactating. (Vaccinating a mom won't boost puppy immunity and can even cause fetus death and stillborn pups.)
- Are from a particularly susceptible breed. (Ask your vet or breeder, or research on-line.)

If your dog is healthy enough to be vaccinated, a holistic vet may help her weather the storm with the appropriate homeo-pathic remedy.Consult a vet trained in homeopathy for assistance *before* you give the shot. *After* the shot is sometimes too late.

The American Veterinary Medical Association says the most common bad reactions to vaccination are mild and short-lasting. (Tell that to Jiggy.) They list fever, sluggishness and poor appetite, and say you should tell your vet about pain, swelling or lethargy lasting a few days. However, if your dog pukes or has the runs repeatedly, or itches all over, or can't breathe, or her face or legs swell up, or if she collapses, they say to call your vet immediately.

Call? Excuse me. In case you didn't know it, there are very few doggy 9-1-1 paramedics to dash into your house to help a dog experiencing anaphylactic shock. Our Mom would race to the vet and call on the way. Unfortunately, your vet will probably give your dog a cortico-steroid shot. It may save her life but give her a lifelong steroid-related immune problem. Still, *alive* is better than *dead*.

Bet you didn't know that dogs have different reactions to different vaccines. *Modified-live* vaccines (MLV's), which offer long and quick immunity, are live viruses that multiply inside of us and can, in rare cases, actually cause the disease they were meant to prevent. Whoops! Bad reactions to MLV's (which include distemper, parvovirus and adenovirus-2) generally happen within 10 to 45 days and may include, among other problems, stiff and achy joints, nervous system disorders, elevated liver enzymes, liver or kidney failure, and autoimmune problems (like Jiggy's hepatitis).

Killed virus or bacterial vaccines, like rabies, Bordetella (kennel cough) and leptospirosis (the "L" in shots like DHLPP), don't multiply like MLV's and have to be repeated more often. Unfortunately, they add all sorts of nasty stuff to boost their effectiveness, so they also cause more bad reactions. According to Dr. Dodds, these reactions *generally* happen immediately or within two days and can include seizures, lameness, allergies, arthritis, and even anaphylactic shock.

When it comes to how dogs are given vaccines, you'd think every dog is Typhoid Mary, infecting everyone she meets. In real-

ity, we'll typically bump into one disease at a time, and those diseases are usually contracted through sniffing, eating or touching. Only tick-borne diseases and rabies are injected.

Outside of a lab, no dog would ever find five to seven diseases at the same time, and yet odds are your dog is getting vaccinated for multiple diseases at once with a polyvalent shot. This witches' brew usually goes by catchy names like DHLPP or DHPPC and may contain vaccines no longer recommended (like coronovirus) and vaccines your dog probably doesn't need. It will also make detective work next to impossible if your dog has a bad reaction.

Worse yet, polyvalent vaccinations are associated with terrible conditions. One of the worst is immune-mediated hemolytic anemia (IMHA), a disease in which the body attacks its own red blood cells. Spaniels, poodles, Old English Sheepdogs, dachshunds, shih tzus, golden retrievers, and several other breeds appear particularly susceptible. (Search for IMHA and your dog's breed on-line for more information.)

The safest vaccines are monovalent (containing a single virus) or bivalent (with two viruses). Don't mistake "single dose," which means "one dose," for monovalent. Your vet may tell you that monovalent vaccines aren't necessary, or readily available, or cost effective, and that it's easier to immunize against multiple viruses at once (which is why polyvalent vaccines exist in the first place).

Mom and I have different ways we would handle a recommendation for a polyvalent shot. My preference is to stamp my paw, toss my ears back and storm out in a huff, my point beautifully made. Mom's method, which will probably work better, is to just ask your vet to go the monovalent (or, at least, bivalent) route. If it becomes an issue, buy your own vaccines and take them in or find a vet who already rejects polyvalents. Your dog has no choice, but *you* do! And your job as our guardian is to protect our bodies, not anyone's feelings.

I know you probably don't want to have to deal with yet another issue, but if you have a small dog, I bet you'll change your mind. Did you know that vaccine manufacturers work off of a "one size fits all" model? Listen, I weigh four pounds dripping wet. My friend and bodyguard, Millie the Mastiff, tips the scales at a big 140. So I ask you: what Einstein came up with the idea that we need the same dosage of vaccine? No wonder these shots can do so much damage to tiny dogs like me and Jiggy. You can try to mitigate this lunacy by asking your vet to split, or "titrate," any vaccine (except rabies, which can't be legally titrated). Dr. Dodds says a split dose still works fine, and that the USDA told her that manufacturers make vaccines up to ten times more powerful than necessary (because vaccines are harmless?). Dr. Pitcairn warns, however, that "giving *half* of 100 billion viruses is still 50 billion" and will not prevent vaccine-induced illness. In response, this dog says, "50 billion!"

Information is power, people. The more you know, the better it is for all dogs. Speaking of which, if your dog has a serious reaction, ask your vet to report it so experts can track it, and then click on our website's link for Reporting Drug Reactions and report it yourself. And never give your dog that vaccination again! (If your dog is at high risk, you might consider using a nosode. More on this ahead.) Alert your dog's breeder so she can warn littermates' parents, too. Some believe reactions run in families.

Think your dog already has problems that might be linked to vaccinations? Consult a holistic vet to start rebuilding your dog's health. (Find one at *dogs4dogs.*)

Learn more about specific vaccines and their reactions, including the new "recombinant" vaccines on the market but still not widely used, read Catherine Diodati's *Vaccine Guide for Dogs and Cats.* It's a little technical, but is full of great facts that could someday save your dog's life. Besides, what are a few big words when it comes to your dog's health?

Deciding Among Non-Core Vaccines Holistic veterinarians like Pitcairn, Goldstein and Allen Schoen have long warned about the dangers of vaccinations. Despite this, a wide assortment of vaccines is available, with new ones popping up all the time. Some may benefit dogs. (If you ask me, and few Humans do, I suspect they mostly benefit stockholders.) To find out which is which, always ask your vet these questions before you prick:

- Does my dog's location or lifestyle put her at grave risk and does my dog have a high risk of permanent damage or death without this shot?
- How many cases of this problem has your vet seen in the past year?
- Is there an alternative? For example, would rattlesnake aversion training help avoid yearly vaccination against rattlesnake venom?
- Is now the best time to vaccinate? Some types have short durations of immunity.
- Does the vaccine protect against most common strains and types?
- Do possible adverse reactions outweigh benefits?

- Has your vet had experience with the vaccine? For how long?
- Does the vet school nearest you recommend it? (Call or e-mail them.)

Question even the most common non-core vaccines. When Mom asked Dr. Schultz about vaccinating dogs going to kennels and dog shows, he told us, "I don't in general recommend kennel cough vaccines, but when they need to be used I prefer the intranasal products rather than the injectable." Unfortunately, to have any effect at all, this vaccine must be given within a week to six months before exposure and, still, immunity's a crap shoot.

You've probably heard the doggy expression, "the cure is worse than the disease." If you hung around me you would hear it all the time. I mean, look at something like kennel cough. It's usually a mild disease. You could even call it a doggy cold, because that's pretty much what it is. Like a cold, it has many strains. And like a cold, it usually goes away on its own. The best thing to do is to keep your immune system strong (by eating right and not over-vaccinating) and stay out of crowded, poorly ventilated places. I think the worst thing to do is to risk the side effects of a "preventative" that may not work and may cause more problems than the disease itself. But then, I'm just a dog (who writes and does research). What do I know?

Same goes for shots for leptospirosis and Lyme disease. A leptospirosis shot protects against only 50% to 75% of strains depending on the vaccine used, doesn't last long, is seldom necessary during cold weather or in non-rural or non-forested areas, and has potentially dangerous side effects. I don't know about you, but I'd want an awfully good reason to get it. The Lyme disease vaccine is also very controversial. Author and vet Dr. Allen Schoen has a great article about it *www.drschoen.com,* click Articles.

If you decide to proceed with any vaccine, do it in the morning on a day when you can monitor your dog's health, especially for killed viruses. Note the date of the shot on your calendar and watch your dog closely for symptoms at least several days for "killed" viruses, and for six weeks after MLV's. Report adverse reactions to your vet.

Puppy Shots Dogs who hobnob with other dogs, or sniff around strange doggy poop, are at danger for the long-lasting parvovirus. Parvo lurks everywhere: in grass and carpets and on vet's waiting room floors. Distemper isn't as durable; it's a dog to dog, or wild animal to dog, thing. Until you've proved your dog's immunity with a titer test, it's safest to keep her inside and away from unvaccinated or sick dogs and from other pups who aren't yet fully immune.

When you bring your puppy home you are going to have to decide how and when to proceed on the vaccination front. I can only advise you to proceed with caution, as there is no one correct vaccine schedule. What you do depends on your dog's health and your own level of comfort with minimal vaccination.

How early should you start giving shots? Unless there's a particular danger, most experts won't vaccinate pups younger than eight weeks. Most still have immunity from their moms until then. Dr. Bob Rogers warns, for example, that vaccinating against parvo at six weeks protects only 30% of pups while exposing the others to parvo at the vet's clinic. (See his link at *dogs4dogs*.)

When you're ready to start with those puppy shots, Dr. Dodds recommends parvovirus and distemper vaccines at 9-10 weeks and 14 weeks (with an optional shot at 16-18 weeks), then one more shot (or titer test) at one year. She uses Intervet Progard Puppy DPV, a bivalent product. Dr. Dodds gives rabies shots as late as allowed by law, at least 3-4 weeks apart from the distemper/parvo shot. She recommends no other vaccinations unless specific circumstances dictate an urgent need.

Dr. Schultz would give one shot for distemper and parvo after 12 weeks of age. Two weeks later he would test titers. If titers aren't strong, he'd revaccinate and test again. He told us, "With the exception of rabies, I have been vaccinating my dogs once with core vaccines then never again." He added that many people wouldn't be comfortable with that schedule and might prefer to vaccinate after 3-, 5-, 7- or 9-year intervals.

Our vet, Dr. Tamara Hebbler, uses monovalent vaccines (like Schering Plough Galaxy® D and Galaxy® Pv.); she says she'd keep her dog inside as much as possible and keep her away from moist grassy areas (especially outside vets' offices). She'd give parvo at 10 weeks and 13-14 weeks, distemper at 11 weeks and 14-15 weeks. She'd revaccinate only if titers tested low.

Some holistic vets don't vaccinate puppies at all. Dr. Pitcairn told us he stopped vaccinating dogs over twenty years ago. Instead, he uses "nosodes" made from the tissues of diseased animals. (He also works hard to keep immune systems strong.) Dr. Paul warns that nosodes have no regulation, oversight or demonstrated efficacy. Dr. Dodds, too, is wary of nosodes, believing they're unproven and will probably remain so.

Permit me a short rant. Why is it that studies of inexpensive, natural substances are never done? Could it be because there's no profit motive? Doesn't anyone care about *health* anymore?

Thanks. I feel better now. Here's some more potential bad news, however. If you get a pup who's had "all her shots," I wouldn't take those as reassuring words. You need to find out what shots she got and how many, and especially how old she was when she got the last shots of parvovirus and distemper. If she was 12 weeks or older, you need to test titers no sooner than two weeks after that shot. If *younger* than 12 weeks, Dr. Dodds advises waiting 3-4 weeks before another shot (2 weeks at a minimum), then test titers two weeks after that shot. The important thing is to make sure you give the last puppy shot at or beyond 12 weeks.

Alert. Some breeds are more susceptible to particular diseases. (Parvo loves Rottweilers and Dobies.) Other breeds, like cocker spaniels, are prone to bad reactions. Ask your vet, or check on-line, to see if your dog needs special handling.

The Rabies Dilemma A rabies shot almost killed our Beagle friend, Snickers. In the middle of the night, she started heaving and having spasms, her temperature shot to 104.8° F and she lost the use of her back legs. Lucky Snickers made it to the vet's just in time. Some dogs aren't so fortunate. In addition to acute reactions, this vaccine may cause hypothyroidism, tumors, arthritis, and allergies, and is linked with behavioral problems like increased aggression, hysteria, barking, and even paranoia. (And no, that's not why I seem paranoid. I'm just very, very careful.) I had to break the news about side effects to Snickers and, I have to tell you, she was none too pleased.

Rabies is the *only* vaccine required by law, and it's done to protect people, not dogs. The law requires rabies shots every three years and, inexplicably, even *every* year in some places! (By the way, the "one-year" shot is no safer than the "three-year" shot.) You're worried about mad dogs? I'm worried about mad people.

There are ways for dealing with crazy laws, though. If your dog is old or sick or immune compromised like Jiggy, and is at low risk for infecting Humans, your vet can help you avoid the shot indefinitely, or at least postpone it, with a *letter of exemption* submitted with your regular license fee and a small additional fee. Some vets also submit titer test results; duration of immunity can be for up to seven years, depending on the type of vaccine used. Letters of exemption work with kennels and airlines, too. If you're living in a state that requires an annual vaccination, I suggest you move. (Mom thinks that's a little extreme, but then, she's not the one facing the needle!) At the very least, get your friends together and write or email your state legislators. We can see no good reason for these archaic laws. Find an advocacy link at *dogs4dogs*.

I'll jump off my rabies soapbox after saying that while there are over 67 million dogs in this country, there were only 117 cases of canine rabies in 2003. Bats, skunks, possums (and even cats) are a lot likelier to infect you. I say, down with discrimination against dogs. No more "mad dog" jokes!

Dealing with Human Resistance If you decide to cut back on vaccinations, and it wasn't your vet's idea, be prepared for him or her to balk. According to the vaccine Task Force, only about 25% of vets have adopted all AAHA

recommendations. (Ah, well, you know what dogs say: to err is Human; to forgive, canine). I also hate to tell you this, but there are still a lot of vets who vaccinate for five or more diseases at once, and give vaccines like coronavirus, or annual shots for core diseases. Maybe we need to sic the SPCA on them. (Okay, so I'm not so forgiving.)

Some of my more suspicious friends think vets keep giving all these shots because they make a lot of money from vaccinations and the annual checkups that come with them. Mom prefers to think it's more an issue of habit, or fear of change, or maybe that vets are afraid you won't come in for that all-important yearly examination. In any event, assuring your vet you'll show up every year, and will replace vaccination with titer testing and regular blood analysis, may help bring about change. If your vet doesn't believe in the new guidelines, or worries about legal repercussions if she changes, offer to sign a form of informed consent and her test titers before, or instead of, vaccinating. In the end, remember: the decision is yours.

Vaccinating outside Your Vet's Office What's worse than getting an unnecessary shot? Getting an unnecessary shot from an untrained layman. Many dog guardians get their dog's "boosters" at a pet store, or buy low-cost vaccines and give boosters themselves, without realizing the great risk. If you're tempted to do this, please ask yourself first:

- Does your dog really need this shot? Maybe your time would be better spent rereading this chapter.
- What if your dog has a life-threatening reaction to the vaccine? Some can cause seizures; others, anaphylactic shock.
- Are you skipping your dog's annual check-up—THE SINGLE MOST IMPORTANT THING TO DO FOR YOUR DOG'S HEALTH? A hidden illness could make vaccination lethal.
- If you're giving the shot yourself, are you sufficiently knowledgeable? Improper storage of a live vaccine can inactivate it. Do you know the reputation of the vaccine seller and his track record? (Beware bargains!) How will you know if a lot has been recalled? Do you know all the side effects? Or how much to give to a small dog?
- If someone else is giving the injection, are they licensed vet techs or temporary help? If they're pushing annual boosters for core vaccines without testing titers first, or unnecessary vaccination for "non-core" or "generally not recommended" vaccines, I say, run!

Vaccines make fun reading, huh? This time you've really earned your treat.

Chiclet's Trivia Treat: *Conspiracy Theorist Alert: Did you know that parvovirus, one of the worst diseases afflicting dogs, didn't exist until the mid-1970's? Within months it swept around the world killing thousands of dogs. Scientists suspect it was likely born from a variation from feline panleukopenia virus, a cat virus, although it may have come from a raccoon, fox or mink virus. Still, I have my money on cats. We've been sworn enemies for ages and this was their revenge.*

Food To Die For

This is the "before" me on an expensive, super-premium "natural" canned food combined with a top vitamin supplement. See my ugly red tears? I'm mortified to have you seeing me look like this, but I've swallowed my pride to help save your dog's life. You now owe me BIG TIME!

It was bad enough that I looked like a canine Vampira when this photo was taken. My blood and urine tests, and Jiggy's, revealed inner scenarios that were even more revolting. I was lacking in Vitamin D, folic acid, phosphorus and chromium. Jigs and I shared deficiencies in B-6, lecithin, calcium, manganese, selenium, and bioflavinoids, plus we both had poor fat absorption and excess sodium. Jiggy, who was on a top "medical" food for his sick liver, showed additional deficiencies in Vitamins A, C, D, and E, digestive enzymes, zinc and copper. Both our foods were labeled "complete and balanced." I'm prompted to ask, as compared to what?

Upon seeing our test results, our new holistic vet, Dr. Tamara Hebbler, convinced Mom to switch us to fresh "people food" and supplements. And guess what happened? Within days of changing our diet, Jiggy's heart-stopping breath (previously a barrier to our romance) became give-me-a smooch-baby fresh. We practically had to leap out of the way to avoid the tartar tumbling from our teeth. Then one fine day we noticed our red tears were gone. My career as a supermodel was back on track.

How can you tell if your dog's food is hurting your dog? Take a good look at her. Does she have red gums, brown teeth, bad breath, smelly ears, ugly red tears or gummy gunk in her eyes? (Hint: she shouldn't.) Does she climb the walls with hyperactivity or languish about like a lump? How's her temper? Pissy? Maybe her coat's dull or sheds in fistfuls? Or she has fleas, allergies, bowel disease, recurring ear infections or parasites, anal gland problems or a musty doggy smell? Does she suffer from arthritis, cancer, diabetes, liver, kidney or heart disease? With so many dogs suffering ill health, something universal has to be at fault. I can't promise you that an improved diet will fix everything that's wrong with your dog, but I can tell you that Jiggy's blood test results improved 50% in just one month. Within *three* months, both of our blood tests were 75% back to normal. Clearly, a good part of the source of our health problems had been lurking in Mom's pantry.

The way this dog sees it, most of us aren't on *health* food diets, we're on *fast* food diets. You can almost hear manufacturers say: "Do you want fries and a shake with that?"

Are things really that bad? Judge for yourself. After commercial food sickened her two dogs in 1990, Ann Martin, author of *Foods Pets Die For,* began a decade-long quest to find out what could legally go into her dogs' food. What she learned was beyond shocking. Believe it or not (I didn't want to), manufacturers regularly serve up proteins from "downer" animals, what inspectors call "4-D": the dead, dying, diseased and disabled. (Why so surprised? Feeding downer animals to cattle is what Mad Cow disease is all about, and cattle are part of the Human food chain!)

Pet foods may legally contain roadkill, zoo animals, and even euthanized dogs and cats. Ann's research uncovered food with traces of the euthanasia agent sodium pentobarbital; sweepings from mill and rendering plant floors; moldy grain; restaurant grease; residual antibiotics and hormones; artificial texture, color and flavor agents; and chemical preservatives banned in *Human* food in the U.S. and in *pet foods* in other countries. If you like real-life horror stories, read an excerpt from Ms. Martin's book at *www.newsagepress.com.*

Okay, you have your yummy ingredients. (Yeah, right.) Next comes processing, cooking at moderate to high temperatures for hours until bacteria and most of the vitamins and enzymes are gone. (Ever wonder why they add back vitamins?) Unfortunately, endotoxins (produced by the bacteria) aren't destroyed, nor are mycotoxins (produced by molds and fungi). In fact, mycotoxins, which are potentially present in all dried foods, have caused at least two manufacturers to recall products after dogs fell ill or died.

Bet you don't know how the dog food industry operates. Well, picture a pack of lions with a carcass. The biggest cats feed first, tear-

ing off the best stuff for themselves. Then the hyenas dig in. After the hyenas come the jackals, and so forth, all the way down to the dung beetles. The same thing happens in the pet food industry. The parent company takes what it wants for you Humans, selling the leftovers (mostly food earmarked as unfit for Human consumption) as food for pets. Ever hear the expression, "The Devil gets the hindmost?" Well, your little angel is that Devil (or dung beetle). This profit-making from refuse and surplus has built a $14 billion a year industry in the U.S. alone. If you want to learn more, go to *www.api4pets.org* and search for "Pet Food." I bet you won't come away hungry.

I have more bad news. You Humans have been sold myths along with the food.

MYTH #1: "People food" is bad for dogs. My ancestors decided to live with *your* ancestors because they wanted to share Human food rather than hunt for their own; in more recent times, your grandparents fed our great, great…great grandparents their leftovers. Anyway, if pet food companies think the food Humans eat is bad for dogs, why do their ads promote "real" beef and "real" lamb? Maybe the "people food" that's bad for us is junk food. And maybe what's really bad about "people food" is its affect on company profits.

MYTH #2: Dogs shouldn't eat fruits and vegetables. Our ancestors were either opportunistic carnivores or scavenging omnivores. (Experts disagree.) They ate meat, game, poultry and fish, plus whatever veggies and fruits they could score inside or outside their prey's tummies. People are always surprised to see Jiggy and me doing tricks for steamed broccoli or green beans or apples. Humans surprise easily.

MYTH #3: You should overlook all that grain in dog's food. Ever see a "scaredog" to keep dogs out of cornfields? Our ancestors ate some grain, but for the most part, they stunk as farmers and cooks. What grain they did eat came, for the most part, predigested in their prey. Never was it genetically altered, chemically fertilized or stripped of nutrients during processing. Companies making grain-loaded commercial dog foods know this, and also know that corn, soybeans and wheat can cause allergic reactions in sensitive dogs, but think you prefer cheap over everything else. *Grrrrrrrrrrrrr.*

MYTH #4: Dogs should eat the same food every day. Allergy specialists will tell you that the best way to give yourself food allergies and nutritional deficiencies is to eat the same thing meal after meal, day after day. Variety's not just the spice of life; it's necessary for a healthy life.

MYTH #5: Variety equals diarrhea. An abrupt change of diet can give us diarrhea, but usually only temporarily. When you're initially changing foods, stretch it out over a week or longer, adding a little new, and subtracting a little old, and watching our poop to see how things work out (so to speak). After an initial week or so of runny poop, Jigs and I began eating something different at every meal. And guess what? No diarrhea. Nowadays we eat pretty much like you do with no gastric upset—because we're mammals just like you.

MYTH #6: Dogs must eat what you put in front of them or they'll become finicky eaters. If something tastes awful, smells spoiled, or makes us feel achy or queasy, how else can we tell you other than to push it away? If we initially turn up our noses at fresh food, maybe it's because we're addicted to fat-laden junk food, just like some of you are. Once we get used to fresh food, we'll love it.

MYTH #7: Dogs' nutritional needs are too complicated for Humans to figure out. Our bodies are so similar to yours that they test your products on us (not something Jigs and I favor), so am I missing something here? If you've managed to stay healthy yourself, with just a few adjustments, you can keep us healthy, too. (On the other paw, if you live on junk food, tequila shooters and cigarettes, better keep us on a good commercial food.)

MYTH #8: The most nutritious food comes in cans and in bags. Highly-processed food is better than fresh? "Meat flavoring" is better than meat? Mom has some real estate she'd like to sell you.

MYTH #9: Quality food is too expensive. Wholesome dog food doesn't have to be expensive, and can be a bigger bargain than processed food even *before* you figure in health benefits. *After* health benefits, there's no contest. If you feed your dog junk, sooner or later she'll probably get sick and require expensive medical care.

MYTH #10: "Complete and balanced" means optimum. Foods can get this designation in two ways: with a chemical analysis (meaning that these foods theoretically meet a certain standard) or by passing feeding trials. Trials are a higher standard, but can ultimately be met by exclusive feeding of the food for six months to six dogs. Even though most of us want to live longer than this, there's no requirement to follow dogs past the initial period (although some companies do). Here's another shocker. One food in a brand "family" might pass the trial and allow the rest of the "relatives" to tag along. I don't know about some of *your* relatives, but considering mine, that idea's pretty scary.

Do you know *exactly* what you're feeding your dog? Are you sure? Remember when Dorothy and her friends thought the Wizard of Oz was invincible until little Toto pulled back the curtain to reveal a befuddled imposter? Well, that's what I want to do. I'm pulling back the curtain on dog food. Grab your cans and bags and let's take a look at those labels:

- Ingredients are listed by descending weight. If numbers one, two and three are ground corn, beef, and corn meal, the food's mostly corn. Great news if you're a crow. If the label reads beef, ground corn, and corn meal, the main ingredient may still be corn because it outweighs the beef. Humans can be tricky.
- Meat means whatever mixture of beef, goat, sheep or swine was available at the rendering plant that day. Poultry is the available birds, anything from turkey to buzzard. Animal could be any dead animal (even a rat or a skunk). Expect that vague words are vague for a reason. *What will Madame have for dinner? Zee chicken breast or zee mystery animal part?*
- Meal means processed and dried at a rendering plant. Bone meal may contain heavy metals like lead. Even Stephen King couldn't make meat and bone meal any scarier than it already is. Dr. Jean Hofve, internationally-

known pet food expert and former official liaison to AAFCO (the Association of American Feed Control Officials) told us this is where the worst stuff shows up. Also, proportions of meat to bone are anyone's guess.

- By-products are basically what's left of a carcass after Humans have taken whatever they can legally eat. Some of this is just icky sounding stuff Humans don't like; most of it is illegal to sell for Human consumption. Poultry by-products get you heads, feet and viscera. Meat by-products get you blood, bone, lungs, spleen, and other fun stuff—but no meat.
- Digest is boiled-down or chemically-degraded flavoring sprayed on low-quality food. Animal digest can be made from any animal from any source. Yum.
- Grains vary from whole grain to dust off mill floors. Expect "feed" quality grains—the stuff they feed to cattle to fatten them up. Corn meal supplies calories. Corn gluten meal is a cheap protein source. Ground corn, brown rice, and whole wheat are whole grains, but what is so much of this stuff doing in dog food anyway?
- Dextrose, maltose, sucrose, fructose, lactose and corn syrup are sugars that may contribute to diabetes and weight gain.
- BHA and BHT are chemical preservatives linked to Human health and behavior problems. Ethoxyquin is a chemical preservative banned in Human food, and banned for pets in most other countrics. Propyl gallate and propylene glycol are synthetic preservatives, too. And don't get me started on artificial colors and flavors. See our *food safety* and *food additives* links at *dogs4dogs*.
- Dinner, as in beef dinner, means beef is at least 25% of the product (excluding water for processing), or 10% of the total weight.
- "With real beef" (as opposed to fake beef?) guarantees that there is at least a whopping 3% of beef by weight,

excluding water for processing. Beef flavor guarantees
only beef taste.

Jigs and I learned the hard way that dog foods aren't necessarily
what they pretend to be. Jazzy packages, sentimental copywriting
and cute dogs no longer fool us. (Did you know that those actor
dogs get paid?) What *would* impress me is pet food company executives eating their brand live on national TV. Now *there* would be
a food worth trying.

Ever play the Claim Game? When an ad claims a product "tastes
meatier," does that mean it is meatier? Meatier than what? Does it
even contain meat? If a commercial quotes results of a study, find the
study on their website; does it match their claim? Is it even there?

A really easy way to check out the exact ingredients in your
dog's food awaits you at a vendor's website: *www.naturapet.com*
(that's natura, no "L"). Click on *Compare Pet Foods* and you can
compare up to four brands at once. As an added bonus, you can
click on any ingredient and see what's lurking behind cryptic
names. Warning: Never attempt this on a full stomach.

You'll find that some commercial foods are better than others,
but they're probably not the ones you expect. And *some* processed
food may be even better than *some* fresh.

So what should you feed your dog? In the next chapter I'll give
you more good food alternatives for your dog than you ever could
have imagined. In the meantime, here's your treat.

Chiclet's Trivia Treat: *Pet food manufacturers go to a great deal of
trouble to make our food look, smell and taste appealing. If we won't eat
it, they can't sell it. But here's the thing. Well, **things**.*

*Although we're not exactly colorblind—we see yellows, blues and
grays—green is colorless to us and red looks yellow. So why are so many
dog foods fresh-meat red? Mom thinks it's to make Humans feel all warm
and fuzzy. I say: you think?*

*You're probably wondering why dog food has such a fabulous
aroma. If we compare our sense of smell to yours, well, forget about it. Our*

*sniffers are about a hundred times better. Walking noses, like blood-hounds, detect smells a **thousand** times better. Give us smell over looks and taste any ol' day.*

As for taste, we can detect sweet, sour, bitter and salty tastes, but culinarily speaking, we're more Ronald McDonald than Wolfgang Puck. And, just for the record, the next time you say, "My dog loves me unconditionally," please remember: we dogs aren't known for our taste.

Food To Live For

Have you ever seen us whimpering and moaning and moving our paws as we sleep? We look like we're running away from monsters, don't we? But we're not. I think you're ready for the truth: we're having a nightmare about commercial dog food. Yes, it's a proven fact. Now that you've read the previous chapter, you'll probably start having nightmares, too. Better run into the kitchen and throw out all those cans and bags, then have a French Poodle advise you on more suitable cuisine. A little *sauté des boeuf avec carottes* would be very nice, thank you.

Okay, I know what you're thinking: the change from *convenient* to *cuisine* seems a little radical. And time consuming. And expensive. You'd like to be a better Mom or Dad, but have neither the time nor energy to even think about your dog's diet, let alone change it (which is what manufacturers count on and why your dog has recurring bad dreams). To make matters worse, after years of being trained to believe that "people food" will kill us, you're afraid you'll change your dog's diet and she'll keel over dead. You probably hate me for learning to type and want your blissful ignorance back. Am I right or am I right? (It's a burden being smart.)

Here's the thing. How quickly (and how much) you need to change your dog's diet depends on your situation. Are you serving meat-flavored cardboard? Organic canned? Something in-between? Anyone out there serving variety? (I thought not.) Is your dog sick or well (or somewhere in-between)? Make no mistake, what you're feeding your dog is affecting her health one way or the other. If you're lucky, she's like one of those hardy old codgers you read about (but never meet) who make it to 103 "years young" while smoking and drinking whiskey and eating fried food every day. But you're probably not that lucky. I suspect only a complete physical check-up and blood profile will reveal the true state of your dog's health (for as you know, we lie about our health so you won't throw us out of the pack).

We dogs have a saying: we are what we eat. If your dog is mostly grains and by-products and preservatives, you'd better act fast. Think of the poor darling as being tied to railroad tracks with a locomotive bearing down. You can take action and feed her better *now*, or stand back and wait for that train.

Fortunately, feeding your dog a healthful diet is even easier than feeding yourself—because we have to eat what you give us (an unpublicized drawback to being a dog). Like you, we need species appropriate food, something similar to what our ancestors ate. It should be high in good stuff like nutrients and enzymes, and low in bad stuff like toxins and antibiotics and chemicals—and yes, with lots of variety. In a perfect world, foods should be fresh, or as close to fresh as possible. In other words, the best food for you is the best food for your dog, with just a few changes. Why don't we start with what's easiest and work up from there?

Quibbles with Kibble My description of doggy health food doesn't sound much like kibble, does it? But kibble is easy and quick and cheap. Your dog gobbles it down. Admit it: *you* love kibble more than your dog does.

Unfortunately, we have more than a few quibbles about kibble, and we're not the only ones. Animal nutrition expert Pat McKay calls dry food "the worst garbage that has ever been perpetrated upon our animals." Tori Rosay, owner of Dexter's Deli health-food stores for dogs and cats, is no kibble fan either. "Want to find the kibble aisle in your grocery store?" Tori asks. "Just sniff. You'll smell the sprayed-on rancid fat and animal digest that makes kibble so tasty. It's kind of a dead body smell, something your nose warns you about but advertising teaches you to ignore."

Let's see, garbage and death. Not the best endorsements.

There's more. Whereas canned food is preserved by the process of canning, most kibble is preserved artificially. Ever think about how many preservatives must be involved to retard spoilage of food left out all day? On top of that, kibble starts as a dried meal whereas canned food is canned fresh. It's exposed to more heat than canned (which does not improve nutrients). But at least kibble helps clean your dog's teeth, right? Ha! That's a greater hoax than crop circles, Big Foot, and the Loch Ness monster combined. Because dogs have teeth made for ripping and gnawing, not grinding, most of us inhale kibble rather than chew it. And even when we chew, a quick crunch isn't brushing.

Many people tell us they like kibble because it can be left out all day, and their dogs can snack on it whenever they're hungry. That's like leaving potato chips out all day for your kids to munch on. And who doesn't know how yummy stale nibbles can be? Even with all those chemicals, no amount of preservatives can help if it gets wet. We're talking mold and bacteria growth. Hello, doctor?

Did you know that because of the way it's made, most kibble can't contain more than 50% meat? That usually translates into corn heavy. Corn, which has the same glycemic index as a Hershey Bar (meaning it raises blood sugar the same way), can contribute to diabetes and obesity. Kibble has also been linked to GDV, a life-threatening bloat common in (but not exclusive to) large-breed, deep-chested dogs. If all this weren't bad enough, Mother Nature likes food to contain lots of water to contribute to keeping our insides moist. It's called hydration and is why Humans walk around sucking on water bottles all day. Don't even think of remedying the water situation with pre-moistened or soft dry food. They're loaded with more sugar and artificial colors and pre-servatives than regular kibble. (Who even knew that was possible?)

Fast, Easy and Nutritious So what do you do if you want to feed your dog something nutritious but still want fast and easy? Think about a raw diet. Yes, I said raw, as in not cooked. Buy your own foods from your grocer or try some of the new super-convenient frozen raw food products; you just defrost them the night before and feed. I know a raw diet sounds strange and scary, but we eat it, and you know how careful our Mom is. We'll talk a lot more about this later.

There are also dehydrated and freeze-dried foods available now that you can mix with meat or kibble. The next best alternative is a good brand of canned food (though probably not the brands you think). Next best is half kibble, half canned. Of course, I'm going to have to ask you to buy a quality product and rotate brands and ingredients. Variety makes our tails wag and does well by our innards. You're probably sick of hearing me say it, but without variety, you're just asking for allergies and nutritional deficiencies. (Want to know what brands we like? New products are becoming available all the time. See our favorites at *dogs4dogs*.)

Something great you can do to add nutrients to your dog's diet is to replace some of the commercial food with "people food." When you cook meat, eggs and veggies for yourself, make extras for us. And when you bring doggy bags home from restaurants, feed the contents to your doggy. (Yes, people actually used to do this; hence, the name.) Just don't feed us the onions or bones or cooked fat—why, we'll discuss later—and remember to wash off fatty or too spicy sauces and seasoning first.

Buying Commercial Foods When checking out brands, know that foods range from *this-stuff-should-be-illegal* to *looks-almost-good-enough-to-eat*. To know what you're getting, scrutinize labels (as explained in the previous chapter) and look for indications of quality. Know that premium means nothing except that Humans will pay more when they see it. Natural means *not chemically altered*, and is better than the alternative, but beyond that it doesn't mean much.

On the other paw, some terms do matter. Accept no less than complete and balanced (meaning it theoretically provides adequate nutrition for your dog) and shoot for words like feeding trials or feeding protocols (meaning dogs actually survived six months eating the stuff). Certified humane means that the food is hormone and antibiotic free, and that the animals were humanely handled. (Hip hip horray!) By law, the term Human quality legally can't appear on labels, but manufacturers sneak it onto websites. Guess the government's afraid you'll eat our food. (P.S. You can have it.) The term 100% Organic means human quality food that's free of synthetic pesticides and fertilizers, hormones and antibiotics, not genetically-engineered or irradiated. Organic means 95% organic, and with organic ingredients means the food is 70% or more organic.

The investigative journalist in me loves the *Whole Dog Journal* (*www.Whole-Dog-Journal.com*). It reviews natural dry and canned foods yearly and accepts no advertising revenues. Search their "Back Articles" (or call 800-424-7887) for recent reviews at a low cost. The WDJ is a great, inexpensive holistic care newsletter, available printed or on-line. We subscribe and think you should, too.

When selecting kibble, buy small bags and store the food correctly (more on this later). Check the expiration date stamp for freshness. If you find a brand showing the manufacturing date, that's even better. Food can hang around the distribution chain for months, even years. Yes, it's more expensive to feed your dog Human-quality kibble, naturally preserved, in smaller date-stamped bags, but it's not as expensive (or heartbreaking) as paying vet bills later. You Humans have a saying that dogs don't have: don't be penny wise and pound foolish.

For the first ingredient on the label, look for something you'd actually consider eating (like lamb or beef) instead of mysterious *animal by-products* or *meat and bone meal*. If the product contains grain, make sure it's a bit player, not the star. And look for whole grains like brown rice or oats. Although you might think it's good to pick brands with lots of ingredients, don't. It makes food rotation and detective work harder. Two places to check out ingredients on-line are *www.naturapet.com* (you were there before, right?) and *www.petfoodsdirect.com*.

As you make changes, do a Nancy Drew on your dog's poop to make sure new foods work for your dog. (Who said detective-work couldn't be fun?) This is a very important part of the transition to better eating. We'll talk more about it in a minute.

People Food: Cooked Mom—who prefers root canals to kitchen duty—reluctantly started cooking for us in an effort to cure Jiggy's liver. His very life was at stake so she really had no choice. Maybe you hate cooking, too. (Mom sends you a *high five*.) If so, won't you at least read this chapter to learn about healthful table scraps and foods we should never eat? I'll make it as painless as I can.

If, on the other paw, you've already donned your chef's hat in anticipation of cooking for your dog, you're surely wondering about the source of Mom's many lip-smacking recipes, what with her hating cooking and all. Well, sometimes she just keeps things simple and sautés some meat and veggies. If she hasn't been to the market lately, she might just scramble eggs or open a can of fish.

Other times, she whips up recipes from *Dr. Pitcairn's New Complete Guide to Natural Health for Dogs and Cat* or Micki Voisard's *Becoming the Chef Your Dog Thinks You Are*. Mom will make extra batches and freeze them; then, on busy days, she can just defrost them (a skill for which Mom has few peers). One day, we all watched a great DVD on food for dogs starring Dr. Pitcairn and Ms. Voisard: *Eat, Drink, and Wag Your Tail.* (Mom drank. We wagged our tails.) You'll find links at *dogs4dogs.*

Now on to the really important stuff. Though dogs, like Humans, can handle a variety of foods, *we cannot handle onions, raisins, grapes, chocolate, sprouted or green potatoes or any moldy foods.* These foods can make us really sick, even kill us. Also limit sugar (which is

as bad for us as it is for you) and avoid MSG and artificial sweeteners (especially Xylitol). Raw spinach, Swiss chard, and rhubarb can be hard to handle, and asparagus, which works for some dogs, gives Jiggy and me the runs. For more "thou shalt nots," visit the Animal Poison Control Center at *www.ASPCA.org.*

Protein sources easiest to digest include boneless fish, beef, lamb and turkey. When you can, add weird foods like venison, duck, tripe and rabbit to give us different nutrients and enough diversity to prevent food sensitivities from developing. Think raw or seared rare. And yes, I know microwaving is convenient, but try not to do it. Vets tell us it turns fat molecules into something our bodies can't recognize.

You know how some people seem to take better care of their dogs than they do themselves? Well, feeding your dog right might be the ticket to your own good health. When Mom started giving more fruit and vegetables to Jiggy and me, the health benefits extended to her and Dad. Now all of us are eating broccoli, green beans, Brussels sprouts, carrots, cooked butternut squash, yams, sweet potatoes, peas, cabbage, snow peas and canned and cooked pumpkin. (Can't wait for Halloween!) If your dog snubs veggies, try sautéing them in a little butter (the real stuff, not margarine) or sprinkling them with flavored oils. Just like Humans, we have preferences and different tolerances.

It's best to lightly steam, freeze, cook or pulverize veggies; this breaks down cell membranes and makes them easier to digest. We're built for predigested veggies in our prey's innards, not for food fresh from the vine. Mom whips up a batch twice a week and keeps them in containers in the fridge so they're available for a quick treat should we do something adorable (which we, of course, do constantly). Unless you mince and mix foods together, it's hard to get us to eat alfafa sprouts, parsley and dark leafy greens. Because of that, Mom gives us (and herself) a green "super food" called Green's First (*www.greensfirst.com*). She mixes it with water and squirts it in our mouths with a syringe (with no needle). Whoops. I almost forgot fresh fruit snacks. (Dried fruits have too much sugar.) We like apples, bananas, berries, mangoes and peaches (though seeds and peach pits are toxic).

Many vets, including our own, recommend little or no grain for dogs, but Dr. Pitcairn told us he's been feeding grains to dogs with great results for more than 20 years. He says that it's not grains that are bad but the "dust" that passes as grain in some commercial foods. If you've been told that dogs can't digest grains properly, he suggests inspecting your dog's poop for evidence. (Dr. P sure knows how to have fun.) If you find whole kernels and grains, he suggests you add a digestive enzyme and try again. Jiggy and I sometimes eat small amounts of cooked oats, quinoa, millet, barley, buckwheat, and brown rice. All are yummy when cooked in broth, flavored with butter or oil, or mixed in with meat.

Grains do have advantages. Compared to meat, they're a cheap source of protein (which is why kibble is loaded with grain). And they aren't contaminated with antibiotics and hormones as meat and poultry can be. It's also better for the planet to serve a little grain directly rather than to load up another animal with grain only to get a little meat in return. Some vegan and vegetarian dogs even eat grains *instead of* meats. (Personally, I think it's their folks' idea, not theirs. Still, I'm all for sparing animal lives. Some of my best friends are animals.) Our research has found more vets *against* vegetarian diets for dogs than *for*. If you're going to try it, you must educate yourself. Otherwise, you could be risking your dog's life. You'll find links at *dogs4dogs*.

What about dairy, you ask? Dogs have had little luck over the ages convincing cows to give us milk. (I think I know why cows are called bossies.) Our ancestors had better luck with chickens and their eggs. Jigs and I have a couple of eggs a week and big dogs can have even more. We prefer ours scrambled or in a veggie omelet, although braver dogs eat them all slimy and raw. Some dogs tolerate yogurt, kefir, cottage cheese, and hard cheese, but many vets suggest avoiding milk products altogether. Dr. Pitcairn, however, finds dairy an excellent food for dogs. If your dog is allergic, he says, consult a holistic vet for treatment.

Certain flavorings are also good for us. Garlic works as well on fleas and other parasites as it does on vampires. Start slowly and increase gradually up to two teaspoons a day for a big dog, bearing in mind that large doses can be toxic. Touches of unsalted butter, ginger, soy sauce and sesame oil add taste to food; sardine and salmon oils might not be your idea of heaven, but we love them.

Supple- One thing I can't bark loudly enough about is the need for cal-
ments cium in dogs!!! Dr. Pitcairn says that a ten-pound dog needs the same amount of calcium as the average Human female. That's a lot of calcium. He also warned us that because our air is contaminated with heavy metals from cars and industry, bones (our traditional calcium source) can be contaminated. He likes bones for teeth cleaning only.

Calcium isn't the easiest thing in the world to assimilate, so selecting the right product is important. Bone meal must be Human quality and *guaranteed* contamination-free. (Try Now Bone Meal Powder; don't use the stuff you organic gardeners spread on your garden.) Jiggy and I use a calcium derived from Irish seaweed from Animal Essentials.

We started with digestive enzymes when we first switched to fresh foods and use enzymes now when we try something new. We also take a good vitamin and mineral supplement and essential fatty acids. Because I have what Texans call a "hitch in my get–along," I also take several joint greasing products and Jiggy does, too. You almost can't start too young if you want to keep your legs working, especially if you have four to maintain. (Find links to many of the products we like at *dogs4dogs*.)

Raw Food Sometimes the best sources for news stories are right in your neighborhood. Of all the dogs I know, two are just brimming with health. One is a terrible flirt named Sweet Pea, a Chihuahua. The other's a chocolate Labrador retriever named Merlin. Although neither is a young pup, both have fabulous hair, are full of energy, and have these eyes that just sparkle. I asked them their secret and they answered in unison: *arf scarf barf*. Roughly translated, that means that they eat BARF.

I'm sure your reaction was the same as mine. BARF sounds like, well, you know what it sounds like and it's not good. Then I learned that BARF is an acronym for Biologically Appropriate Raw Food, or Bones and Raw Food, depending on who you talk to. Personally, I think it would garner more converts if they called

it something that sounded a bit less nauseating, but it seems to be catching on anyway.

Opponents to BARF say bacteria and potential dangers from bones and parasites present insurmountable problems. *Proponents* pooh-pooh naysayers, saying dogs eat poop, for heavens sake, and clean each other's private parts. They say our short intestinal track and abundant hydrochloric acid help protect us from bugs that would bring Humans to your knees.

Advocates say BARF brings us closer to our wolf roots, and that it offers fewer vet bills (from improved health); decreased arthritis and allergies; healthier teeth and gums (and better breath);

fewer and firmer stools; fewer parasites (including fleas); and decreased doggy odor. (Odor? Dogs have odor?) BARF supporters also report a more appropriate rate of growth for puppies along with proper muscle development in the neck and jaw. There's anecdotal evidence, too, that it helps prevent GDV (bloat).

When our vet prompted Mom and me to start researching BARF, we learned that Sweet Pea and Merlin were just two of a growing group of dogs forsaking kibble and canned dog food for this new old diet. Most of them eat between 50% and 75% protein and bones (with raw organ meat and eggs twice weekly), along with plenty of veggies and sometimes grains. If you watch your dog's eating habits, he'll probably tell you what he needs.

For better digestion, warm up cold food in a double-boiler or a plastic bag immersed in hot water. No nuking, please! If you're worried about bacteria (most experienced BARFers aren't), serve whole rather than ground meats, soak them twenty minutes in food-grade hydrogen peroxide (1 tablespoon per pint of water), then rinse and serve, or sear them. Food expert Dr. Jean Hofve recommends freezing meat at 4° F for 72 hours before use. We think it's wise to avoid raw salmon and pork because of concerns over parasites, but we know lots of people who don't.

Drs. Pitcairn and Martin Goldstein and most other holistic vets we consulted endorse raw feeding. Many other vets, especially those with no experience BARFing, warn against it. New ideas scare most Humans. In the immortal words of Joe Friday, I've tried to give you "just the facts." Now you need to do some research and decide for yourself.

Jiggy and I began our transition to BARF at the urging of our vet, Mom switched us from canned food and kibble to home-cooked people food to what we eat now: fresh organic meat that's either raw or lightly seared, some cooked food and occasional pre-packaged frozen raw. It took Jiggy one gulp of raw lamb to decide he'd found heaven. I try never to appear too eager myself. It's a diva thing. But after a few days, even *I* was chowing down on raw lamb and turkey and chicken.

SCARED POOPLESS

That frozen pre-packaged "raw food" we mentioned contains a variety of ground meats, veggies and bone; you can find it at health-oriented pet stores, some Human health food stores, or on-line. Primal Pet Food comes in small nuggets you defrost as needed. Halshan has one-pound meat and vegetable combos you rotate from day to day. OmasPride, too, offers great variety. (Note: When traveling, lots of our friends eat Innova's Evo, a grain-free dry food based on raw feeding principles.)

As more and more companies jump on the raw food bandwagon, we hope you'll remember that there's nothing magical about the word "raw." Raw only means *uncooked*. It doesn't mean organic, or properly handled, or good for your dog, or anything else. It's up to you to find *quality* raw foods, from USDA sources, preferably with no antibiotics and no hormones.

If you're buying fresh meats from your butcher, don't worry about expensive cuts. Melt in your mouth tenderness is completely lost on most dogs. (But not on Jiggy and me, of course.)

Want to hear a wild story? Nola, a dog rescuer who's been feeding her dogs BARF for five years, sometimes partakes of freebies from a barrel of fresh deer meat left by hunters. One night she went to the barrel only to realize she had forgotten her plastic gloves. With seven hungry dogs waiting at home, Nola went barrel diving with her bare hands and filled several big bags full of meat, bloodying herself and her clothes in the process. On her way home with a trunk full of meat, she was stopped at a vehicle checkpoint and asked to explain her bloody hands, shirt and jeans. When the officers asked her to open the trunk, she told them all about BARF. The police let her go and Nola said it was worth it. When she arrived home with the fresh meat, her dogs proclaimed her to be the best hunter in the whole wide world!

A small warning for you: when dealing with raw meats, please be mindful of hygiene. (You Humans have wimpy digestive systems and can't handle all those bugs.) No slobbery kisses for anyone (especially toddlers) right after we eat. Wash your hands, utensils, kitchen counters, floors and our bowls after contact with raw flesh. Don't leave food down longer than 15–20 minutes. Leftovers should be tossed out or refrigerated, then cooked for the next meal. We can handle raw, but not spoiled.

When Mom started feeding us BARF, she had a lot of help from on-line "user's groups." Go to *www.groups.yahoo.com* and search for BARF, and I bet you'll find a group you like. (Check out a group's Message History to see how active they are and sign up for a daily digest if you're too busy to read lots of emails.) Two groups Mom has found helpful are *Toydogbarf* (for little guys like us) and *K9Nutrition*, but there are lots of groups for specific breeds and locales.

People who prefer books (my favorite kind) might like Kymythy Schultze's *Natural Nutrition for Dogs and Cats,* Carina Beth MacDonald's *Raw Dog Foods,* and Susan K. Johnson's *Switching to Raw.* If you want even more information, try classics like Tom Wolfe's *Raw Meaty Bones* or any book by Dr. Ian Billinghurst. Also, Dr. Pitcairn has a new edition of his book in which he discusses BARF in detail.

Transi- For a healthy dog, the switch from the best commercial food to a
tioning home-cooked or raw diet should take only a week or two. But if
Your Dog you're transitioning from flavored cardboard to a smorgasbord, my advice is to go slow. Start by mixing a little good food into the old. If we gobble it down with no tummy upset, great. Gradually add more. If not, go slower. And don't forget to add digestive enzymes and maybe a little yogurt with probiotics. (Also check out colostrum; see our index.)

After years of consuming chemicals, mystery meat, refined carbs and nutrient-poor food, your dog's body is likely full of toxins. As nutritious foods start their healing, toxins will head for every available exit. Don't panic. You want to encourage this cleansing, not suppress it with drugs or a return to crummy food.

Toxins may exit in the form of clear gray goop in our eyes, increased or red tearing, pudding poop, mucus in poop, skin sores, runny noses, itchiness, or increased shedding. During our own transition the whites of Jiggy's eyes turned red. I thought red eyes gave him a rakish look, but Mom panicked. Was it pink eye? Demonic possession? She considered calling an exorcist, but ran him to our vet instead. Dr. Hebbler, seeing no ulcers on his eyeballs, suggested natural eye drops and patience and that worked just fine. It was another symptom of his detox.

During transition from canned food to home cooking, we did have the runs on and off for a few weeks. Mom used a meal of cooked yams, sweet potatoes or pumpkin to help firm things up. (Surprisingly, these same foods help with constipation as well.) A bland meal like boiled chicken and rice also made our unhappy tummies feel better. Had our diarrhea continued, or been severe, Mom

would have called our vet. But luckily, before long, our trots stopped. That was about a year ago. Since that time, Jiggy and I have been the picture of health, and our blood work proves it. We have the runs only occasionally and cure them with yummy yams.

Sometimes a day or so of fasting before the switch helps, too. In fact, some BARFers routinely fast dogs once a week, giving them just water, or bones and water, to let their innards rest. (Toy dogs shouldn't fast more than 12 hours, though, because our speedy engines idle so fast that our blood sugar might plummet.)

Warning. Dogs most in need of better vittles are also the ones who should transition most carefully into BARF. (Mother Nature loves irony, doesn't she?) Dogs who have bowel problems, or suffer from pancreatitis, need an especially slow transition and perhaps a diet low in fat until they improve. Sedentary dogs should be wary of too much protein; high-meat diets require more elimination. Also old, ill or immune-compromised dogs might need some immune support before eating raw (we did) and should consult a holistic vet before they start. (Find a vet at *dogs4dogs*.)

Because of our hypothyroidism and Jiggy's icky liver, our vet wanted Mom to cook for us and take supplements for a few months before trying BARF. When Mom did start us on raw food, and we didn't immediately drop dead, she tried more. Client testimonial (unpaid and unsolicited): we are so glad that she did.

Dem Bones If dogs were better singers, you might hear us singing a chorus of Dem Dry Bones. You know the words: the toe bone connected to the paw bone, the paw bone connected to pastern, the pastern connected to the . . . Well, you get the idea. Stop singing.

The most important thing to know is that *bones must be served RAW!* Cooked bones can splinter in our throats and intestines, leading to impaction or perforations.

Bones come in two varieties: those you chew and those you gobble up. The chew variety includes raw beef knuckle bones, but they're a little large for small dogs. Give Jiggy a rib or chop bone and he'll Zen out for hours. (I don't care for bones myself; they get my whiskers too messy. Just look at Jiggy after a session with a lamb chop bone! I'll tell you what I chew later.)

Not all bones are created equal. Cow leg bones, especially marrow bones, can be tough on teeth. Veterinary dentist, Dr. Brook Niemiec, says that they can brutalize back teeth and damage may go undetected leading to pain and infection, even systemic disease. Big bones come from older animals,

are harder to chew and are more likely to be contaminated by pollutants. Young bones (from lamb or chickens), and bones from organically raised animals, are safer. Most BARFers recommend raw chicken necks, backs and wings, or turkey necks and backs (but not poultry leg or thigh bones which sometimes splinter). Seems it's not poultry bones that hurt you, but *cooked* poultry bones. (Another feeding myth bites the dust.) Kitties kill and eat raw bones in the form of birds and mice whenever they can. Think they're tougher than we are? Fat chance!

Your vet may warn you that bone chunks can get stuck in your dog's throat or intestines, and they can. So can fake bones, rawhide treats, balls and small toys. It pays to be careful. (In case you ever need it, you can find links to sites explaining the doggy Heimlich maneuver at *dogs4dogs*.) Here are some bone tips:

- Always supervise chewing and don't feed chunks that might be swallowed whole.
- Grind up or crush bones for beginners, and increase quantities gradually.
- Don't feed fish bones unless they're soft and tiny (like sardine bones).
- Wrap and refrigerate bones not being chewed and toss them after several days before they get too hard.
- Feed bones outside in an area *safe from predators* or inside where you can clean the floor. Some people foster crate-love, and limit mess, by feeding bones in a towel-lined crate. Others feed bones on old sheets.
- Separate dogs in a multi-dog household to prevent jealousy and fighting. Some of my friends have snapped at loved ones trying to take bones away, so take care. If you think your dog might be aggressive, have a trainer help you practice giving bones, then taking them away, and immediately giving them back until your dogs willingly surrender them.
- Always insist on proper bone etiquette.

Lots of Mom's friends were really scared when they first started feeding raw bones to their dogs. Her friend Nola said she did Poop Patrol by flashlight every night looking for bone fragments in her dog's droppings. Mom's friend Beth said, "I used to stare at my Waldo after he'd eaten a bone. I was afraid it was going to be like the movie Alien, with this bone shard ripping out of his belly." Fortunately, there were no fragments or shards anywhere—just happy dogs eating bones. Jiggy attributes bones to helping him find "his inner wolf." I can see it, can't *you*? There's something so primal, so attractive, about a dog with a bone.

Food Service Tidbits There usually aren't too many leftovers when it comes to fresh (and canned) diets, but when there are, seal them (if they're left out less than half an hour) in a container in the fridge. To aid digestion, bring them back to room temperature before serving by immersing a bag in warm water. Toss leftovers after a few days where your dog can't Dumpster dive after them. Here are some more tips:

- Protect against life-threatening bloat by keeping bowls at floor level. A Purdue University study showed that elevated bowls more than double the risk.
- Place food dishes where your dog has his flank protected and can see into the room. He'll feel safer, and may eat slower and more carefully which helps with digestion and GDV. Also, startled dogs are more prone to bite. This removes the startle factor.
- Limit chow time to 15-20 minutes. At first, we may poke around and end up hungry, but in a jiffy, we'll learn the lesson.
- Pick up the dish, dump or refrigerate leftovers, then wash the dish in hot, soapy water, rinse and put it away. Licked clean isn't clean.
- Separate puppies and adults and seniors.

- Heavy glass and U.S. ceramics (which are lead-free) make great dishes; just keep an eye out for jagged edges. Stainless steel is easy to clean, but can give dogs a mild shock in some circumstances or can stick to their tongues in freezing weather.
- The *Whole Dog Journal* suggests storing kibble in the original bag inside an airtight, or at least varmint-proof, container; storing food directly in plastic isn't a good idea unless the container is certified food safe. Also, if there's a problem with the food, you'll need lot numbers.
- Store food indoors (not in the garage) during hot weather; heat can destroy kibble and make your dog sick. Before refilling a container, swish it in hot, soapy water and dry thoroughly. Dumping new food into a dirty or damp container, or on top of old food, can spoil the new stuff sooner.

Quantities How much should your dog eat? Let's throw that question back at you. How much, in pounds or cups, will you eat tomorrow? Don't know? How could you? It depends on a lot of things: your appetite, available foods, activity level, and your size and build. The same goes for your dog. The amounts listed on cans and bags of foods are just estimates and can be way off the mark. One manufacturer even suggested feeding small quantities to make his food look more economical—like we wouldn't eventually figure that one out! Another upped suggested quantities to sell more food. And they say dogs are dumb animals.

If you must have a measuring stick, try giving your dog daily portions equaling 2–3% of body weight (or one pound of food for a 50 lb. dog). Little guys with fast metabolisms can eat as much as 4–5%. This is great info for the three of you out there who have scales and actually use them.

In the beginning, Jigs and I ate larger quantities of fresh food than we had of commercial. I suspect we were starved for nutrients. Once our bodies healed, we ate less than we had before.

Now Mom figures quantities by whether we're leaving food in our bowls or pestering her for more. She also checks our weight monthly. For years I've been lugging around the same four pounds. Just can't seem to lose that extra ounce. Jiggy's remains a lean, mean, eight-pound love machine.

Puppies need three meals daily, evenly spaced, all they can eat, and many vets suggest keeping small amounts of baby food readily available should they show signs of low blood sugar (such as wobbling, lethargy, or even collapse). This is especially important for toy puppies, the canine equivalent of hummingbirds. Grown-up dogs, especially small dogs and those at danger for GDV, do well with two meals a day. Jigs and I get our two meals plus veggie snacks at Tricks-for-Treats time.

Age Groups Tori Rosay says people come into her store all the time and inquire about where they might find foods appropriate for their "senior" dogs. She always asks them back, "When you're in a grocery store, where do you find the foods appropriate for people in *your* age group?" Customers invariably laugh and shake their head. They realize that Humans, after weaning, eat pretty much the same foods no matter what their age (but only because no marketing genius has dreamed up "senior" Human foods yet. Well, there *is* that one drink.) Kids and pups use up more protein and fat than grown-ups, and seniors might benefit from eating more eggs, but other than that, feeding differences for BARFers are mostly about *when* and *how much,* not about *which* foods.

By the way, feeding time is a good time to remind your dogs who's top dog. At our house, we have to sing for our supper (actually, lie down for our supper; Jiggy is tone deaf). Mom points at the floor and waits for us to assume the position before she serves up the goodies. And it's fine by us. Obedience is our job. Besides, handouts are demeaning.

Snack Time Dogs, like Humans, love snacks. As a reward for good behavior a smidgen of something wonderful is, as Chihuahua's say, *fantástico.*

Unfortunately, commercially available treats are usually full of preservatives, artificial flavors, and baffling substances like meat and bone meal, animal by-products and animal digest. Personally, I'd just as soon snack on cockroaches. At least they'd be fresh.

Fortunately, we don't have to resort to cockroaches. Jigs and I do our entire comedy routine for steamed broccoli flowers, green beans, carrot chunks, or a soupcon of dehydrated liver. (Because livers filter the body's toxins, only organic will do; as Hannibal Lecter could tell you, one must be very wary of whose liver one eats.)

Other dogs (including Jiggy) may get me for telling you this, but I think we should get treats only at appropriate times and places. Most important, don't let us circle like sharks while you're cooking—unless you think boiling water, heavy skillets, and sharp knives are suitable playthings for dogs. Our vet says she's treated more than a few scalded dogs and never wants to again.

Here's something else we find important. Before offering a treat, Mom says to ask yourself: what behavior am I encouraging, and is this a smart thing to do? For example, if we're shaking because we don't want a bath, comforting us with a treat only

teaches us to shake. Mom's on-line friend Rita's motto is NILIF: Nothing in Life is Free. Her dogs earn every morsel by sitting, lying down, staying put or whatever. Only if they perform a desired task do they get their treat. (Yes, I've mentioned this before. Humans learn best with repetition.)

Want to know my favorite thing to chew? Merrick Natural treats, especially their "Flossies." These look like corkscrews but are actually all natural dried USDA cow tendons with no preservatives, additives or artificial colors. Jigs was ready to perform back flips for Tori after she introduced us to their Texas Toothpicks, but Tori never asked. (Find a link to Merrick at our site.)

Of course, if you'd rather, you can find orange and green and purple treats filled with delicious chemicals and loads of calories. Some dissolve down to a size perfect to lodge in our throats which, as luck would have it, is when they're soft and gooey and taste their very best. Why not give us something natural instead? (Hint: Nylon doesn't grow on trees.)

Some treats are made of refined flour. Preservative-free whole wheat biscuits are okay occasionally if your dog's not plump or sensitive to wheat (although, these days, most dogs are one or the other.) Mom won't let us near pig's ears and hooves; most are treated with artificial colors, flavorings, and preservatives, and our Dr. Niemiec warns that hooves are way too hard and might break our teeth. Besides, they're gross.

Attention rawhide lovers! Rawhide chews are on our don't-even-think-about-it list. According to the American Animal Hospital Association, rawhide chunks have been known to get lodged in our throats causing choking and even suffocation. Even when they make it down the throat, pieces have been known to lodge in our intestines, causing gastritis or a dangerous blockage requiring surgery.

When Mom used to feed rawhide to her Yorkies, she found gray puddles of upchucked rawhide everywhere. If that's not nasty enough for you, rawhide is usually treated with bleach (to make it white) and some imported rawhide is even treated with arsenic! Humans, what are you thinking?

Well, that's enough about us. Here's a trivia treat for you.

Chiclet's Trivia Treat: *In 1891 Charles Cruft, an ambitious salesman working for Spratt's Dog Cakes, founded the first Crufts Dog Show, now the largest dog show in the world. Cruft thought that if he could encourage the breeding of purebred dogs, he could increase the sale of dog* *food. (What a notion!) When he died in 1938, his widow took over the show. Later, she sold it to the Kennel Club which has run it ever since.*

Wondering about that dog cake? It was developed in England around 1860 by an American electrician named James Spratt. While in London selling lightning rods he noticed sailors throwing leftover biscuits to hungry dogs and set about designing a biscuit containing wheat meal, beetroot, meat and veggies. Commercial dog food was thus "invented" by a lightning rod salesman. To me, that explains so much.

Stop Pest-ering Me

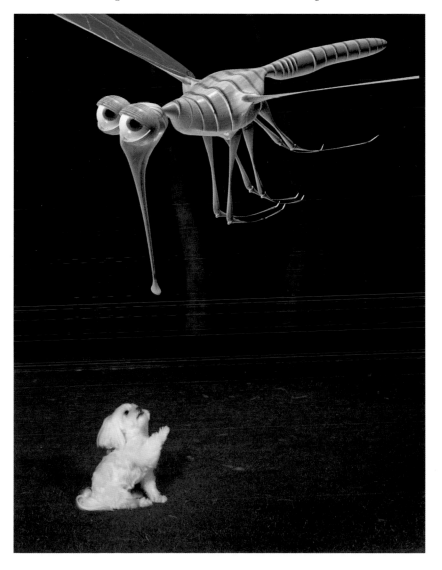

As I walk out to center stage, the lights dim, and a sole spotlight illuminates my troubled face. With anguished voice, the torment spreads over the four pounds of my flesh that weigh so heavily upon me. I begin:

SCARED POOPLESS

To medicate, or not to medicate: that is the question:
Whether 'tis nobler in mind to suffer
The slings and stings of outrageous mosquitoes,
Or to take arms against a sea of heartworms,
And by opposing end them?

All right, I suppose those lines might not be quite as eloquent as Hamlet's soliloquy, but for dogs they're a lot more pertinent than that "to be or not to be" stuff.

You see, when dogs see skeeters we get nervous. The appearance of those winged bloodsuckers means it's time for another heartworm decision. It's not like our vets are of one mind either. Some believe the benefits of heartworm medication outweigh the dangers; others say the medication is toxic.

Shakespeare might not have pondered these things, but have you ever wondered about the heartworm preventatives, flea preventatives, tick preventatives, and the dewormers you give your dog? You do know that they don't really *prevent* pests, don't you? They *kill* pests, kill them dead.

You think you're helping us, I know, and maybe you are. You trust that the companies making these products love us dogs and have only our health and well-being at heart. That's what their commercials say, isn't it? You probably also think there's some watchdog agency making sure products are safe for us. I hate to tell you, but it wasn't until 1996 that the EPA even started to evaluate our pesticides. Dig a little deeper, like this reporter, and the story only gets worse. Did you know that one heartworm "preventative" was sold for years before the FDA "suggested" it be voluntarily recalled because of its propensity to kill dogs along with the worms? We could do without such a permanent cure, thank you.

Consider all those diet pills and arthritis meds for Humans that, whoops, caused strokes and heart attacks. Consumers didn't know the dangers of those chemicals, just as you probably haven't considered the dangers of all the chemicals you're now using on us.

I wonder, would you blindly swallow potentially toxic chemicals, or spread them between your shoulder blades or those of your children, without considering the potential danger? Think about it: if a product tells you to wash your hands immediately after use, dispose of it carefully, keep it away from children, and call poison control if anyone consumes it, do you really think it's completely safe?

I beg you to examine the labels and study the warnings. While it's true that some products are safer than others, you should still be considering dangers when giving *any* pesticide to *any* dog, and especially if they're sick, old, really young or pregnant. And know that some breeds have a harder time with drugs than do others. (Learn how to research active ingredients in PREVENTING THE PREVENTABLE or at *dogs4dogs*.)

The Chase for Your Wallet Pest control companies promote products to vets and consumers stressing benefits and soft peddling (or not even mentioning) potentially dangerous side effects. You know those Human drug ads on television where they speed through the potential side effects at the end? I wish dog advertisements had to do the same (although the commercials would probably run too long and be too scary).

We dogs have to depend on you to make our health care decisions. We can only hope you'll be skeptical, and that you'll ask questions. If the answers you get sound like advertising copy, presume they are. Don't take my word for it. I'm a dog, for heavens sake. Use all that excess gray matter you Humans are always bragging about. The truth will set you free and it might save our lives. Ah, that's what Shakespeare would do.

Avoiding Toxic Overload Don't ever combine pesticides without consulting your vet. "A common way that toxicity can develop is to give your dog a flea bath, place a flea collar on him/her, use a topical flea product and use a flea bomb in your house," say the folks at *www.petplace.com*. "All these will combine together and could easily result in toxicity."

Toxicity is a big word. How about illness or death? Add to the above potions your heartworm medication and a monthly dewormer—well, how'd you like *your* body to have to contend with all that?

So what are you supposed to do? Many of you believe there are few alternatives. You don't want a flea or heartworm infestation, and you're afraid of ticks. Your pest control products are easy to use, and they work fast, too. In some instances, they might even be the best choice. You can, however, take steps to increase safety if you do the following:

- Use toxic chemicals only when there is no effective safer alternative.
- Use pesticides only during the pest's "season."
- Use the smallest effective amounts spaced as far apart as can provide protection.
- Prioritize pests. Heartworms are potentially deadly for dogs in mosquito country. Fleas seldom are. High-rise dwellers rarely have tick problems.
- Think garlic. Consider gradually adding garlic to food (up to 2 teaspoons a day for a big dog). Too much garlic can also be toxic, so take care.
- Improve immune system function. Healthy dogs have fewer pests. Author and vet Dr. Steven Blake, who uses no chemicals in his practice, recommends a raw or partially raw diet, bovine colostrum, minimal or no immunization, and natural repellents as needed.
- Outsmart those darn bugs. Keep your dogs indoors at dawn, dusk and night during mosquito season. Clean up poop. Eliminate standing water. Put screens on windows and doors and keep your dog out of pest danger zones like kennels.
- Use natural repellents. Dr. Blake says, "No wolf ever went to a chemical plant for a flea/tick or mosquito repellent." I'm pretty sure he's right. His alternative is essential oils. Dr.

William Kruesi recommends natural botanical insecticides like Neem and citronella as a spray and shampoo to control fleas and ticks; for mosquitoes, black flies, and other flying insects, he uses as "Buzz Away." Go to *dogs4dogs* for links to Doctors Blake and Kruesi's sites and choices.

Hearts and Worms Heartworms are weird little creatures with a bizarre lifestyle and deadly habits, and those are the nicest things I can say about them. A bad infestation can kill us, although it's not the automatic death sentence you've probably been led to believe. In fact, author and vet Dr. Martin Goldstein sees heartworms as less of an epidemic than the "disease-causing toxicity" of heartworm medicine. What it comes down to is picking your poison, and that's a decision you'll need to make for yourself.

How do we get heartworms? It's not that easy. First of all, heartworms are a seasonal problem. According to the University of Pennsylvania's veterinary school website, heartworm larvae need two weeks of day or night weather above 80° F (27° C), and no temperatures below 57° F (14° C), if they're to develop. Ask your vet about your local heartworm season; if you're traveling elsewhere and need a heads-up, click on the maps at *www.citadeltm.com/Heartworm.html* for approximate start and stop dates across the U.S.

Even if the weather is perfect, things have to go just right. A female mosquito has to bite a dog hosting baby heartworms (called microfilariae) and suck them in. If the weather is right, the babies then evolve through several stages inside her; at the third stage (L3), they migrate into her mouth. (An appetizing thought.) If Madame Skeeter bites a Human, the L3s die; if she bites a dog, the L3s celebrate and eventually migrate to the dog's heart where they have their own babies. These worms will die off, probably causing little or no problem, *unless* the dog is bitten by another L3-carrying mosquito. That's when things can go south fast. Learn more about these scary creatures at *www.heartwormsociety.org*.

If you and your dog live where there are no mosquitoes (that is, in heaven), then you don't have to worry about heartworms. Otherwise, they're something you have to carefully consider. Your dog is especially at danger if he's an "outdoor" type living in a hot, humid mosquito-infested swamp, but "indoor" dogs living in penthouses can be infected, too. (To see a scary map of the spread of heartworms in this country, see the link at our site.)

Prevention: The conventional route

There are certainly persuasive reasons to use heartworm "preventatives." If you do take this route, please:

- Make sure your dog gets a blood test (preferably an "antigen" or "occult" test) to be sure he isn't already infected. Giving "preventatives" to an infected dog is dangerous.
- Select a product protecting against heartworms only.
- Check for product safety and watch for side effects.
- Give as few doses as possible. Dr. Don Hamilton, in *Homeopathic Care for Cats and Dogs*, says monthly meds kill larvae injected in the previous six to eight weeks, and "are

effective if given at six-week intervals, and possibly even at seven- or eight-week intervals." Author-vets Dr. Richard Pitcairn and Dr. Allen Schoen told us essentially the same thing. If you opt for this "less is more" treatment, mark dosing dates on your calendar and don't miss them.

- Treat only during your area's "heartworm season." Dr. Hamilton suggests starting, "six weeks after the first mosquitoes appear . . . giving one dose after the end of mosquito season." Over a six-month heartworm season, this saves your dog two or more doses of pesticide. Don't treat year round unless necessary.
- Treat (or don't treat) as appropriate if you travel or move.
- Select the right product. Go to *www.veterinarypartner.com*; click the Health tab, search for Heartworm, and then click Heartworm Preventative Comparison.

Prevention: the natural route

Some holistic vets, like Dr. Blake, use only natural methods to protect against heartworm, especially in areas where mosquitoes are a minor problem. Others use a combination of natural and chemical methods. Talk with your vet and make the decision. Good steps to consider taking include:

- Testing for heartworm antigens twice a year if you're not using chemical treatments.
- Researching information on combating heartworms naturally. Check out sites like *www.holisticanines.org, www.preciouspets.org/heartwormprevention.htm*; and *www.theherbsplace.com/heartworm.html*.
- Doing something about mosquitoes. Go after the source instead of the disease. Research "pets" at *www.mosquitozone.com*. *The Whole Dog Journal* suggests checking out *www.mosquitomagnet.com, www.fightwestnilevirus.com,* and *www.mosquitocontrolsystem.com*.

Flea What can you say about the creature that spread the bubonic
Bag plague? You can say, "No fleas, please!" I'm told that the shortest
poem in the world is entitled "Fleas," and the entire text is: "Adam
had 'em." If Adam did have 'em, he probably had the same opinion
of fleas that dogs have: they are literally a pain in the butt. If your
dog is a-scratchin' to distraction along the back third of her body,
there's a good chance she has fleas. (If she's scratching mostly at her
ears, she might have an allergy, ear mites or sensitive skin.)

Before treating for fleas, check your dog for evidence. Look
especially above her tail for a peppery substance; that's what flea
poop looks like. (It turns red in water from doggy blood—a fun
experiment to try.) If you're looking for further proof, try comb-
ing your dog with a flea comb onto a white towel, or just wear
white socks around the house and see what shows up.

The adult fleas on your dog, which are just the tip of the flea
infestation iceberg, deposit eggs and poop on us dogs, and then
everything topples onto your carpets, sofas and beds providing a
scrumptious buffet as the hungry little larvae hatch. And you
thought fleas were disgusting.

Dogs shouldn't be surprised that most of the fleas found on us
are usually "cat" fleas. That's just another piece of evidence for my
Cat Conspiracy Theory. (If cats didn't control the media, you
would undoubtedly have heard more about this.) The only poetic
justice in all of this is that cats suffer from fleas as well. You
two-legged sorts do, too.

Fleas can live in houses and yards year-round, depending on the
climate (the little beasties prefer temperatures between 65° and 80°
F), but there are certain times of year they're particularly prevalent.
Find your flea season index (provided by a company selling flea
products) at *www.nofleas.com*. To rid fleas from your lives, and ours,
Humans must address the entire problem in a manner that's both
safe and effective. As pirate dogs are wont to say, "Aye, there's the
rub" (not to mention the itching and scratching).

Some dogs don't do well with flea medication treatments.
"Mild" reactions include fatigue and lethargy soon after application. Some dogs have seizures. If your dog has a reaction, wash off

the medication if it's fresh, and call your vet immediately. You might need to cut dosages, change brands or methods, or better yet, go natural. You might even have to rush to the vet, depending on the severity of symptoms.

Nature's way

A weekly bath, and frequent use of a flea comb, can solve many flea problems without having to resort to chemicals—if you'll actually do it. Dr. Pitcairn recommends steeping thinly sliced lemons in hot water overnight, then rinsing or spraying your dog with the lukewarm liquid. Dr. Blake recommends a natural flea and tick collar. See *dogs4dogs* for information.

Only five percent of a flea's life cycle is spent on your dog. It's up to you Humans to figure out where they're hiding the rest of their lives. (Hint: they're everywhere.) Frequent vacuuming of carpets is one of the best ways to end the flea cycle. So is frequent washing of bedding (yours and ours). Dr. Blake also sprays a mist of oil of wintergreen in his home three times a year. Go to *dogs4dogs* for all sorts of flea links that offer holistic approaches and give you some natural products options that purport to offer the same benefits without the chemical drawbacks. Incidentally, don't try magic. It doesn't work.

Maybe your flea problem is starting in your yard. Those little suckers are good at ambushing us dogs. To treat the outdoors, try beneficial nematodes, small wormlike creatures that go nuts for flea eggs and larvae. Or try diatomaceous earth from garden centers (but not from pool supply stores).

Chemical warfare

Flea treatments, which are hard on fleas, can also be hard on dogs. Some of the flea medications seem to have a "take no prisoners" philosophy. We can only hope it stops at the flea and doesn't extend to the unwitting host, although warning labels aren't exactly reassuring. Since puppyhood, I've been hypersensitive to topical flea meds, and we've been afraid to use any chemicals on Jiggy (because of his bad liver), so we don't use any. And guess what? We don't have fleas. Who says clean living doesn't have its benefits?

Check out the various chemical flea-control products at *www.veterinarypartner.com*. Chemical flea shampoos, dips, and powders, can be harsh and should be avoided. Most collars, except herbal ones, have dangers, although some clever Humans put them in vacuum cleaner bags to kill fleas as they vacuum. In our research, Advantage® and Frontline® are the two chemical products holistic vets like most (or perhaps more accurately, dislike least). These products work quickly and, with minor infestations, can be used only as needed.

Older products, especially those containing organophosphates or carbamates, can be hazardous to our health, and the health of our Humans. They're sometimes sold cheap and it's easy to guess why. Follow our links at *dogs4dogs* and read more about these insecticides, *especially* if you have young children. You should also be aware that toxic chemicals masquerade under many names. Hey, if Humans could call the most advanced intercontinental missile of its time "The Peacemaker," you know they must have creative names for scary chemicals.

Ticking Ticks carry a host of deadly baggage, including Lyme disease,
Bombs babesiosis and ehrlichiosis. If you live in a tick-infested area, you'd better check your dog head to toe whenever he returns from The Great Outdoors—which could be really fun if your St. Bernard makes daily visits to his lady love on the far side of the woods.

Where Lyme disease is a problem, know that the vaccine for this illness is, to say the least, controversial; the American Animal Hospital Association suggests using it only if Lyme disease is a proven problem in your area. Other vets say don't use it at all. Read more about this from Lyme-country vet Allen Schoen at *www.drschoen.com;* click Articles. By the way, some *Humans* vaccinate their dogs thinking it will somehow protect Humans from Lyme disease. It won't.

Dr. Bob Rogers writes: "a Preventick collar, unlike most other collars, paralyzes the tick's mouth parts preventing transmission of disease." He adds that these collars contain amitraz and "should be used with extreme caution, as they are toxic if chewed on or swallowed by a dog or children." It may seem weird that I mention a "toxic" product, but in some areas ticks are a terrible problem and some believe that a removable collar is safer, and more effective, than the vaccine. Read about "Amitraz toxicity" at *www.petplace.com* if you're considering it.

Worms How'd you like to take a toxic substance every month to kill a parasite you don't have now and may never have had? Me neither. We say, if it ain't broke, why fix it?

If you see your dog scooting her bottom across the floor, or if she has persistent diarrhea, have her checked for worms. If you see something that looks like angry spaghetti in your pup's poop or vomit, think roundworm. If you see "rice," think tapeworm. There are other worms you can't see without a microscope (and trust me, you wouldn't want to), which is why you should pop fresh poop into a bag for your puppy's first vet visit and her yearly check-ups thereafter.

Puppies get worms from their moms, thank you very much. Dr. Don Hamilton says a mild infestation of worms may be Nature's way of teaching our immune systems how to fight. Apparently it works, because a CDC study says that most healthy puppies clear worms on their own.

A *bad* case of roundworms, however, can cause diarrhea and vomiting, and sometimes weight loss and a pot belly, and in very severe cases, even death. A vet can determine the degree of infestation. Stool tests aren't foolproof, but if they show a heavy infestation most vets would suggest a chemical wormer to fix the problem. After that, go to work to make your dog's immune system stronger, starting with a better diet.

Tapeworms, contracted by eating fleas or infested animals, look like flat white rice hanging around our poop hole or on feces. Whipworms, says Dr. Pitcairn, often lie dormant causing no symptoms, but can cause watery diarrhea in unhealthy dogs. Blood-sucking hookworms, which hang out especially in the southern U.S. (why couldn't they just eat grits like any other self-respecting southerner?) are contracted through the skin or licked off paws from poop-contaminated soil or sand; they can cause bloody stools and even anemia. While not bothering grown-up dogs much, they can be deadly to puppies. Watch out for them in crowded kennel play areas and dog parks.

Giardia, a common protozoan parasite, comes from contaminated water or feces and causes diarrhea. The American Animal Hospital Association recommends against vaccinating for this parasite. See your vet or consider the product at *www.hannasherbshop.com*.

Dr. Blake says his patients have had good luck with an herbal wormer called Parastat (800-370-3447). Other holistic vets recommend chemical wormers—the least toxic available—for bad infestations. See what your vet thinks.

Our consultants like wormers you ingest, rather than those you inject, to send meds straight to the problem. Never buy cheap wormers in pet stores or on-line unless you're sure they don't contain organophosphates (second warning to watch out for the camouflaged chemicals that can be harmful to both dogs and Humans). Buy the right kind of wormer for your dog's kind of worm, and don't combine wormers (including heartworm meds) without consulting your vet.

After deworming, improve your dog's health with natural remedies to prevent persistent problems. Give your dog digestive enzymes and probiotics and make sure your dog's diet is fresh and nutritious. Dr. Hamilton's homeopathic care book is a great place to study holistic methods, as is Martin Zucker's *The Veterinarians' Guide to Natural Remedies for Dogs* and *Dr. Pitcairn's New Complete Guide to Natural Care for Dogs and Cats.*

If you Humans out there have been complacently reading all this information about worms with the mistaken notion that "it's only a dog problem," wake up and smell the poop. Most worms can be contracted by Humans through feces or poop-contaminated soil. If that doesn't prompt a poop patrol, I don't know what will. (After the patrol, don't forget to wash off shoe bottoms and your hands.)

Reporting Reactions We dogs understand that sometimes you have to fight fire with fire, but please be careful with the poisons you give us. For product alerts and recalls, go to *www.epa.gov/pesticides/alerts.htm.* And please, if your dog has a bad reaction, report it to the manufacturer as well as the Environmental Protection Agency (800-858-PEST). To report other drugs, go to *www.dogsadversereactions.com/fdareporting.html.*

We don't want anything *pestilential* out there on the marketplace. (I know Nietzsche said, "What doesn't destroy me makes me stronger," but it's the *destroy me* part I worry about.)

Speaking pestilentially, here's your treat.

Chiclet's Trivia Treat: *Fleas can complete their entire life cycle in a few weeks or can drag it out for a few years. The five stages of life are egg, larva, pupa, adult, and whoa-mamma-does-that-itch! What causes the itchy fifth stage? Flea spit.*

SCARED POOPLESS

Flea saliva softens dog skin to make feasting easier. The bad news is that flea spit can be very irritating and highly allergenic. It's what causes all the itching and scratching that makes you rush out to buy flea meds.

Flea Allergy Dermatitis, a problem of highly spit-allergic dogs, is the latest doggy FAD. Flea . . . Allergy . . . Dermatitis. FAD? Get it? Do I have to spell out everything for your species?

Death by Teeth

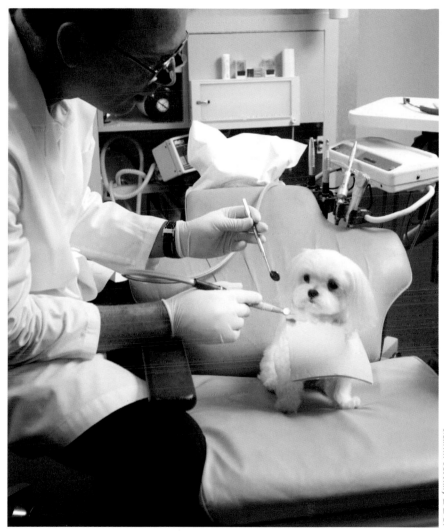

Martin Abelar, DDS.

One of my favorite bedtime stories is Mom's version of *Little Red Riding Hood*. It differs slightly from the story most of you have heard. It does feature a little Human with the unfortunate name of Little Red Riding Hood, and she is visiting her Grandma in the woods. The villain is the same as well, although Mom usually introduces the Wolf by referring to him as "that hairy drag queen who wears old women's clothes." (Yes, Mom is weird, even for a two-legger.) The dialogue is much the same: "What big eyes you have," says Little Red Riding Hood, to which the Wolf offers his immortal reply, "The better to see you with, my dear." Where Mom's story deviates from the original is that in lieu of saying, "What big teeth you have," Little Red Riding Hood says, "My, what awful looking teeth you have. That yellow-brown color tells me that you're probably already suffering from dental disease."

That really throws the Wolf who was ready to pronounce, "The better to eat you with." Instead, all the Wolf can manage is, "What?"

All the while this dental savvy Little Red Riding Hood has been looking at the Wolf's teeth, sadly shaking her head, and making "tsk, tsk" sounds. "It's apparent," she said, "that you have serious periodontal problems. Your gums look inflamed. Have your teeth been aching?"

The chagrined Wolf nodded.

"Open wide," commanded the bossy little girl, and the Wolf complied. "Just as I suspected," said Little Red Riding Hood, "You have an abscessed tooth, and I don't like the look of that mass. It might be an oral cancer."

"Cancer?" asked the scared wolf.

"If you don't have it removed," said the opinionated (but in this case correct) little girl, "it could become life threatening. When was the last time you had your teeth professionally examined and cleaned?"

"Why, never," answered the Wolf.

"No wonder your pack booted you out," said Little Red Riding Hood. "All wolves and dogs should have a complete dental exam at least once a year."

"But . . . but . . . no one ever told me that," stammered the Wolf.

"With breath like yours," said Little Red Riding Hood, "the other wolves were probably reluctant to come near you. Now, get out of my grandma's clothes. You know she hates your wearing them. And go make an appointment to see a Board Certified Specialist in Veterinary Dentistry."

The Wolf reluctantly removed the Laura Ashley print dress (returning it to the indignant grandmother who had just awakened from a nap on the sofa), and left to log on to *www.AVDC.org* to find a veterinary dentist. With oral cancer a possibility, he knew he needed a specialist.

At this point Mom always concludes the fable with, "Although the tumor was benign, the Wolf needed a lot of work on his teeth, but the kind veterinary dentist managed to heal his choppers in no time. The dentist also convinced the Wolf to brush daily and to eat a more balanced diet with lots of fresh food and plenty of variety (but no more little children). Then they all lived happily ever after. The End."

Know what Mom does after the storytelling? She brushes Jiggy's and my teeth. It's routine for us now, so we don't mind. There was a time, though, when brushing our teeth was like, well, *pulling* teeth. That was before our vet convinced Mom to brush Jiggy's teeth daily for three months to see if it would help his sick liver. (Boy, was she looking forward to that!) But when his blood test came back looking much better than normal, Mom kept brushing his teeth, and mine, too.

Our friend, Dr. Brook Niemiec, a Board Certified Specialist in Veterinary Dentistry and a Fellow in the Academy of Veterinary Dentistry, wasn't at all surprised that Jiggy's health improved with daily brushing. He says it happens all the time. You see, the bacteria that cause periodontal disease don't know they're supposed to stop at the gum line. Instead, they hop right into the bloodstream. Although the kidneys and liver help filter the bacteria, they sometimes do so at the cost of micro-abscesses and decreased organ function. Bacteria can also attack our hearts, lungs and brains, and when our bodies are constantly fighting infection we can end up with a chronic disease like Jiggy's hepatitis. Dr. Niemiec says most Humans don't realize that dental care is one of the most important things you can do to maintain or improve your dog's health. He also says you have to start early. He's never seen a dog over the age of two without some dental disease. Not even one. Jiggy's teeth were pitiful at 11 months. (If your dog has bad teeth, go get some blood tests. Maybe something systemic is going on.)

Evaluating Your Dog Big dogs with big teeth (and big spaces between them) generally have fewer dental problems than little dogs with squeezed-together teeth. In our experience, dogs eating healthful diets, especially those on BARF diets (you did read my food chapter, didn't you?) are much more likely to have healthy teeth and gums than those eating the same ol' highly processed food day after day. Does that tell you anything about the first step in improved dental health? It's DIET, people! DIET! Nothing changed our teeth and gums as much as good food did. We can't promise you the same results, but it's worth a try for just for your dog's good health.

Mom asked friends from her on-line nutrition group about their experience with raw food, bones and teeth. Nola, who has seven dogs, said: "Their teeth are very white and there's no build up of any kind . . . never has been. There's no bad breath, either." Mary noticed some improvement in her dogs' teeth after feeding raw food along with marrow bones and beef ribs; she noticed a huge change when she added neck bones (lamb, veal, chicken, turkey). Pauline said, "Our older Beagle mix came to us with hor-rid breath and tartar near the gum line. We started the BARF diet six months ago and already she has sweet breath and no tartar on her teeth." Mom has dozens of stories like this but The Gator (our editor) said "enough!" He can be *so* rude.

Detecting Problems What if your dog's teeth look like the Wolf's teeth, caked with tarter and plaque, with gums red and inflamed? Here's a newsflash, people: our teeth throb and ache just as yours do. Maybe this is why your dog's been so cranky lately. Or why he's suddenly refusing crunchy food. Or won't play fetch. Short of pawing at our mouth or refusing to eat, we have few ways to alerting you to the sorry state of our teeth and gums.

However . . . if you'll just pay attention, you Humans can detect lots of our dental problems. If your dog's kisses smell of dead fish, or the gum over even one tooth is red, inflamed or bleeding, or her teeth are yellow-brown rather than snowy white, your dog is already suffering from dental disease, is very likely in pain, and needs you to take action now.

You can help us fight oral cancer, too. The American Veterinary Medical Association says that oral cancers are common in dogs and encourages Humans to watch for "a mass on the gums, bleeding, odor, or difficulty eating." Their website also adds, "Since many swellings are malignant, early, aggressive treatment is essential." However . . . UC Davis Vet School warns that cancers may look like "non-healing, ulcerated sores instead of the 'typical' prominent masses." Dr. Niemiec says he has saved countless dogs' lives by finding and removing tiny oral cancers before they became life threatening. If you pay attention, maybe you can find one in time, too.

Although all dogs are susceptible to dental problems, little guys like Jigs and I have to be especially vigilant. (I know I mentioned this before, but I'm the author. I can do what I want.) When Humans breed us down to tiny sizes, we still have to pack 42 teeth—which can only be so small—into a downsized jaw. Our teeth end up looking like toothpicks packed in a box. Unfortunately, this overcrowding causes cleaning problems that inevitably lead to gum disease. Another problem of pint-sized dogs is that baby teeth sometimes don't fall out, causing grown-up teeth to come in at weird angles; Dr. Niemiec says this condition (called retained deciduous teeth) needs to be treated immediately. It will not cure itself and will lead to serious gum disease.

Dr. Niemiec also warned that the inside of the upper canines (the vampire teeth) can be prone to bad dental disease that can cause a dangerous infection in our nasal cavity called an oral/nasal fistula. Our friend, Buster, had a fistula that caused him to lose his right eye. Be especially wary of all these problems if you have a

Dachshund, Yorkie, Poodle, Schnauzer, or a Maltese (who are otherwise perfect). Dogs with pushed-in faces, like Pugs and Bulldogs, may also have bite problems that need extra care. If you want to take a bite out of doggy dental care problems, see Dr. Niemiec's website *www.dogbeachdentistry.com*. (He really is a peach of a guy. Because he sees so much canine suffering resulting from poor dental care, the good doctor currently provides free training for Southern California vets and their staff!)

Fixing Problems Not many years ago, Humans laughed at the thought of dental care for dogs. Some of them still do. Why suffering and disease seems funny, I don't know. (Glad I got that off my chest.)

The first step towards healthier teeth and gums, assuming you've already made any necessary upgrades in your dog's diet, is a dental check-up, and if necessary, a good professional cleaning. But here's the thing. Before you plunk down good money for a teeth cleaning, find out exactly how cleaning is handled in your veterinarian's office. Bogey, a Cocker Spaniel we know, was handed to a vet who passed him to off to an assistant with a tooth scaler and an automatic toothbrush. For this she paid $250! And Bogey experienced a lot of pain. Most vets would never do this, but you need to be careful.

We dogs need to see a vet with experience in doggy dentistry. This may or may not be your everyday vet. Did you know that dentistry, the hands-on instructive kind, is taught at only about half the vet schools? And that just 15 years ago, it wasn't taught at all?

Good doggy dental cleaning (called prophylaxis, which means prevention of disease) is more than just scraping teeth. The process entails:

- Cleaning visible surfaces. This is mostly cosmetic.
- Under-gum scaling of the outside and inside of the teeth. *This is the most important step and vets say it must be done under anesthesia.* Instruments are sharp; ultrasonic scaling

equipment is wet and noisy. Humans will sit still through this because it's good for them. We won't. To us, it's scary and it hurts, and what hurts, might kill us.

- Polishing. Scaling abrades the tooth surface. Polishing smoothes it and helps keep plaque from sticking, which increases the time between visits.
- Lavage (flushing debris out of the crevices).
- Detection and treatment. This requires using a probe and maybe x-rays. If necessary, extractions are performed and growths are removed.
- Charting. You can't tell the players without a program and you can't tell the progression or regression of your dog's teeth without charting.

I can just hear you saying "yeah, but . . ." It's the anesthesia thing holding you back, right? It can be dangerous, and adds a lot to the cost? It's a dilemma for us, too. So what's a dog to do? Get a thorough cleaning under anesthesia? Or go the anesthesia-free cleaning service route? Let's examine both sides of this controversy.

The Vet Route When was the last time you had a "deep cleaning" by a dental hygienist? It wasn't fun, was it? You submitted (reluctantly) because you knew it was good for you. Unfortunately, most of us dogs don't have dental hygiene adequately explained, and don't understand the benefit of having strangers poking around in our mouths. In fact, the mere idea of a sharp, scaly thing being thrust sword-like around our mouths scares most dogs poopless, and you know how scared that is! Even holistic vet and author Richard Pitcairn, someone you might think would favor anesthesia-free cleaning services, believes you can't satisfactorily clean the teeth of a dog who's awake.

If you're considering using one of those doggy teeth cleaning services that seem to be popping up everywhere, including at grooming establishments and even pet stores, please be careful. Put yourself in our place. Would you trust your teeth to someone who was unlicensed, and whose business was not only unregulated but, according to the American Veterinary Medical Association, illegal (at least in the United States and Canada)? Cleaning without a vet on premises is considered practicing medicine without a license. Many vets think such services are "irresponsible and dangerous." One even called it, "Animal cruelty, plain and simple."

On the other paw, more and more vets are offering this service in their offices. (Humans are so confusing.) I guess some vets want

to control the quality of the process. Others figure that if you can't beat them, you might as well join them. Still others see the profit potential.

Unfortunately, superficial cleaning of a diseased mouth, according to Dr. Niemiec, is like painting over rust. He said he sees clients all the time with teeth sparkling white from cleanings by these services, but with gums diseased and teeth broken or cracked.

That said, the veterinary route is often imperfect, too. To see if your vet is the right person for the job, you have to ask:

- Is there an anesthesia specialist? Will they be placing a catheter and administering IV fluids? Hint: these questions should be answered yes. (Read my ANESTHESIA ANXIETY for the information you need.)
- Who'll actually perform the procedure? Don't presume your vet will. It's more likely a tech will do it. Find out how much training and experience the tech has.
- What's the antibiotic policy? When teeth are cleaned, bacteria are released and aerosolized into the bloodstream. Dr. Niemiec suggests I.V. antibiotics at the start of surgery. If there's significant disease, or extensive work is done, he may want to continue meds at home.
- Does your vet have the capability to take dental x-rays? Your dog can have a broken tooth root your vet can't see. It can be very painful and packed full of dangerous bacteria. This is particularly common in dogs who chew on hard bones or hooves, and dogs that fight. (Dental x-rays are more detailed, offer a smaller dose of radiation, and are less expensive than standard x-rays.)
- If your vet's price seems out of line (high or low), ask why. You've called around, haven't you, to find out the going rate?
- Ask to see their dental charts. If they don't do charting, how can they detect changes or rate the effectiveness of home care?

You should also make sure your dog has a blood test *no earlier than a month before cleaning*. Some vets offer to skip it, but we wouldn't. You don't want to give anesthesia to a dog with a hidden illness.

Mom says she likes to kill two birds with one stone. I used to think she just didn't like birds, but then I realized that she means that as long as we're getting our teeth cleaned we might as well have our annual blood tests done, too.

Anesthesia-Free Cleaning Services You probably want to know what I, as a consumer activist dog, think of anesthesia-free dental cleaners. Well, first of all, these people need a catchier name. Second, some of these service providers are *much* better than others; they range from former dental hygienists certified to work on Humans, to people with only a weekend's worth of training. (To clean Human teeth, you need at least two years of training and a certification exam.) Have a preference for which group you'd want working on your teeth? The big thing to remember is that there's no certification and no regulation in this business. The establishment providing this service may be doing it for the love of dogs, or the love of money. Go where you trust the proprietors. Remember: you are the inspector—the only inspector.

Before you put your dog's mouth (and body) in their hands, make sure they screen for health problems, especially heart disease. Bacteria released during cleaning could cause deadly endocarditis in susceptible dogs unless they're on antibiotics. Kathy (owner of Houndstooth, a cleaning service using former dental hygienists) insists that you watch her inspect your dog's mouth before she begins so she can tell you what she sees. Maybe your dog needs a good cleaning under anesthesia first and shouldn't return to her for a few months.

Most teeth cleaners don't want you to observe, saying your dog will be too difficult to manage if he sees his Mom nearby. Kathy disagrees. She tells new clients: "Don't leave me alone with your dog. You don't know me. Don't assume that I'm safe. Don't trust me because you like me. I haven't yet earned your trust." She says that if the cleaner is experienced and talented, she should be able to handle your dog even with you there.

Before cleaning starts, ask for proof of liability insurance (for injury the cleaner causes and injury your dog causes). Dogs have been seriously injured, even died, having their teeth cleaned both by vets and others. With the latter, it's mostly because of the way they were secured. Some establishments use bite bars, restraints, and mummy wraps; dogs are hurt struggling to get free. (Can you blame them?) Conversely, some establishments relax your dog using a variety of products from flower essences to natural calming products. Kathy uses none, saying it's all about attitude.

Kathy does several things we like that we haven't seen elsewhere: she uses magnifying glasses and a forehead-mounted light that makes healthy teeth look blue and tartar look yellow. (Ever had your own teeth cleaned in a dark back room?) She also modified her instruments to make them safer when dogs wiggle. After cleaning, she gives clients a full report and invites you to have your vet check your dog's teeth after she cleans them. If she missed something, she'll fix it for free. We think you should expect no less.

Home Care No matter how good the professional teeth cleaning, that relentless enemy plaque begins to form just 24 hours later. No, doggy dentures are not the answer. If you Humans help us, we can stave off bacterial growth. Brushing our teeth daily, or at least three times a week, gives us the best shot at good health. But even if you just brush once a week, you reduce our toothy plaque by 75%! That's not incentive enough? All right, we'll throw in a few fresh-as-spring kisses after every brushing. How's that?

Mom has even managed to make brushing a bonding experience. At first I hated it, but she cajoled me into it with rubs, scratches, and food bribes, so now I've grown to like it. Mom might have had an easier task with Jigs and me if she'd started brushing our teeth when we were pups, but she didn't know she was supposed to, so we were adults when she started brushing. Through trial and error Mom found the best ways to deal with our teeth. In order to spare other dogs from having to be dental guinea pigs, she has a few suggestions. Okay, more than a few. You know Mom.

The first thing you need to do is assume that leadership role. Be calm, but firm. Bribes always help so dip your finger into something your dog loves: applesauce, banana baby food or some yummy enzymatic doggy toothpaste. Offer up that finger and then start massaging our gums. As your dog relaxes, which could be immediately or weeks later (just kidding—sort of), wrap gauze around your finger, dip it in toothpaste, and have at it. Go very slowly, don't fight, and always be gentle. And stay relaxed. If you get tense or frustrated, we'll get tense and frustrated.

When your dog's ready, advance to a super-soft child's toothbrush or one of C.E.T.'s duel-end brushes (the small end works for me). There are plenty of products on the market, including a nifty little brush that slips on like a ring, and brushes that purport to brush three sides of your dog's teeth at once. Go to our site for links you can get your teeth into (or at least your dog's). Mom cut down the bristles of a child's toothbrush (so the bristles didn't splay) and it worked great. Just make sure the bristles feel soft. And, just like Humans do, clean brushes after every use and replace frayed brushes.

One reason I've come to be a tooth brushing enthusiast is that Mom found some nifty toothpaste: C.E.T. poultry flavor. (Who wouldn't like chicken-flavored toothpaste?) All she has to do is take off the cap and I'm there ready to lick it from the tube. Whatever you do, don't substitute people paste; it's meant to be spit, not swallowed, and might give us a tummy ache. Besides, we need a paste containing enzymes to make up for, uh, imperfect brushing.

Some people say that if your dog sees toothpaste as food, she might fight brushing. They suggest using aloe gel on your brush, or dipping it in a mixture of one part hydrogen peroxide to three parts distilled or filtered water. Or squirt on the peroxide mixture if you like, and then brush. That doesn't sound like much fun to me, but if your dog's a fighter, I suppose it's worth a try.

Believe it or not, Jiggy and I line up for the brushing. Mom takes care of our teeth right after dinner and rewards us with a broccoli treat. (Bribes are great.) You can even do it before dinner, signaling to your dog that food is about to come. Humans need to brush after eating to prevent cavities, but cavities aren't much of a problem for us.

If despite your best efforts your dog wiggles too much, try loosely swaddling her in a towel or blanket as you would a Human infant. Then she can't use her legs as crow bars. Just don't bind her up like a mummy. That's dangerous! If love, bribes, and swaddling still aren't enough, try one of the dental wipes available at pet stores instead of a toothbrush. If that works, go back and try brushing in a few weeks. And make sure your brush's bristles are really soft. Also consider that your dog's gums may be sore; maybe he needs professional attention prior to you starting in on the personal touch.

Begin brushing, a few teeth at a time, then work up to the whole mouth, not forgetting those two teeth tucked behind the big rear molars. (Bet you didn't even know they were there.) Our dentist says not be too discouraged if you can only brush the outside of the teeth; unless you have a small dog, that's where the biggest problems are.

To more easily do the inspecting and brushing, Mom sits Indian fashion and cradles me in her lap and then slips her index finger into my mouth to keep it open while inspecting my teeth and the roof of my mouth. Mom never used to do this until one day she found she'd been brushing an abscess in Jiggy's mouth. Ouch! It had been hurting him like crazy, and he'd wiggled a lot, but not wanting to disobey Mom he just endured the pain. Boy, Mom sure felt guilty. Jiggy even extorted a few extra treats out of her.

The moral to all of this is if your dog isn't easily submitting to brushing, look for a source of pain. Mom's niece, Stacey, found a sliver of wood imbedded lodged in her stick-fetching Lab's mouth. Dogs don't have hands. We need your help. So when it comes to our dental care don't give us the *brush-off.* (If I promise not to make any more bad puns will you promise to take care of your dog's teeth?)

Other Options If you can't or won't brush, Dr. Niemiec recommends squeezing on a gel or liquid containing 0.12% chlorhexidine gluconate. Your vet can get one from C.E.T., which also makes an Oral Hygiene Rinse for use with or without brushing. There are also doggy dental cleansers, as well a new product line called OraVet which applied once a week makes a waxy barrier so plaque can't stick. How cool is that?

There are lots of chews on the market that purport to reduce plaque and calculus, but we'd want to see proof before shelling out good money. Many artificial bones or pig hooves are way too hard for us to safely chew. We say: never let your dog chew on anything harder than a tooth's surface.

If your dog chews bones (other than raw chicken or turkey necks), check frequently for broken and cracked teeth. By the way, a broken tooth with exposed pulp (the pink inner tissue) is really painful and will abscess sooner or later. Your vet may give you the option to wait until it does, but don't. It hurts now and you are absolutely going to have to fix it one of these days. In the meantime, we'll be suffering.

Doggy Breath Some Humans try to mask the problem of their dog's bad breath with breath fresheners. We ask you not to cover-up halitosis but to investigate instead. Remember Mom's Story about the Wolf? Gingivitis can cause bad breath, and brushing and professional cleaning are the first step in taking care of the problem. If halitosis continues, consider improving your dog's diet. Especially, switch from corn-based dry food. Once we tossed out the commercial food our bad breath disappeared (and Jiggy and I no longer faced the indignity of some Human scrunching up her nose and saying, "Ooooh, doggy breath").

Hollywood Smiles Just about everything dentists do for Humans, veterinary dentists can do for your dog. Services include capped teeth, orthodontia, root canals, crowns, and repairs of broken teeth. Oh, lucky us.

Pulling Teeth In the case of us dogs, diseased gums may be worse than no teeth at all. If our teeth get really bad and you can't afford to fix them, and you've tried brushing and a raw diet and nothing has worked, most vets would advise you that the best thing is to just let them go. This does not mean letting them rot out. Nothing could be crueler or more damaging to our bodies. Teeth must be professionally extracted using antibiotics, anesthesia and pain killers.

Oh, and if you save that tooth, and put it under your dog's pillow, maybe the tooth fairy will bring your dog a treat. It always works that way at our house!

You can have *your* treat now if you promise to brush after reading it.

Chiclet's Trivia Treat: *If you look inside our mouths, you'll find our incisors in front: six above, six below. We use them for nibbling and grooming. Next to these are our canines, which are great for grabbing, puncturing and scaring mean people. Behind the canines are the premolars: four above, four below. We use premolars to rip meat from bones and to have our way with chew toys.*

Behind the premolars are the molars, two above, three below. These are our crushing teeth and are great for crunching green beans and snow peas. We have two molars above and three below. Most people think the large molar below is the last tooth, not realizing there are two molars behind it. Because they're hard to see, let alone brush, these "hidden" molars are often besieged by periodontal disease.

All my research has left me with one question: why do wolves and Humans and dogs have canine *teeth when only horses have* wolf *teeth? What's up with that?*

WHY WE WON'T
HAVE SEX

Okay, birds do it, bees do it, and supposedly educated fleas do it. (I will state my bias right now: there is no such thing as an educated flea.) Anyway, the facts of life according to my Mom (who is otherwise fun) is that dogs *shouldn't* do it. What?!?

This point first came up on the occasion of my six-month birthday. That's when I first heard the S-word (*spay*). Some friends had been invited over to the house for a party and I, as usual, was perched on her lap (also known as my throne) so that I could more easily accept the admiration and praise of all the Humans in the room.

Suddenly, Mom announced, "Next week, I'm taking Chiclet in to have her spayed." Since she kind of whispered the spay word, I knew something important was afoot.

"Why on earth would you do that?" asked a guest cradling a third glass of wine in her own lap. "Chiclet's such a beautiful dog. She just *has* to have puppies. Everyone will want one." (Clearly, wine hadn't impaired her senses.)

Didn't I swell up with pride? *Moi* as matriarch to generations of little me's? Then Mom explained that pups weren't in the best interests of either me or the planet. Mom's friend made one of those suburban faces (the kind usually presented to Human backs), then said to me, "I don't know about you, Chiclet, but I think your Mom sounds suspiciously like Cruella De Vil."

Cruella De Vil? Mom? All dogs know that name from the famous horror flick, *101 Dalmations*. Mom *does* have this weird black and white hair—just like Cruella. While I sat there wondering just whose lap I might be perched upon, the Humans laughed. Neither Jiggy nor I got the joke. What was funny about Cruella De Vil, the would-be serial killer of puppies who wanted to make a coat out of Dalmatian hair?

Was Mom a puppy hater, too? Or could there be other reasons, hard as it was to believe, to deprive the world of little Chiclets and Jiggys? The Disney movie version of doggy motherhood seemed so fun, but then, Disney executives worship a mouse. Their view of life could differ from mine.

Mom (who still hasn't satisfactorily explained her black and white hair) said that instead of thinking about the fun of having 101 puppies, I should consider the 101 reasons NOT to have puppies. Turns out, Mom knew better than I did. (I hate it when that happens.) Here are her reasons:

1. Every year three to four million dogs and cats are euthanized in shelters—an average of one every nine seconds—and that's only in the United States. People who think their own dog's adorable pups will find homes have completely missed the point. When an *infinite* supply of dogs meets a *finite* supply of loving homes, something's gotta happen to the leftovers. Humans seem to like disposable diapers and disposable razors, but why do they put up with disposable dogs?

2. Spaying makes us healthier. When they took out my female equipment (which I wish I'd thought to auction on Ebay), I was no longer at risk for ovarian and uterine cancers. It's a myth that dogs are healthier if allowed to have one season or heat. (The real term is estrous cycles, but Humans are big into euphemisms.) Spaying before puberty reduces the chances of getting breast cancer to almost nothing. Bet you didn't know mammary tumors are the most common

tumors in girl dogs and that almost half are malignant. I sure didn't (but then again, prior to writing this book, the total sum of my sex education came from that Dalmatian movie).

3. Spaying a dog at any age prevents pyometra, a horrible condition where our uterus fills with pus. Shall I explain further? I thought not.

4. Three little letters that might convince you if the "pus" word didn't. I'm talking P-M-S. Think your dog doesn't get it? Think again. I doubt the Human females in your life chew up sofas, scratch doors, and howl when they gets PMS. They do? Whoops! Well, so do dogs.

5. Two more words of importance: Unplanned pregnancy. My friend Matilda was a "mistake." Her mom, Gwendolyn, an aristocratic Golden Retriever, was supposed to make pup-

pies with Tad, the handsome purebred Golden she'd had a crush on for years. That was before Nature intruded in the form of Gus, an Australian Shepherd. Answering the call of the wild, Gus vaulted an eight foot fence and pushed through a window. Poof! went the family's plans to finance a vacation by selling purebred puppies. They had to beg people to take the little darlings. Even Fort Knox isn't secure from male dogs on the track of a hot-to- trot female dog.

6. "Intact" males help you get sued. Don't neuter your male dog, and be irresponsible enough to let him roam, and get a

quick course in responsibility when your dog knocks up the neighbor's poodle. People have sued and won for vet bills, loss of potential puppy sales income, and damage done to their homes (breaking and entering).

7. "Intact" males are three times more likely to bite than neutered dogs. If your dog puts the bite on someone, you're the one who's going to get bitten hardest. Think a pit bull has big teeth? They're nothing compared to a plaintiff's lawyer's.

8. It's a myth that sterilization is expensive. As my southern friends say, that dog just won't hunt. The real expense comes if you *don't* spay or neuter. If money is holding you back, find links to low-price options at *dogs4dogs*.

9. Oops, she did it again. If your dog does get pregnant and has unwanted pups, know that some amazing organizations will take in those pups as well as sterilize the canine parents at little or no cost. Be responsible and stop this cycle! Ask the folks at your local humane society if there's a place like this in your area.

10. Cute puppies don't always find homes. What part of millions of dogs dying every year in shelters didn't you understand? There are too many unwanted puppies and dogs. You can't see me, but I'm growling. I'm showing teeth.

11. Puppybirth is no way to show kids the miracle of life. Unfortunately, miracles seldom materialize on cue. Puppies pop out in the middle of the night. Deliveries have "complications." Pups are stillborn or die shortly after birth. Sometimes, you see agony and blood. Sometimes momma dogs die. You know how Bambi starts out all nice? Things change. Your "miracle of life" could end up more gruesome than *The Texas Chainsaw Massacre*. And your lucky kids get

to watch! Click on the Miracle of Birth link on my website for the most incredible thing you'll ever read in your entire life (not counting this book).

12. Puppies aren't profitable. If profiting from breeding is your business plan, you might as well file for Chapter XI right now. Do the words *emergency Caesarian section* mean anything to you? (Does $1,500? That's the minimum cost.) What about blood transfusions and I.V. lines? How about puppy "intensive care?" Your "profit" can end up costing you thousands of dollars.

13. Neutered males don't care that they've been neutered. Here's a newsflash for the men out there: few dogs are Hugh

Hefner wannabes, nor do they miss their randy days when breeding ceases to be a possibility. No male dog I've ever met had a name for his privates. Hormones, not fantasies, make dogs breed. Don't anthropomorphe.

14. Male dogs without testes are healthier. Neutered dogs have no testicular cancer, increased protection from prostate cancer, lessened aggression and little or no desire to roam. Neutered dogs also miss the fun of sexual frustration. Think about his exercising that frustration on your boss's wife's leg. Cut off that testosterone supply and his sexual problems go away (although he may still yearn for your boss's wife's leg unless you neutered him soon enough).

15. Your dog can get a sexually transmitted disease. You probably think Humans have cornered the STD market. Nope. Better have a talk with your dog about canine sexually transmitted disease. Sexually active dogs need to watch out for brucellosis, canine herpesvirus (CHV), and canine transmissible venereal tumors (CTVT), among others. It's a jungle out there.

16. No more "marking" territories. Jiggy, who was neutered at six months, never "marked his territory." That saved Mom lots of cleaning up. Like many males who are neutered young, Jiggy "squats" (yes, like a girl) instead of lifting his leg to pee. Isn't it nice when males don't feel the need to prove themselves with macho leg lifting? And, because Jiggy doesn't go around marking his territory every six inches, he's much more amenable to peeing on command in a designated spot.

17. Maybe not 101 puppies, but how about 24? Tia the Mastiff recently gave birth to 24 puppies. Four died. (There's that fun miracle of life thing again.) *The Guinness Book of World Records* lists three other "lucky" dogs who've had 23 puppies each. This is littering in the fullest sense of the word. And think of the joy of disposing of the pups who don't make it. And finding homes for all the pups who do. And getting your vet's bill into record books.

18. But you want a dog just like Max. If you're breeding to duplicate your dog, forget it. Heredity's a crap shoot. Just take a look at those weird siblings of yours. And your parents. And have you forgotten your strange Uncle Jack?

19. It's a myth that sterilization makes dogs fat. Too little exercise and too much food make dogs fat. These are things controlled by you, not your dog's hormones.

20. Spaying and neutering shows community spirit. Rounding up, housing and destroying stray dogs cost your community mucho bucks. In California alone, these costs top $50 million yearly. If Humans were more responsible, maybe that money could be spent on, say, schools? Or law enforcement? Or dog parks?

21. Save money by sterilizing your animal. Many localities try to encourage sterilization by reducing license fees for sterilized dogs. Now that's enlightened governing!

22. Male dogs have no innate right to be studs. Do you have a Dog Juan or a dog? The American Kennel Club says, "The only responsible reason to make puppies is to improve the breed." Truly responsible breeders (none of whom turn out

pup after pup for profit) know genetics and their dogs' bloodlines and work to breed out inheritable health problems (like bad hips and knees and a tendency to get diseases), and are experienced midwives and nannies. If your dog is invited to be a stud, before getting too flattered, consider what happens if those puppies never find homes. Are you willing to take on that duty?

23. "Indoor dogs" get pregnant, too. Few housedogs spend every minute of every day inside the house. Where there's a male dog, there's a way.

24. Sterilization is safer than not sterilizing. Most vets will say it's more dangerous *not* to do it. While any surgery carries dangers, sterilization is safer than ever because anesthetic

techniques have greatly improved. (I've written a chapter all about it.)

I know I promised you 101 reasons to spay or neuter your dog, but The Gator (that editor guy) cut me off. According to him, I've made it "abundantly clear" that sterilizing makes sense. I hope he's right. Remember, for every puppy who finds a home, another dog awaits death in a shelter.

And if my polite "carrot" approach hasn't worked, here's a stick. Recently CNN reported the story of a Florida man who, unable to find homes for his dog's seven puppies, decided to shoot them. He'd already murdered three of them when one of the surviving pups got his paw on the revolver's trigger and shot the man. (The pup claims it was an accident, but I'm not so sure.) The four surviving pups were taken to a shelter where they've been seen practicing on the target range. So what's the moral of this story? I say, there *is* such a thing as poetic justice. *Mom* says the moral is that the momma dog should have been spayed. Jiggy agrees with both of us.

Have my exquisite prose and sales skills convinced you to sterilize your dog? If not, at least promise to go to my site and follow the link "For Breeders." It'll take you to a site where you can read the code of ethics for your dog's breed. You can also use this link to read about canine reproduction. Or, if you'd rather, I can ask Mom to go over the other 76 reasons to spay and neuter. (It might be more fun to just sterilize your dog.)

For those of you treating dog population control responsibly, here's your treat.

Chiclet's Trivia Treat: *Male dogs in a funk over losing their testicles can rejoice. Now there are Neuticles prosthetic dog testicles. (No, I'm not kidding.) They have this catchy slogan: "Looking and feeling the same," which I have to say creeps me out. This whole thing sounded nuts to me until Mom explained that males use testicles for decision making.*

Anyway, there are many sizes of Neuticles and they're available in rigid and soft, which also creeps me out. A pair of the large currently goes for $87, while the petite (like any male who wants fake testicles could ever bring himself to order petite) goes for a bargain $73. This company even makes Neuticles necklaces and key chains. What will they think of next? (Don't answer that!)

Preventing the Preventable

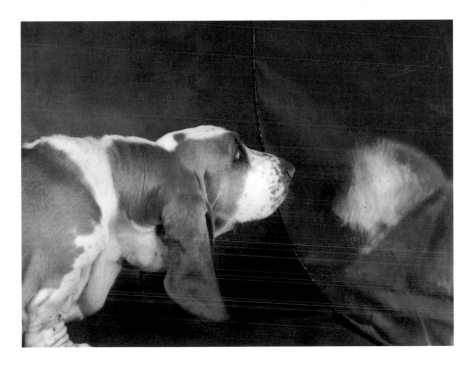

See the mirror in the picture? It's magic. I made that discovery while my friend Bubbles the Basset hound was primping in front of it. As nothing much surprises me anymore, I decided to chat with the mirror. I asked, "Mirror, mirror on the wall, what's the best health remedy of all?"

And the mirror replied, "Prevention is the best medicine."

Because she was engrossed in her reflection, Bubbles didn't take notice of the talking mirror. "An ounce of prevention," the mirror added, "is worth a pound of cure."

"But I weigh four pounds," I said, "and Jiggy weighs eight, so we'll need at least twelve ounces of cure."

**12
Pounds
of
Prevention**

The mirror wasn't done talking in proverbs. "Hearken to reason," it said, "or she will be heard."

"Mom says something like that," I said to the mirror. "She thinks the best preventative measure is an annual check-up. Cornell University Hospital for Animals even recommends dogs seven and older get *two* check-ups every year to prevent the cancer that plagues older dogs. Because our life span is much shorter than yours, two years between check-ups could be as much as 20% of our entire lifetime."

"It costs more to do ill than to do well," the mirror said.

"Tell me something I don't know," I said. "All the vets we know say early detection of potential problems usually means easier and less expensive treatment, and may even spell the difference between life and death. That's why every canine and Human in our family has at least one yearly CBC blood test. We dogs get a heartworm test, too. If something shows up, we fix it pronto. If nothing shows up, we celebrate. Broccoli for everyone!"

"Do not look where you fell," said the mirror, "but where you slipped."

"That's why Mom changed our lifestyle," I said. "She hoped to heal Jiggy once and for all and to take him off corticosteroids forever. Mom knew that steroids would do a lot of bad things to his body (see *dogs4dogs* for more about steroids and how to avoid them). Mom was also hoping to find a way to get us through our second knee surgeries without totally stressing our systems. That's when she went in search of and found our holistic vet, Dr. Tamara Hebbler.

"Snow White is the fairest of all," the mirror said.

"Don't know her," I said, "but for my money I'd take Dr. Hebbler. She changed our lives."

The mirror didn't answer, which was just as well. One can talk to inanimate objects only so long without feeling silly.

After Dr. Hebbler did all sorts of tests on us, she and consulting vet Dr. William Kruesi decided a complete change in our diet was in order, and recommended specific supplements for specific problems. (Find consulting vets, and their recommended tests, at *dogs4dogs*.) The results were almost magical—maybe not magic-mirror magical, but magical just the same. We were shocked at how fast our health improved. For Jiggy, nutrition and supplements did in a few months what pharmaceuticals had taken more than a year to do.

That isn't always the case. Although holistic methods often work quickly on acute symptoms, long-term problems often take longer to work than pharmaceuticals. That's because healing an entire body usually takes longer than suppressing a symptom. Of course, the necessary blood tests and supplements aren't cheap, but we think of them as an investment in lifetime health. Keeping your dog on drugs forever isn't cheap either, nor is treating a disease that might have been cured early or prevented.

Happily, one part of Mom's prevention program is free. It's our "monthly massage check-up." She rubs me and Jigs all over, checking us for lumps, heat, ouchy spots (a technical term) and asymmetry in our bodies. Remember, the more you know about your dog, by sight and touch and smell, the easier it is to keep her healthy. *The Healing Touch for Dogs: The Proven Massage Program for Dogs,* by Dr. Michael W. Fox, has a great chapter on using massage for diagnosis. We also like Dr. Allen Schoen's article at *www.drschoen.com* (click Articles).

Another good "read" is Dr. Martin Goldstein's book, *The Nature of Animal Healing.* It taught us the difference between suppression and healing, how vibrant health scares off fleas and diseases, and how some popular meds may shorten our lives.

Homeopathy

When we went holistic, we added some really strange stuff to our diet and health regime. For example, Jiggy and I became converts to homeopathy, a non-pharmaceutical way to cure illness using the highly-diluted energy of a substance. It works on the premise that if a substance causes a symptom like, say, nausea, the energy of that substance will also cure it. (The mirror just said: *seek your salve where you get your sore.* Anyone know how to shut a mirror up?)

We take homeopathic remedies all the time and they seem to work well for us. Give remedies orally fifteen or more minutes away from food, tap water or other meds, into what Dr. Don Hamilton calls a "neutral mouth." If possible, work with a holistic vet. Giving the wrong remedy can make matters worse. If such a vet isn't available, go to *www.wholehealthnow.com* or *www.drpitcairn.com* and click Homeopathy. Or read Dr. Hamilton's comprehensive manual, *Homeopathic Care for Dogs and Cats.*

Colostrum

We also take bovine colostrum, a powder made from the fluid produced by a mamma cow's mammary glands in the first 72 hours after calving. Colostrum is a hot new (and age-old) weapon in the battle against immune suppression. Dr. Steven Blake calls colostrum "by far the most exciting discovery I have made in the past 29 years." (And that includes meeting me!) Learn more at *www.thepetwhisperer.com* and *www.symbiotics.com.*

Flower essences and other remedies

Now, don't get weirded out, but these things can be really useful. (If you can handle a mirror talking to a dog, this will be child's play.) You hear me talk about Rescue Remedy a lot. It's a Bach flower essence used for calming, but there are other essences for other things. For best results, take these essences as you would a homeopathic. (Read more at *www.drschoen.com*; click Articles.) Dr. Jean Hofve (*www.spiritessences.com*) has the only vet-developed line we know of. (Find other links at *dogs4dogs*.) If you're interested in aromatherapy, check out *www.thepetwhisperer.com.*

Finding a Special Vet "Since you like proverbs so much," I told the mirror, "here's one for you: *It is no time to go for the doctor when the patient is dead.* You need a good vet long before we get sick. That's why Mom is so thorough about vetting our vets."

The reflection in the mirror began to ripple, as if someone had tossed a pebble in the middle of still water. "Ask me about Snow White," it said.

"I already told you I don't know her," I said. "She's white, huh? Is she a Maltese?"

"Ask me who the fairest dog of all is," demanded the mirror.

"As if we both don't already know," I huffed. Then I summoned Bubbles the Basset, and we took our leave of the mirror. Who has time to look into a mirror, let alone talk to one, when you're busy researching a book on dog health and safety?

Okay, back to vets. Mom says vets come in two flavors, allopathic and holistic, and that we couldn't get along without either. *Allopathic vets* practice conventional medicine. They believe in the healing power of pharmaceuticals and surgery, and think that disease mostly comes from outside agents like germs. They're especially great when we're bleeding or have a broken leg or bad knees. More and more allopathic vets also employ some holistic principles or work closely with holistic practitioners.

Holistic vets treat the whole animal and her environment, believing that disease comes from within, and that only the animal

herself can cure it. (This is me consulting with our holistic vet, Dr. Hebbler.)

You'll find that holistic vets are big on natural, minimally invasive methods. Virtually all these vets were trained in conventional medicine before deciding that cures using nutrition and stress reduction offered their patients more alternatives. You'll find a listing of holistic vets at *www.AHVMA.org* (search by zip code). Homeopathy experts can also be found at that site, or at *www.theAVH.org*. If you want a local vet who studied with Dr. Richard Pitcairn go to *www. drpitcairn.com;* click Referrals.

Many Humans (and dogs) are finding success with other non-traditional forms of medicine. Find a chiropractor for your dog at *www.animalchiropractic.org*. If you can't find one near you, know that some chiropractors for Humans have taken courses in animal chiropractic; you'll have to call around. Acupuncturists can be found at *www.IVAS.org*; also check out the Chi Institute (*www.TCVM.com*) for graduates of Traditional Chinese Veterinary Medicine. If you're in the market for an herbalist go to *www.VBMA.org*. Other non-conventional specialties (including Reiki, Ozone Therapy, Nutrition, Kinesiology, T-Touch and many others) can be found at *www.AHVMA.org*.

Talking to your vet

As you now know, we dogs mask our ailments and we hate to complain. So when we go to the vet's, you have to be our translator. Not only that, you have to be our advocate and record keeper.

Mom keeps a health notebook for both Jiggy and me. You probably think this is a waste of time and that your vet will keep records for you. That's what we thought until one of our previous vets lost a huge chunk of Jiggy's file. Notebooks are great for writing observations and helping you remember symptoms. For example, a few notations about the date and situation leading to "runny poop" might not be the kind of eloquent entry that excites biographers, but it could be the beginning of the realization that your dog is allergic to beef (or your mother-in-law).

Record questions to ask your vet, then record the answers. List the what and when of vaccinations, titer testing and treatment protocols. Write down appointments, rechecks, and reminders (then translate them to your appointment book or into a computer file, or both). Keep a diary of illnesses, accidents and treatments. You think you'll remember three years from now that Max had a bout with ear infections that was cured by Remedy X, but you won't. And if you switch vets, or are traveling, you'll have all relevant information at your fingertips.

Vets and money

Mom says vets need to understand your financial situation and your degree of willingness to spend money to care for your dog. Some vets recommend tests and treatments most people can't afford. Even more vets, it seems, hold back on suggesting costly treatments presuming you'll find them too expensive (a concept I find hard to grasp). To decide how to proceed with a health problem, Mom always asks, "If this were your dog, and you loved her dearly, *and money and time for nursing were unlimited*, how would you proceed?" That generally gets the vets to spill all the options and helps Mom come to an understanding of what can be done, what should be done, and when it should be done.

At the vet's

Your vet's office can be a very dangerous place. No matter how hard they try to keep it clean, disease lurks everywhere. Parvovirus thrives on benches and floors. Some guy who just cleaned drool off his sick dog's face wants to pet your cute puppy. And the "Germy" Shepherd next to you is sneezing sputum all over the place. If *that* weren't bad enough, that big dog in the corner is eyeing all the small dogs and thinking *hors d'oeuvres*.

The safest place for your dog is in a carrier or on a leash in your lap. If your baby's too big for that, at least keep him away from other animals. No touching noses to say, "Howdy." No sniffing around outside where everyone pees and poops. If you have a puppy or a senior, this advice goes ten-fold.

After the vet

Ever leave the vet's office wondering just exactly what she said? Now you can access a resource vets have been using for almost 50 years: *The Merck Veterinary Manual*. It's available as a public service at *www.merckvetmanual.com*. Just click the "Index" tab at the top and search for your subject.

Weighty Problems You two-leggers have a saying: *you dig your grave with your own teeth.* (Sorry, that magic mirror and her proverbs are sort of contagious.) As usual, Humans don't seem much inclined to listen to their own time-tested truths. As Humans have gotten heavier, so have their dogs. Studies say more than 25% of us are overweight. Unfortunately, studies also show that almost half of our Humans think we look absolutely perfect. As we dogs like to say: *love is blind.*

So, is your Poopsie porky? Viewed from above, she should have a waistline. (Even Scarlet O'Hara would envy my tiny waist.) Viewed from the side, Poopsie's cute little butt should tuck under and her tummy should tuck up. There should be a little padding

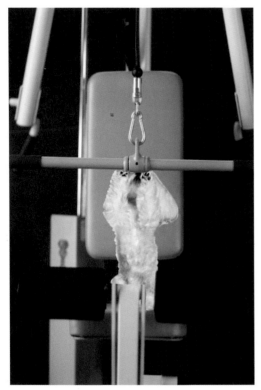

over her ribs, but no thick slathering of Crisco. The idea is to feel ribs but not see them. If this doesn't describe your Poopsie, don't blame her. It's unlikely she's the one with the can opener.

Do you love your dog? Do you want her around a long time? Well, lean dogs live longer than fat ones. A 14-year-long Purina Life Span Study followed 48 Labrador Retrievers throughout their lives. One group pigged out at a continual doggie buffet; another group ate the same kind of food, but 25% less. And guess what? The dogs on restricted diets lived up to 15% longer. That's a gain of several extra years or even more, depending on a breed's lifespan. (Read this study by clicking the Pet Institute tab at *www.purina.com*.)

Slim dogs are less plagued by osteoarthritis, and suffer less ligament damage. And guess what? The study showed a link between excess canine body fat and the development of chronic health conditions. Even moderate plumpness put dogs at increased risk for cancer, diabetes, hypertension and reduced liver and gastrointestinal function. And the longer we stay plump, the more risk we face. Being heavy even puts us at greater risk should we ever need surgery—which being heavy also makes more likely.

You Humans have complete control over whether our waistline expands or not, being our personal trainers and all. Would you love your trainer if she let your body go completely to pot? I think not. And since there's no Jenny Craig weight loss program for dogs, it's up to you. I suggest the following:

- Have your vet draw blood for a Thyroid Panel. (Purebreds, especially, are often hypothyroid and this can lead to other health problems.) Send the panel to an expert on reading it by breed, like Dr. Jean Dodds. (Link to her at *dogs4dogs*.)
- Note your dog's exact weight and weigh her weekly. Otherwise, you won't know week-to-week if your weight reduction program is working.
- Measure your dog's food. No eye-balling.
- Cut out products based on corn and other refined carbs. Consider switching to a raw diet with veggies. Think Atkins for Dogs.
- Feed your dog small meals three or more times a day.
- Count everything caloric that enters her mouth as food. Treats of broccoli or green beans won't hurt, but if you're slipping her a burrito under the table or giving her five or six doggy biscuits for dessert, Poopsie may never see her toes again. Remember: a moment of biscuit on the lips, a lifetime on the hips.
- Resist advertising ploys. For years, Humans have been consuming "diet foods" and yet 65% of Humans are overweight. Think diet food for dogs is really the answer? Simply put, quality food and portion control are better bets. If you're looking for additional help, know that some vets recommend flower essences and/or vitamins for overweight dogs. Check out our links at *dogs4dogs*.

Exercise

When you begin an exercise program for your dog, remember, *slow and steady wins the race*. Your dog will take on more than he can safely handle just to please you, but don't let him.

Outdoors, always take a water bottle along. If we're panting, we're getting hot. If we can't stop panting, we're in trouble. Our vet says she takes extra water to all doggy gatherings; there's inevitably some dog there who's dangerously overstressed. If we do overheat, apply water or rubbing alcohol to our ears, belly and feet, and offer some cool (but not too cold) water to drink.

When selecting exercise regimens, try to "double-dip" when you can. When we go someplace with stairs, Mom makes us wait at the bottom until she calls, at which time we go bounding up. We get exercise and a lesson in discipline to boot. She also tries to make exercise fun. We play fetch and, of course, Jiggy plays soccer. Mom has him thinking he's World Cup material. Personally, I'm skeptical, though do I love a guy in a uniform.

Can't handle the exercise yourself? Consider recruiting a neighborhood kid. Some of the little darlings can be bribed to walk us after school. Or how about a retired neighbor who takes long therapeutic walks every day? Maybe she'd like company. And then there's always group exercise at doggy daycare. Speaking of groups, even two dogs can keep each other well toned. Jiggy and I wrestle for fitness day in and day out. Sometimes he even lets me win.

Skinny dogs

Humans like to say: you can never be too rich or too thin (although they seem more willing to work on the former than the latter). Anyway, when it comes to dogs, you *can* be too thin. If your dog's ribs and breast bone are her most prominent features, she's already there.

After our knee surgeries, Jiggy and I shrank down to almost nothing. Mom had been so afraid we'd gain weight from lack of exercise that she overlooked our weight *loss*. Fortunately, we fattened up in no time with increased portion sizes and more frequent meals.

If your dog is losing weight but eating and exercising the same as usual, see your veterinarian right away (especially if the weight loss has been rapid). Take a poop sample with you and have it checked for parasites and other icky stuff. If your dog is getting older, try upping food quantities or, better yet, improving the quality of her food.

Preventing Poisoning Jigs and I think of our home as our sanctuary, but for too many dogs it's just a potential crime scene. (Think they'll ever do a *CSI: Dog?*) We canines get poisoned every day. Why? Ever hear the fish saying: *the bait hides the hook?* Sometimes, poison looks like fun.

As Dad says, the best offense is a good defense. (He especially likes to say this during football season and following disagreements with Mom.) One great offense is to post the following numbers by your kitchen phone and program them into your cell phone: your veterinarian, an emergency pet clinic, and the ASPCA Poison Control Center (1-900-443-0000 to charge it to your phone or 1-888-426-4435 to bill it to your credit card).

If your dog has collapsed, or you have any other reason to think she's been poisoned, be prepared to make a mad dash to the closest open vet's office, taking the poison container with you. Here are some of the usual suspects.

Poison pills

Like Human babies, we'll eat anything that's fun to chew and lots of stuff that isn't. Prescription meds can be lethal, but so can over-the-counter meds like acetaminophen (Tylenol, Datril, Liquiprin and others). Ibuprofen (Motrin, Midol, Advil and others) can be fatal in large quantities. That said, never ever leave out pill bottles or packets. And don't expect us to be deterred by childproof caps. For us, they're just a fun challenge.

Baits

I understand not wanting rats in your rumpus room or bats in your belfry, but efforts to eliminate pests may also eliminate your dog. Virtually all product labels warn that vermin control products are unsafe for pets and children and can make us bleed inside, just as they

make rodents bleed to death. (What? You thought that stuff was just an overdose of sleeping pills?) Because of that, NEVER STORE POISON BAIT WHERE WE CAN REACH IT, especially not near food or dog treats. Bait tastes great. That's why rodents eat it, and why we like eating it, too.

If you use an exterminator, frequently remind dispatchers and service personnel (who have a higher turnover rate than their prey) that you live with a dog. Make sure they don't leave baits where your dog can reach them. When we were last at our vet's, we saw a Dachshund who'd eaten long-forgotten rat bait that had fallen off a roof. We don't know whether or not the Dachshund survived. We do know that her Mom couldn't stop crying.

Some dogs see slug and snail bait as a perfect between-meal snack. It sent one friend of ours into convulsions just last week. (Fortunately, he lived.) Escargot is yummy, but also potentially deadly if snails have previously dined on snail bait. (Buy one of the "animal-safe" baits, but still be careful.) Some dogs with indiscriminate palates even like ant pellets. If you've spread any bait outside, keep your dog indoors for days. If you find Fido chowing down on any bait, call your vet immediately.

Gardens and plants

Though dogs are great diggers and unparalleled bone planters, we're generally not heralded for our gardening skills. That's probably just as well because gardens are fraught with danger masquerading as pesticides, fertilizers, insecticides and weed killers. Dogs who play in chemically-laden gardens often have a higher rate of cancer than other dogs. Herbicides like 2,4-D are particularly dangerous. Even cocoa shell mulch is dangerous for dogs. Don't let us play where you have sprayed or spread, and remember that chemicals linger. If your dog rolls in something she shouldn't, put on gloves and attempt to wash away the offending substance before your dog licks it off. Labels should tell you when the area is safe, but personally, I'd wait longer. As a precaution, also check with your local park department for dog park's fertilizing and weed killing schedules.

Sometimes what you plant can be just as dangerous, or even more so, than the chemicals you apply. Outdoors plants like azaleas, bird of paradise, foxglove, oleander (and many others) are poisonous to dogs. (Speaking of dangerous, lawnmowers, weed whackers, and virtually all power lawn tools intrigue us. Do us a favor and lock us up when you're using them.) Avid gardeners might also want to check out Cheryl S. Smith's *Dog Friendly Garden, Garden Friendly Dogs*.

Just like their outdoor counterparts, *indoor* plants can also cause pain, vomiting, and even death. Problem plants include caladium, corn plants, most lilies, philodendrons and Christmas mistletoe and Poinsettias. For more culprits, follow our links at *dog4dogs*.

SCARED POOPLESS

Household dangers

Come into my parlor said the spider to the fly. Unwittingly, Humans offer the same dangerous invitation to their dogs. And it's not only the parlor that's fraught with danger.

Kitchen and laundry products can be particularly hazardous. If products are dangerous for Humans (check the label), they can probably do us in as well. You know how caring parents of toddlers baby-proof their houses? Caring doggy parents should do the same.

Even seemingly innocuous items can make us sick. In the bathroom, safely store away toothpaste (especially if it contain Xylitol), depilatories, creams, cosmetics and cleansers. While you're at it, put away your razor blades and disposable razors. My personal vice is those little plastic caps on disposable razors; they're one of my favorite snacks.

You already know, I hope, about doggy-proofing your garage. Traditional antifreeze (which contains ethylene glycol) is deadly but we love its sweet taste. Newer, safer brands (like Sierra) contain propylene glycol. (Store these safely away, too.) There being no accounting for taste, some dogs even like motor oil, gasoline, paint, and paint thinner. Few dogs know the proverb *do not drink poison to quench a thirst.*

Here's something else you may not have considered. Even your house itself can be dangerous. Homes built before 1978 may have a dangerous problem with lead in peeling paint. Call 1-800-424-LEAD for more information.

For another poison prevention tip you need go no farther than your dog's watering bowl. First of all, your dog needs a plentiful supply of purified water. Tap water, with all of its low levels of chemicals and bacteria, can be a slow poison. Isn't that why you Humans drink your fancy water?

Second, beware of polluted water sources. On hot days, we take our water wherever we can get it: fountains, ditches, saucers under plants, street gutters and standing water that might be contaminated with road grime, chemicals, pesticides, algaecides or bacteria. If you wouldn't drink it, don't let us.

All right, I admit it: some dogs have been known to drink out of toilets, but it's not like you Humans aren't known for doing some very peculiar things, too. There's a simple solution to the toilet-water problem: shut the toilet lids and the bathroom doors, and keep full water dishes around the house. Never use in-tank toilet bowl cleaners; they can be poisonous.

Your "vices"

Coffee, alcohol, tobacco products and "recreational" drugs can make us sick as a dog. And their effects can scare us. Enough said? If not, know that I'm acquainted with a few DEA dogs and might be tempted to drop a dime.

Pharmaceuticals

Before giving your dog *any* medication, check it out. (We'd do it ourselves but we have trouble with small print.) Don't presume something is safe just because it's on the market. Think about all the Human meds that have been recalled after people started dying or having serious side effects. Then think where dogs rate on the FDA's food chain. A few minutes of your time before the fact can save you a fortune at the vet or the pet cemetery. Here's what to do:

- Actually read package "Warnings" and "Side effects." You need to know what to expect in the way of a reaction that's rare, delayed or looks harmless but isn't.
- Check out *www.dogsadversereactions.com.* This site has lots of information on common medications known to cause problems.
- Search on-line for the product name and active ingredient.
- Read about side effects reported to the FDA at *www.FDA.gov/cvm/index/ade/ade_cum.htm.* Scroll to Cumulative Summaries, find a drug's active ingredient (listed on the package) and click the alphabetic link. Note: This reporting is voluntary, and thus, incomplete.

- Research the drug info at the Drug Library at *www.petplace.com* or click on the Drugs tab at *www.veterinarypartner.com*.

Reporting bad reactions

If you don't bother to report bad reactions, manufacturers can't fix problems and vets can't treat us properly. So if your dog has an adverse reaction to a medicine, contact your vet, the drug manufacturer and the FDA (*www.fda.gov/cvm/adereporting.htm* or call 888-FDA-VETS). Also see the reporting information at *www.dogsadversereactions.com/fdareporting.html*. Be an activist. Help keep all dogs safe.

Stop Stress Stress is sometimes described as the unseen poison. I wish I could tell you that dogs aren't susceptible to stress, but I'd be lying. In fact, I'm feeling pretty stressed right now trying to get this book finished. I think a tummy rub might help.

We dogs experience pretty much the same gamut of emotions that Humans do, including grief, anxiety, loneliness, annoyance, frustration, anger and fear, and they affect our health negatively just as they affect yours. If there is dis-ease in our household, the seed of disease is growing in our bodies. Count on it.

Fortunately, there are antidotes. According to one old Latin proverb, the best physicians are *Dr. Diet, Dr. Quiet, and Dr. Merryman.* Now that's good advice for any dog. If we're facing short-term situational stress, you might consider slipping us some Rescue Remedy, Stress Relief Plus for Pets or Mellow Out Pet Relaxant (from Oxyfresh). Some dogs swear by these products. Long-term stress requires a stronger constitution and a less stressful environment.

Reducing stress

I've heard that the only difference between a shiny diamond and a lump of coal is that the diamond had a little more pressure put on it. Let me *stress* that what's good for coal is *not* good for dogs. The more stresses a dog faces, and the longer she faces them, the more likely she is to contract a major disease.

Have you heard about all those studies showing that people who live with animals lead longer and healthier lives? Well, I haven't seen any studies showing the same for dogs, but I'd like to think that's true. Nevertheless our lives, like yours, are filled with stresses we'd live longer without. In addition to those mentioned elsewhere in this book (like poor food, over-vaccination, over-medication and such), we'll be healthier if you:

- End rejection: we dogs live to please. Imagine having the object of your adoration reject you on a daily basis. Think hugs, not shouts. Think kisses, not cold shoulders.
- Reduce inactivity: a fit dog is less prone to injury, and has a healthier digestive system and heart. Heart disease, in case you didn't know it, is a major killer of dogs.

- Reduce exposure to environmental stresses such as continued loud or jarring noises, air pollution, and known allergens.
- Reduce long exposures to sun: dogs with thin coats, fair skin and those with summer buzz cuts are susceptible to skin cancer. Apply sunscreen and shade liberally.
- Reduce exposure to second-hand smoke: second-hand smoke is as bad for us dogs as it is for you and can cause lung infections, respiratory problems, and even asthma and lung cancer. So please stop smoking, for your sake and ours.
- Reduce exposure to unending heat or cold. We like temperate temperatures just as you do. Don't leave us anywhere we'll cook or freeze. And if you sleep indoors, we should sleep indoors, too. We're pack members. We're family.
- Reduce exposure to chemicals: in addition to herbicides, pesticides, road grime and other potentially carcinogenic substances, consider safer alternatives to floor cleaning products. You know how we like to eat off the floor.
- Reduce isolation: leave us alone hour after hour, day after day, and we'll waste away. Unrequited love is probably the biggest stress of all.

With your help, we can prevent the preventable and lead long, healthy lives. In honor of that magical mirror, here's one last proverb to leave you with.

Chiclet's Trivia Treat: *Of all the Human sayings Mom has read to me, my favorite comes from the Latin. These words have been placed on parchment and chiseled in stone, and speak of a bond that goes back for thousands of years:* Qui me amat, amat et canem meam. *The phrase means, Who loves me, loves my dog too. Translators often shorten it to, love me, love my dog. What a wonderful proverb that speaks to our special relationship.*

Combating Major Medical

When I was a mere fifteen ounces of canine potential, I used to hear Mom bemoaning this mysterious Major Medical. At the mention of his name, Jiggy would growl. We kept hoping the Major would get demoted or court-martialed or shipped overseas, but he kept hanging around. Major Medical was bad news.

Now that I'm three pounds heavier and loads wiser, I know that major medical isn't a person. (You never made a mistake when you were a kid?) One thing hasn't changed, however. Major medical is still bad news. Fortunately, when it comes to your dog's health, there are ways to "demote" major medical and promote better health and well-being.

Now, you know that I'm not a vet, right? I don't even play one on TV—yet. I have, however, survived the boot camp of Major Medical, and I never miss *ER*. With the best of them I can bark out, "Stat, people! She's seizing! We need to intubate her and put in a central line!" Unfortunately, only canine nurses seem to understand me.

Because Jiggy and I have both been under the knife three times, and because Mom spends an inordinate amount of time with vets, I've picked up a lot of medical information pertinent to dogs. Since I'm also the only dog in the world (not to mention the cutest) speaking out on canine health care, I've gained a certain reputation in the field. You can call me Dogtor Chiclet, DVM (Dogtor of Vivacious Medicine). Humans, scared for the health of their beloved dogs, have been writing all sorts of letters to *moi* asking for advice. If your own dog is preparing to battle major medical—cancer, surgery, heart problems or whatever—my prescription for you is to read the upcoming letters. The Dogtor is in.

Dear Dogtor Chiclet,

My vet wants to do exploratory surgery next week on my four year old dog Sam. I'm feeling pressured to make a quick decision even though his illness isn't life-threatening. This is all rather overwhelming. What should I do?

Pressured in Poughkeepsie

Dear Pressured,

Where's the fire? If Sam doesn't require immediate surgery, do your research first. Repeat after me: the vet is not always right and the first answer you get is not always the right answer. You need a second opinion, and maybe even a third, before proceeding.

Our Maltese friend Sophie, who kept toppling over, was told she probably had a brain tumor and needed some expensive tests. A Human friend suggested they seek a second opinion first. Sophie's "brain tumor" turned out to be a pinched nerve! A veterinary chiropractor gave her one "adjustment" and she's been fine ever since. Of course, it could have been a tumor, but why not check out simpler alternatives first?

Your job as our guardian is to ask questions and stand up for our welfare. We can't do it for ourselves. (When we try some jerk usually slaps us on the behind.)

Always take notes at consultations. Ask about options. Bring along a pushy friend if you're easily spooked or swayed. Maybe acupuncture, diet change, supplements, or physical therapy will prevent or delay your dog going under the scalpel. Maybe there's a cheap alternative to an expensive test. Or a natural alternative to toxic medicine. Investigate everything, learning a little here, a little there. As a wise old dogs like to say: don't leave all your pee on the first tree.

Dogtor Chiclet

Dear Dogtor Chiclet,

My vet told me that my six year old Cocker Spaniel Cinder needs to have an anterior cruciate ligament procedure. She recommended a board certified surgeon to do it. Cinder only has a little limp for goodness sakes! Isn't that ridiculous? It's not like I'm made of money.

Skeptical in Saskatchewan

Dear Skeptical,

That little limp can mean big pain. And if your dog has a torn or stretched ACL, her joint instability may eventually lead to degenerative joint disease. Your vet sounds as if she is looking out for Cinder's best interests.

Regarding the board certified surgeon: expertise is expensive. But even more expensive is a job poorly done by someone with insufficient experience. When our primary vet said I needed knee surgery, she recommended a board certified surgeon in another practice to cut on my ultra petite knees. We eventually interviewed two specialists from different practices and followed the advice of The American College of Veterinary Surgeons—that is, we asked how often each surgeon performed this surgery, whether special equipment was necessary (and did they have it?), what should the typical outcome be, and what follow-up care was required. (You can read more at *www.ACVS.org;* click Health Conditions.)

Since you're worried about spending all that money (which is weird since we dogs do fine without any money at all), ask for detailed estimates from at least two surgeons. When Jiggy and I had our knee surgeries, there was a $1000 difference *per dog* in estimates between our first and second opinions! Even if you feel more comfortable going with the high-bidder, a second bid can be a negotiating point. Also, don't be afraid to ask if there's any wiggle room in the estimate or if you can pay over time. And did you know that if your vet is a member of The American Animal Hospital Association, you may be eligible for financial assistance (*www.AAHAhelpingpets.org/home/*)?

Don't let money prevent you from getting necessary surgery. Sometimes vets work pro bono for truly needy patients or know an "angel" who'll help. Jigs and I once attended a "fundraiser" pizza party with Mom to help pay for my friend Goldy's (a Golden Retriever) ultimately successful operation. Most Humans don't like to see dogs suffer. I hope you prove to be one of those Humans.

Dogtor Chiclet

Dear Dogtor Chiclet,

My brother's 10-year-old dog Lucy just died of cancer, and now I'm worried about my dog Lacy. You see, Lucy and Lacy were sisters. What should I do?

Scared in San Diego

Dear Scared,

I'm so sorry about Lucy. According to the Morris Animal Foundation, cancer kills half of all older dogs. Half! Can you believe it? Though it's not the automatic death sentence you might think it is, clearly it's better to prevent cancer than to treat it.

Be watchful for cancer in Lacy, but don't drive yourself crazy. She might have very different risks than Lucy had. Did you spay her early? Sterilization decreases cancer risks. Do you give her good nutrition, and work hard at eliminating stresses like passive smoke, insecticides and herbicides?

To learn more about cancer detection and prevention, read the terrific information at the website of Cornell University Hospital for Animals (*www.vet.cornell.edu/cancer/prevention.html*). While you're at it, keep an eye on Lacy's peeing and pooping habits, always looking for changes. Mom watches ours like a hawk (and yes, she needs to get a life). Also look out for the American Veterinary Medical Association's cancer warning signs:

- Abnormal swellings that persist or grow

- Sores that don't heal
- Weight loss
- Loss of appetite
- Bleeding or discharge from any body opening
- Offensive odor
- Difficulty eating or swallowing
- Hesitation to exercise or loss of stamina
- Persistent lameness or stiffness
- Difficulty breathing, urinating, or defecating

I hope you haven't seen any of these things in Lacy. If you have, see a vet!

Dogtor Chiclet

Dear Dogtor Chiclet,

My vet tells me my 10-year-old mix-breed Teddy has heart disease, and it's breaking my heart. I don't want to see Teddy suffer. Would it be kinder to just put him to sleep?

Heartbroken in Houston

Dear Heartbroken,

Whoa, pardner! If your 70-year-old Dad had heart disease would you just put him down? The American Veterinary Medical Association says 3.2 million dogs have "some form of acquired heart disease," *acquired* being the operative word. Degenerative atrio-ventricular valve disease (DVD) is the leading cause of doggy heart failure and causes 75% of all canine cardiovascular disease.

The chances of getting heart disease increases with age and studies show 93% of dogs between nine and twelve are affected. Still, just as there have been advances in treating Human heart disease, there has also been progress in treating dogs. Nowadays, there are veterinary cardiologists and cardiac surgeons. Need a pacemaker for your dog? No problem. (Go to our links at *dogs4dogs* for more information.)

Before you even consider playing *Taps* for Teddy, you should try to determine the extent of his heart disease. If Teddy is in the early stages, he might be helped with a special diet high in antioxidants and low in toxins. You might also be able to help him with a vet-approved exercise regimen. Even if his disease is more progressed, Teddy might surprise you and improve or stabilize enough to have many more years of good health. Want some hand-holding? Go to *www.groups.yahoo.com* and search for Canine Heart Disease. For an informative read, go to *www.drschoen.com* and click on Article.

Dogtor Chiclet

Dear Dogtor Chiclet,

My dog Harley has the Big C and I haven't a clue what to do. My vet recommends this horrific sounding operation; friends say I should skip it and just give him pain meds. What should I do?

Baffled in Butte

Dear Baffled,

Dogs have as many kinds of cancers as Humans do, and most are treatable. The first thing you should do is seek out a cancer authority (preferably someone who's completed an oncology residency at one of the top universities with cancer centers, like Colorado State, Tuffs or Cornell), and then get a second and even third opinion before proceeding.

Different vets have different philosophies and approaches, so find a vet whose plan makes sense to you. Your dog may need chemotherapy, surgery, or radiation, and will definitely need top notch nutrition, appropriate supplements and buckets of love.

If Jiggy and I ever get cancer (which we're trying really hard not to do), Mom says we'll call the internationally-renown cancer specialist Dr. Greg Ogilvie from Angel Care Cancer Center in San Marcos, California. His website (*www.cvsangelcare.com*) is packed with information and has links to lots of other sites. When it comes to treating cancer, you need to bring out the big dogs. Even canines know: you don't scare monsters with puppies.

There are a lot of dedicated people out there trying to turn "the Big C" into "the Little C." At *dogs4dogs* we have links to a number of sites (including universities and veterinary cancer specialists) that offer canine cancer information. One of our favorites, *www.caninecancereawareness.org,* has plenty of practical care tips and loads of information. There are also on-line support groups; one of the biggest is at *www.groups.yahoo.com;* search for Canine Cancer. For information on clinical trials, go to *www.vetcancersociety.org* and click Clinical Research Trials.

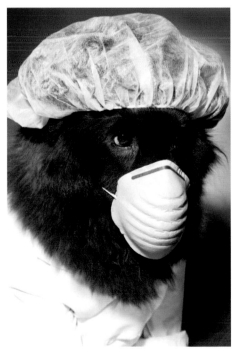

If you're looking for a holistic approach to treating cancer, you might consult Dr. William Kruesi at *www. crvetcenter.com*, or Dr. Nancy Scanlon at 818-784-9977 or *www.drnancysplace.com*. (Both do phone consultations.) I'd also recommend that you read Dr. Martin Goldstein's *The Nature of Animal Healing* and *Dr. Pitcairn's New Complete Guide to Natural Care for Dogs and Cats*. Whatever you do, don't fall for too-good-to-be-true "natural" formulas touted in suspect sites on the

Internet. And remember: the word "holistic" isn't magic and requires no certification to use.

One more thing. Make sure your dog's diet consists of a variety of fresh foods (preferably organic, with all meats hormone-free), purified water, essential fatty acids and no refined carbohydrates. Just be sure to consult your specialist before changing diets or adding supplements. And give Harley a big hug from me.

Dogtor Chiclet

Whoops! I almost forgot your treat (which is actually neither trivial nor a treat).

Chiclet's Trivia Treat: *Next time you have a heart attack, thank dogs if you survive. In 1933, Johns Hopkins physician William Henry Howell, together with professor of electrical engineering William B. Kouwenhoven, discovered that a heart sent into fibrillation by a shock could be restored to normal rhythm with a countershock. It was an unlucky dog whose heart showed them the way.*

Later, G. Guy Knickerbocker, another engineer, noticed a small rise in a dog's blood pressure when he pressed electrodes into position on the heart. Was it possible, he speculated, that pressing rhythmically on the chest could cause the blood to circulate? From that observation, Knickerbocker and Kouwenhoven led the way to cardiac massage, the technique that would become key to cardiopulmonary resuscitation.

We suspect that dogs, as well as Humans, have benefited from this research, but we'd feel a lot better if the dogs involved had been volunteers. "Anyone want to get shocked? Raise your paw!"

ANESTHESIA ANXIETY

Trust me on this one: counting sheep doesn't help dogs fall off to sleep. Shepherds and collies want to go herd those sheep; greyhounds want to run with them; golden retrievers want to play with them. They *scare* Jiggy and me. No, sheep don't work. When it comes to surgery, there's only one way to put us to sleep, and that's with anesthesia. (Okay, C-SPAN does make us drowsy, but doesn't quite put us under.)

As a veteran of three surgeries, you'd think I'd have no qualms about anesthesia. After all, I've "been under" three times and have lived to write about it. As a dog journalist, however, I needed to get answers to important questions. Join me now as I begin counting answers backwards from one hundred. Relax. Don't fight it. This is a short but important chapter. Afterwards, you can sleep.

One hundred, ninety-nine, ninety-eight. . .

I would like to be able to tell you that anesthesia is 99.99% safe. After having checked high and low, though, the only thing I can say is that I'm 99.99% sure that there are no reliable statistics addressing doggy anesthesia. Still looking for reassurance, I checked (Mom did the talking) with Dr. Peter J. Pascoe, Professor of Veterinary Anesthesiology at the University of California-Davis School of Veterinary Medicine. In regards to anesthesia safety, Dr. Pascoe said anesthesiologists like to say: "There are no safe anesthetics, no safe anesthetic procedures, only safe anesthetists."

Not exactly a reassuring saying, is it?

Dr. Michael Paul, former president of the American Animal Hospital Association, didn't comfort me either. Comparing anesthesia to flying a plane, he said: "Dangers arise on takeoff and landing and are almost always Human error. It's the same with anesthesia. Induction and recovery are the touchy parts. Doctor and technician error are responsible for almost all deaths of healthy anesthetic patients." He added, "In most cases, however, the risk of not doing a procedure is far greater than the risk of doing a procedure under anesthesia."

I wish he hadn't used the words *deaths* and *healthy patients* in the same sentence. Anyone need a sedative? I know I do.

Mom says you can cross your fingers and hope things go well, or you can ask questions and make informed choices. Since I don't even *have* fingers, I vote for informed choices.

Seventy-five, seventy-four . . .

The If your dog has previously had problems with anesthesia, or has
Safest relatives who have, or if she has any health problems or allergies to
Patient meds, be sure to tell your surgeon. Surprises of this kind aren't fun. The goal is sweet dreams, not permanent dreams.

Dr. Paul says that heart, lung, kidney and liver problems that alter metabolism can send anesthetic risks off the chart. Obesity is a problem, too. That's why Drs. Pascoe and Paul and all our other vet friends recommend a thorough check-up and blood test. Some vets offer to skip the blood test to save money. Don't. Dr. Pascoe says that blood work reveals hidden disease, allowing them to investigate further and to use the appropriate anesthetic technique for the dog's condition.

To ensure that your dog is a good candidate for anesthesia, veterinary dentist Dr. Brook Niemiec, who estimates he's done 20,000 anesthetic procedures without a death (now those are the kind of stats I've been looking for), requires a blood test and urinalysis no earlier than a month before dental work. For dogs over six, he adds a three-view chest x-ray (which also screens for lung cancer). Some vets also order an electrocardiogram.

Fifty, forty-nine . . .

The Dr. Paul says, "Modern anesthetic agents are generally extremely
Safest safe with wide margins of safety." Our knee surgeon, Dr. Dhupa,
Anesthesia says they're far safer than they were fifteen years ago.

General anesthesia may be injected or inhaled. For very short procedures, injectables may be useful and are no riskier than inhalants, says Dr. Pascoe, who also uses them when particular medical problems rule out gas. In some circumstances, he even combines them with gas. If a dog has liver or kidney disease, though, injectables are out because of how they're metabolized.

SCARED POOPLESS

Vets like using inhalants because amounts given us, and thus their effect, can be altered quickly. (Sevoflurane and isoflurane are the newest inhalants, by the way, replacing halothane.) Effects of some newer injectables can also be reversed, but you have to give another drug to do it. Before getting gas, we need a sedative to calm us down (talk about a *Catch-22*); agitated dogs may require more anesthesia and this could increase potential problems. We also need a short-acting anesthetic to get that endotracheal tube down our throat. Gulp! This tube helps keep airways clear and is especially important for flat-faced dogs like Pugs, Pekinese and Bulldogs.

Twenty-five, twenty-four. . .

The Safest Procedures How do you know if your surgeon uses the latest and safest procedures? Ask:

- How do they monitor bodily functions during surgery? Dr. Pascoe says *the most important thing is having someone solely dedicated to administering anesthesia and monitoring our progress.* This person, who should be an experienced registered vet tech, must monitor blood pressure. This is vital. And to ensure our breathing is okay, they must also watch blood oxygen and carbon dioxide levels.
- When inducing sleep, do they titrate to effect? That is, do they ease into the process, giving maybe a quarter dose, noting the effect, then giving another quarter and so on until they get the desired effect? This helps hypersensitive dogs and decreases the chances of a long-lasting anesthesia hangover.
- Will they place a catheter and administer IV fluids? Fluids are especially important for surgeries lasting more than half an hour. *Small dogs, which need a "mini-drip," are especially in need of a catheter.* If blood pressure plummets, doctors have to immediately shoot meds into tiny shrunken veins. If no catheter's in place, life-saving meds may be delayed.
- Do they offer pain control? It's cheaper not to, but come on! Do you know anyone who would willingly go

138

through surgery without pain meds? And we need meds before we hurt, not just after. We especially need them during long procedures.

- How do they keep dogs warm? Dogs lose heat during surgery. *Small dogs, especially, become vulnerable to hypothermia.* An electric heating pad can cause burns. A circulating water blanket is safer, and some places use snuggly warm air blankets, too.
- Do they regularly use a stretcher, especially for big dogs? Big fellows have been paralyzed (temporarily and otherwise) while being moved.
- How will your dog be monitored during the potentially dangerous recovery period? We need to be kept warm and have a tech watch us closely until our vital signs normalize and we can stand up without toppling over. (Note: Injectables take longer to recover from than inhalants.) Because some dogs awaken violently, make sure they don't just throw us into a cage and disappear. Post-op thrashing permanently paralyzed our spaniel friend, Sparky. Poop happens.

Ten, nine . . .

This hasn't been so painful, has it? And don't worry; the anesthesia we gave you should wear off shortly. Want to learn more about anesthesia and drugs? Go to our links at *dogs4dogs*.

Dad likes to tell about the time they put him under for surgery. When he awakened, Mom was at his side. He opened his eyes, looked at her, murmured, "You're beautiful," and then he drifted back to sleep. An hour later he opened his eyes again, and Mom was still there. This time he said, "You're cute." Mom asked him, "What happened to 'beautiful?'" And Dad said, "The drugs are wearing off."

Good thing Mom has a good sense of humor.

Two, one . . .

I thought writing this chapter would put me to sleep by now but I find myself still wide awake wondering what *sheep* count when they can't fall asleep.

Chiclet's Trivia Treat: *Oliver Wendell Holmes, Sr. (doctor and father of the famous U.S. Supreme Court Justice, Oliver Wendell Holmes, Jr.) was asked in 1846 to name the process of using ether to eliminate pain during surgery. He suggested "anaesthesia," meaning "no feeling" in Greek.*

Who invented anesthesia is a controversy that still rages. Two dentists and two physicians claimed the discovery in the mid-1800's. The heated controversy even made it to Congress, with no resolution.

Recreational use of nitrous oxide (laughing gas) and ether clearly influenced the discovery. When a monument was proposed to honor the inventor, and no one could decide who that should be, Holmes suggested that that the monument have the inscription, "To Ether," a tongue-in-cheek reference meaning "to either."

Dogs, as far as I can tell, had nothing to do the discovery. When it comes to drugs, we say: Just Bark No.

Surgery Is A Pain

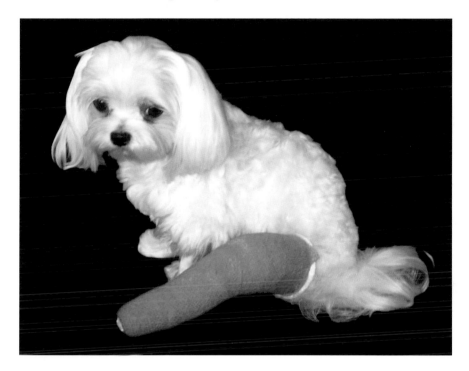

This is how I looked after my first knee surgery. Do you like my hangdog expression? So much for pretty in pink, huh?

As a survivor of three surgeries, and as Jiggy's bunkmate during his four, I can say without equivocation: surgery is a real pain. It's not the slice and dice that irks me; it's that Humans make the entire process so much tougher than it needs to be. Your dog is luckier than we were. She can benefit from our successes and you can learn from Mom's mistakes.

How? By realizing that the best directors of the doggy surgical experience are like the best movie directors (though it's best if they don't run around the operating room shouting "Cut!"). Before committing to anything, they read the entire script (this chapter plus ANESTHESIA ANXIETY and portions of COMBATING MAJOR MEDICAL). They expect the best and plan for the worst. And they know that what they do before and after the main event can make the difference between success and failure.

Pre-Cut Think of "pre-cut" as your pre-production time. Assuming your dog is not having emergency surgery, you can be methodical and organized.

Make sure your dog has the proper tests so your vet can select the right anesthesia. Pick up the pre-surgical instructions as early as possible, then follow them to the letter. If you have any questions or qualms address them immediately. Also pick up, read, and sign the pre-surgical consent form. This terrifying document warns that your four-legged friend might die, or have to be put to sleep, if something goes wrong during surgery. Your dog will look to you for leadership; this means no emoting on the set, no showing fear, and NO CRYING. If you melt down in front of your dog just prior to her operation, she's likely to get spooked, and that's no way to start surgery.

As director, you have overall responsibility for the props and sets. One prop to get sooner rather than later is your dog's "Elizabethan" collar. (Jiggy calls dogs wearing them "cone-heads.") This lampshade-like collar keeps us from eating our bandages and stitches (alas, the only fun thing to do after surgery). Get it from your vet early and consider redesigning it. Collars are usually a pain to put on and take off for meals and cuddling, and if you have a tiny patient, it probably won't fit right. Mom refitted ours with Velcro and taped the collars' necks to make them more comfy. High budget directors might consider buying their diva a deluxe Pet Botanics E-Collar. I like them because they're transparent and we can see our meds coming in time to hide.

When getting ready for the scene where the patient comes home after surgery, remember to prepare a doggy sick room. Stars have their own trailers, you know. We don't need luxury (although it couldn't hurt), but confining us to a crate after surgery is a good idea. To you it might seem cruel, but we dogs love the security a cozy crate brings, especially when we're under the weather. I lounged in mine even when Mom left the door open. It was like having my very own condo or movie star trailer.

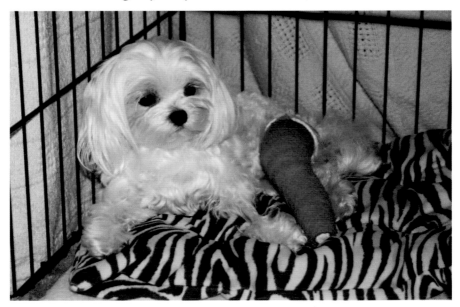

Cushion our crates with something easy to walk on but also easy-to-clean (like a sheepskin pad or folded blanket; not a lumpy pillow). Keep us out of direct sun and away from heat and drafts. If yours is a wire crate, cozy it up by covering three sides with a light blanket. And don't forget a no-spill water dish with clean water. (My agent spelled all this out in my contract.)

You might also consider doing the following:

- Give your dog a good multi-vitamin. Insist on human-quality ingredients with no wheat, corn, yeast sugar, artificial preservatives, flavoring or coloring. Shop for quality, not price. A vitamin your dog can't assimilate is money wasted. (See *dogs4dogs* for suggestions.)
- Dr. Pitcairn recommends that you add a daily dose of 10,000 IU Vitamin A, 100 IU Vitamin E, and 250 mg. Vitamin C for three days before, and three days, after surgery.

- Ask your surgeon about Arnica Montana (found at the health food store, in Montana and elsewhere). Arnica decreases bleeding and swelling, and speeds healing. Both Jigs and I took one bead of 30C homeopathic Arnica the night before surgery and the morning of it. (Big dogs can take three.) We took it orally (15 minutes removed from foods or meds) every two hours for several days after surgery, then three times daily for the rest of the week. Our surgeon, Dr. Sarit Dhupa (I call him "Dr. Super Dhupa") thought it helped a lot; we had little swelling and almost no bruising.

- Keep your dog calm. If your dog gets the yips at the mere site of a vet, consider spiking drinking water with Rescue Remedy for several days before surgery. Four drops on the tongue, or rubbed on our ears, on the morning of surgery may take the edge off. Use it for a few days afterwards, too. You have your relaxants; we have ours.

- Plan to pick up your dog when you have time to play nurse. You may have to give meds three times daily for up to a week, so plan accordingly.

- Have your dog practice "going potty" on command. As a good director, you should have already rehearsed this scene over and over. When your dog is hurting and you're dog-tired, you'll want him to complete business on cue. Don't worry that your dog will ask, "What's my motivation?" This isn't method acting. Even an "extra" can pee and poop on demand. (Warning: avoid peeing near the vet's office—the Grand Central Station of peedom; you don't want your dog catching anything just prior to going under the knife.)

- Prepare a potty area. You may have to carry us, or wait while we hobble along, so make this area convenient to our sick room. And make sure we're safe from predators. Even big guys are sitting ducks when they're disabled.

- Weigh your dog. Your dog could go from skinny to plump, or vice versa, during convalescence. Take action to help keep weight stable.
- Take measurements. Dogs lose muscle during convalescence, especially after knee or hip surgery. Jigs and I did. Physical therapist vet Dr. Claire Sosna recommends measuring an affected limb, and its mate, just before surgery, and then again before exercise begins. Measure the exact same spot on the two legs, say, three inches above the knee after knee surgery. Then you'll know how much we'll need to work to get our fitness back, and when we're ready to play!
- Teach your dog to love the crate; she may need confinement for a while after surgery. Leave the crate open in a favorite room, toss treats inside, and then leave the room. Before long, you'll need bribes to coax your dog *out*. Does the name Pavlov ring a bell?
- Prepare for your dog's increased mobility. As we get a little better, we'll need a slightly larger bedroom. Mom made us a "suite" with some flexible fencing around our crates.

Because we love our car carriers, and because they're comfy and small, Mom asked our surgeon if we could camp in them before surgery, and after post-op recovery. The nurse placed them open, side by side, inside a big cage. That made our stay not quite so scary.

Know what else we liked? Into each of our carriers Mom stuffed one of her socks (freshly worn and smelling of Mom). Some moms and dads sent old shirts instead. To us, those socks were better than a sachet of "forget-me-nots." It reminded us of home and the family we love. Just be sure to tell the surgical techs that you don't mind if your "sachet" gets ruined. If they think it's their job to keep it clean, they might just fold it and put it away.

Post-Op (or what directors call the "Final cut") Movie buffs say that great films are always made in the cutting room. After all, the cut is where everything comes together. It's the same after surgery. What comes after the principle action is as important as what comes prior. So before you snatch us up into your protective arms to take us home, plan your success:

- Read the post-surgical instructions. Sometimes they're pretty obtuse; don't hesitate to ask a "dumb" question. Your dog's life might be riding on the answer.
- Get all required meds. Make sure the instructions on the bottles and the handouts agree. Ask about common side effects and what to do if they occur. Find out when our next dose is due and learn how to give it. Know that some meds need refrigeration; others don't. Some pills can be crushed; others must go down whole. Learn what to do if you miss a dose. Never given your dog a pill? Get a demo or ask if they have liquid meds you can squirt in by syringe. Incidentally, when using a syringe, know that "3 ml" is the same as "3 cc." Another Human mystery solved by a dog.
- Make follow-up appointments and ask if there's a charge. Knowing that appointments are free, which they usually are, makes it easier to show up—which you must! If you

remove bandages or stitches yourself, make sure you
report your dog's condition to the vet or a surgical tech.
- Take us home in a carrier or crate or a strong person's arms.
This is not time for us to get jostled or fall off the seat.

Okay, once you've done all the above, it's time to gather up
your wounded friend. This, of course, is the time for the big
close-up where you give your dog a smooch and whisper, "I love
you." *The End*? Not so fast. In real life, the difficulties may just be
beginning. Remember in *Rear Window* when Jimmy Stewart was
convalescing in a wheelchair and being stalked by a murderer?
Even with Grace Kelly looking after him, Big Jimmy had big
trouble. Your dog can have trouble, too.

Convalescence

Quiet on the set! The best medicine after surgery is sleep, so give
us plenty of peace and quiet. We can sleep through anything—but
shouldn't have to.

You've heard rumors about drugs on the set? After surgery,
there may be plenty. Vets typically prescribe antibiotics. Because
those bug killers zap good bacteria along with the bad, Mom gave
us probiotics (live beneficial bacterial cultures) to restore our
healthy intestinal flora. Find these good "bugs" in your health
food store's fridge. Just be sure to give them at a different time of
day than you give the antibiotic, and to continue them several
weeks after the antibiotic runs out. (If we had to do it all over
again, we'd probably start on colostrum, too, to boost our
immune system.) All this is important for a great recovery and our
long-term general health.

Besides antibiotics, we'll probably have pain meds and maybe
something for inflammation. (Ask your holistic vet for natural sub-
stitutes.) Keep a close eye on how we react to these meds, as they
can sometimes do more harm than good. If you spot any unusual
behavior or symptoms, check the notes you took about common
side effects. Also click the Drugs tab at *www.veterinarypartner.com*, or

see the Drug Library at *www.petplace.com*. If your intuition tells you to call the vet, call. Better to be known as "that pushy paranoid pooch parent" than "the quiet person whose silence killed her dog."

Bandage care

With all our bandages and wrappings, it might look as if you're directing a sequel of *The Mummy*, but a horror flick is the last thing you want. When it comes to bandage and wound care, follow your

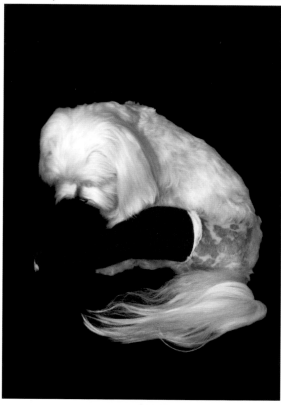

vet's instructions precisely. Bandages that get wet from urine, dew, poop or whatever, invite infection and must be immediately removed. A plastic bag over a leg bandage helps in wet grass, or if your dog is a wayward piddler. Just don't leave it on for very long.

Slipped bandages must be removed, too, as should bandages that cause our toes or other body parts to swell or that seem to be otherwise causing us distress. Call your vet immediately if icky stuff from the wound starts soaking through. And once the bandage is off, watch for swelling or discharge at the incision site. As long as our temperature is below 102°F, ask your vet if you should carefully wash the wound with mild soap and water. (Find more tips on wound care at *www.cvsangelcare.com/html/ac_surgery.htm*.)

Health watch

Sometimes, even with the best directors, it's not all, "Lights, cameras, action." Behind the scenes the unusual, the unexpected, and the unwanted can occur. Watch out for:

- **Excessive lethargy.** If we're acting listless and won't eat, check our temperature. If we have a fever over 102°F, contact your vet immediately.
- **If we're shaking,** we might need to go potty, especially if it's been a while. If we don't go when asked, and we keep shaking or get worse in any way, call your vet.
- **If your dog turns up her nose at food,** honor her decision for a day or so. Fasting allows us to funnel energy to healing rather than using it for digestion. If we continue snubbing food, ask your vet for some Science Diet® Canine a/d. It's designed for dogs recovering from illness, injury or surgery. Our vet told Mom to add some to our normal diet, along with a little cooked brown rice, because we were losing too much weight. She warned us against high caloric supplements made mostly of sugar (sucrose, maltose, dextrose, etc). We needed nutrition, not a sugar high.
- **If your dog won't drink water,** slowly syringe in small quantities from time to time.
- **If your dog is particularly ravenous,** it could just be boredom talking. We need nutrition, affection and attention, not recreational food. Better to occupy our minds than our jaws. Go to *dogs4dogs* for some links to neat toys. (Warning: these toys are meant for dogs; Humans should not appropriate them for their own use.)
- **Many dogs get constipated after surgery.** Don't make us have to strain when we're in pain. A little cooked sweet potato or canned pumpkin (but not pie filling) will usually do the trick. If your dog's still poopless after a few days, tell your vet.

Because being separated from our Humans is a pain too great to bear, Mom let us spend the night in crates near her and Dad's bed. During the day Jigs and I stayed in a fenced-off area where we could see Mom most of the time. We might have been down, but we weren't out.

Humans like to say *an idle mind is the devil's workshop*. Mom made use of her captive audience and occupied our minds at the same time by reinforcing obedience commands and teaching us a few tricks. (*Sit, stay* and *lie down* were permissible, but she was too superstitious to risk *play dead*.)

Rehab Dr. Dhupa says most Humans get their dog romping too soon after surgery. Some feel lonely for their four-legged playmate; others feel guilty over having made their buddy suffer. But remember: you're supposed to be the responsible one. Yes, we'll jump through hoops for you but, please, not right after surgery.

We dogs have a saying: the spirit is willing, but the flesh is weak. Although our wounds heal faster than yours, we also lose fitness faster. Jiggy the Jock tried a three-legged leap onto the bed just two days after his knee surgery; Mom caught him in mid-air, averting disaster. Thereafter, she kept us confined in a small area away from the bed. When we were allowed on the bed, she kept us on short leashes. Dr. Dhupa had scared Mom with a story about a recuperating Dachshund patient who jumped off a bed and broke his back; he says post-surgical accidents happen *way* too often.

Begin exercise with care as well. If your surgeon says to start with short walks, that means one block every day this week, two blocks next week and so on, not one block today and the Boston Marathon tomorrow. If your dog's body even whispers *whoa*, cut back. Two months after surgery, I twisted my knee in a tussle with Jiggy and had to go back on Arnica Montana and stop exercising for two weeks. Had Mom not taken this action, I might still be gimpy today. How embarrassing would it be to limp down the red carpet at the Oscars when they make that movie of my life?

Why do we try to do more than we should? Dr. Dhupa thinks our *seemingly* rapid healing is Nature's way of protecting us from predators. Our ancient brain knows that a limping dog is easy prey. Unfortunately, our theatrics fool our Moms and Dads as well, so please don't second guess your vet's instructions. Always err on the side of caution.

Speeding up healing

We met our holistic vet, Dr. Hebbler, *after* the surgeries on our left knees but *before* the surgeries on our right knees. She gave us several nutrients (Kaprex and Ligaplex) to help our knees heal, and switched us to natural foods. And guess what? Our right knees healed much faster, and hurt much less, than our left ones had!

If your dog still isn't healing as fast as you or your surgeon would like, and you miraculously have some money and energy left, you might try an acupuncturist or physical therapist. Dr. Sosna and other therapists have water exercise tanks now that make rehab a breeze. I know some lucky dogs who swear by this therapy, and some Humans who claim their dogs really benefited. You can also take matters into your own hands (literally) by gently massaging your dog to bring healing blood to the surgery site. Just give us a few days to heal before you start, and please don't squish our wounds.

My favorite director (Mom) must have been thinking about my modeling and acting career because when my incision began to heal, she started swabbing it with a little Vitamin E oil several times a day. Not only did my wound heal faster, I don't even have a scar! Now if only the paparazzi would just leave me alone....

Well, the movie is over and it's finally time to say "Cut!" I hope the word isn't so frightening now. Surgery will always be a pain, but it doesn't have to be scary. With your good directing, it can have a happy ending.

That's a wrap, people. Time for a treat.

Chiclet's Trivia Treat: *In 2003, competitors accused Danny the Pekinese of cosmetic enhancement after he won Crufts Best in Show. Since then, there has been a rash of requests for doggy facelifts, eyelifts, rhinoplasty, chin lifts, eyebrow correction, tummy tucks and, of course, Botox to reduce wrinkling. (Yes, really.)*

Some procedures have a medical basis (such as when folds of skin around the eyes or private parts cause repeated infections). Other procedures are performed solely to impress friends or to win shows (even though it violates the rules).

What about the surgical risks, people? You won't risk anesthesia to clean our teeth but will risk it for a cuter nose? And they say **dogs** *are perverse.*

Emergency, Emergency

Since there is no Doggy 9-1-1, guess what? *You* are our Doggy 9-1-1.

You don't need to be a knight in shining armor to rescue us, but you do need to do some planning. For example, do you keep a canine first aid kit and book where you can find them at a moment's notice? Are all those *important* numbers (your vet, the nearest 24 hour emergency clinic, and Animal Poison Control) posted by your kitchen phone and programmed into your cell phone? Do you know what vet you'd go to in an emergency, and exactly how to get to get there? Have you printed out (and studied) instructions for doing the doggy Heimlich maneuver?

Please tell me you answered a resounding *yes* to all these questions.

Uh-oh. It's awfully quiet out there. Since I don't hear anyone replying (even with my spectacular sense of hearing), you'd better read on. This chapter won't take the place of a first aid manual, which you should get, or common sense, which you should already have. It will, however, sensitize you to the general ways to keep us alive in an emergency.

Fast Aid Doggy first aid kits are plentiful these days. Buy one on-line or in pet stores, or make up your own. Most kits contain antiseptic wipes, gauze bandages, and insect sting wipes, but you also need small needle-less syringes to give meds, an antihistamine like Benadryl, 3% hydrogen peroxide (USP), saline eye wash and artificial tears (because even Lassie wouldn't cry on command). We also recommend keeping on hand the holistic remedies mentioned ahead in STINGS. Find more options at *dogs4dogs*.

Muzzle before Moving Severe pain makes dogs cranky. Sometimes we snap or bite just to tell you to be careful not to hurt us more than we're already hurting. So if you, in your supreme wonderfulness, ever rescue me or one of my injured friends and we're in pain, apply a muzzle before moving us. We don't want to hurt you, but we might get confused and screw up.

If you have a chronically-cranky dog, *buy* a muzzle. Otherwise, make one with a necktie, scarf, soft leash or whatever's handy. Pantyhose, maybe? Gauze? You'll want a loop over the bridge of the nose (near my eyes), under the chin, and around the back of the head. Tie the ends in a bow, not a knot, so you can

154

release it easily. Remember: the goal is to keep your dog's mouth shut, but not so tightly that he can't pant. Don't leave the muzzle on any longer than necessary.

Gravity Don't worry, this isn't the part where we talk about Isaac Newton, an apple and physics. We're talking about how gravity may be one of your best defenses in an emergency situation. If you want blood flow from a wound to slow down, elevate the injury higher than the heart. If you want blood to flow away from the heart, as with a poisonous bite or sting, try and keep the injury lower than the heart.

Bleeding To keep blood flow to a minimum, immobilize the animal and the injured part as much as possible. If we're bleeding a little, apply pressure to the area with a cool, wet gauze pad. Wrap the area with a bandage (but not too tightly), and don't use anything that will get stuck in the wound. If possible, use gravity to slow blood flow (see above). Get us to the vet.

If you see squirting blood, we have a severed artery. Apply firm pressure and get to the nearest emergency facility fast.

Vomiting The first time Mom saw me hurl, she canceled her dinner plans and stayed home to watch me doing my deathbed routine. As I weighed only 31 ounces at the time, milking her pity wasn't all that tough.

Mom has since wised up when it comes to our upchucking. The thing is, we canines are into vomiting. If something offends, it's outta there pronto! It's Mother Nature's way of compensating for our indiscriminate eating habits. You do need to call your vet, however, if we continue vomiting three or four times, or if we seem sick, spit up blood, or have a fever.

Stings The other day, some sneaky little bug stung Jiggy's back paw. Jiggy screamed bloody murder and started licking frantically at his ballooning foot so Mom rushed him to the vet. On the way there his eyes got red and swollen and watery, and then he vomited all over me (talk about a bad hair day). Fortunately, we got him to the vet fast. They gave him a shot of Benadryl and, much to Mom's chagrin, a shot of corticosteroid. They also insisted on watching him for a few hours to make sure he didn't stop breathing. After he did a good job of breathing for a few hours, we went home, washed the vomit off me and lived happily ever after.

Stings can be life threatening, so always err on the side of caution. If you want a happy ending to your dog's close encounter with a bug, be prepared to act as follows:

- If your dog's mouth or throat starts to swell, rush her to the *nearest* vet. Call on the way and tell them what happened. This could be a matter of life and death. Seconds count.

  For sting and bite emergencies, our vet has us use holistic remedies from our health food store. For bee stings, she recommends Apis 30C. For spider bites and other stings, it's Ledum 30C. (Note: for animal bites, use Ledum 30C and Arnica Montana 30C.) Keep these on hand, storing them at room temperature.

  After the sting, she says to immediately give three to five pellets (depending on your dog's size). Just tuck them into the pocket between your dog's gums and cheek. Do this three times, five minutes apart, while someone else is driving you and your dog to the vet. She says that by the time you get there, the emergency may well have passed, saving you a ton of money and saving your dog the long-term immune system problems inherent with the inevitable corticosteroid shot. (If your dog is still in distress, or if it will make you rest easier, go ahead and see the vet.) Back at home, continue your remedy three to four times a day for three to five days.

- If you don't have any holistic remedies, but you do have Benadryl, administer a size-appropriate dose (of plain Benadryl containing diphenhydramine only) and get to the vet. Why not call your vet now and ask what dose your dog will need? Write it on the bottle with an indelible marker. Jig and I use Children's Benadryl because we're so tiny.

- If your dog is showing no signs of an allergic attack, and you detect a stinger still in the wound, try to carefully knock it out with the edge of a blunt knife or credit card. If you pull out the stinger with tweezers, you may squeeze more poison into the wound. Clean and dress the bite with an antiseptic ointment. If the wound swells, apply ice (wrapped in a towel) for 10 to 15 minutes, being careful not to freeze the skin.

Snake Bites I am very suspicious of any creature without legs and consequently am not that fond of snakes. To my thinking, they appreciate us even less than cats do, and that's saying a lot. If you live in snake country and find your dog trembling, agitated, drooling, vomiting, or with dilated pupils, think snakebite. Look for swelling, especially on the face or legs. Most venomous snakes leave two fang marks. Here's what to do until you can rush him to the vet:

- Muzzle your dog and keep him quiet. Call ahead to your vet and tell them you're coming.
- If you can, apply a cold pack (not ice) to the bite.

- If the bite's on your dog's leg, bandage it. Think compression, not tourniquet.
- Do not cut the wound or try to suck out the poison, no matter how many TV westerns you've seen.
- Take the snake with you if you've killed it. (Be careful!) Otherwise, bring a description. Three are obvious: a rattlesnake has rattles; a cottonmouth has a white mouth; a copperhead has a copper head and is brightly colored and patterned. Coral snakes have red, yellow and black rings (red and yellow, kill a fellow).

If you live in an area rife with snakes you might consider enrolling your dog in a course on snake avoidance. (Check online for a class near you.) You'd think "once bitten, twice shy," but those snakes can get you when you're just sniffing around, minding your own business. There's also a new rattlesnake vaccine on the market, currently available only in California, which some recommend for dogs that have previously had antivenin for snakebite. (Investigate it thoroughly before giving it. Our vet recommends against it.)

Garbage Can Syndrome Think dogs can gulp down road kill with a toilet water chaser and still want to boogie? Think again. There's a condition nicknamed Garbage Can Syndrome, so named for an illness brought about when, well, you figure it out. GCS causes a rise in liver enzymes and can be very serious.

If you see an upturned garbage can and your dog doesn't look so hot, call your vet with the symptoms and be prepared to take him in.

String Emergency If you see string or ribbon or yarn hanging out either end of a dog, resist the urge to pull it. You could perforate our intestines and kill us. Instead, call your vet.

Burning Issues If your dog experiences a first or second-degree burn (the kind of burns that sting but aren't life-threatening), immediately immerse the burned area in cool water (not cold water or ice) for 10 to 15 minutes and get him to the vet. If the dog's face is burned, apply a clean, wet sterile dressing. Do not apply butter to any burn. If the burn is severe, do not immerse in water. Cover with a wet sterile dressing (not butter or ice) and rush to the vet. Keep the burned part elevated if possible to reduce swelling. If your dog is unmanageable because of the severe pain, muzzle him.

Major Sniffles After a great walk with Mom and Jiggy one spring afternoon, my nose started running, and running, and then gushing. You would have thought someone had turned on a spigot in my head and couldn't turn it off. My whole face was soaked. I snorted and sneezed and shook my head till it rattled, but my sinuses kept flooding. I ran to Mom and blew some sputum her way. Nothing works like spewed mucus as an attention-getter. Mom retrieved her first-aid books but couldn't fix me. While she read, I ran around in circles (creating a race-track oval of phlegm) and then hid in the closet.

A thorough examination by my vet showed that my vital signs were stable and my nasal cavities weren't swollen. The vet said it *could* be an allergic reaction, and it *would* be $62. Mom got instructions for using Children's Benadryl (which she keeps for emergencies) if I got worse. I didn't.

Poisons If your dog has collapsed and you suspect poisoning, grab the poisonous substance and rush to the vet. Call on the way and tell them what your dog ingested. Take the bottle or a sample with you.

If you catch your dog in the act, call your vet or poison control. Tell them what your dog ate or drank, and how much. The

SCARED POOPLESS

ASPCA National Animal Poison Control Center is on duty 24 hours every day at 888-426-4435 (or 900-443-0000 if you want to bill it to your home phone). A fee ($50 as of this writing) may apply, although follow-up calls are free.

Poison Control or your vet may want you to induce vomiting right away. They'll probably tell you to give 3% hydrogen peroxide one tablespoon of at a time or less (depending on his size) until he starts vomiting. It's important to know that your dog should not vomit up all poisons. (Caustic chemicals can cause more damage as they come back up, collapsed dogs may choke, and there may be no benefit to vomiting up a poison that has been inside your dog too long.) You need a good medical book (the ASPCA produces one) or live medical advice to determine when, and when not to, induce vomiting.

Emergency Situations If you live in a part of the country that experiences fires, hurricanes, earthquakes, floods or tornado or terrorism—that is, everyplace on earth—you need an emergency plan for your dog. I know you're busy, but if you love us . . . . (A little emotional blackmail can be very effective.)

Most "people shelters" won't accept pets, so you need to find out where to take your dog in the event of an emergency. Call your local animal shelter for information. (Find the shelter nearest you at *www.pets911.com* or 1-888-Pets911). Do it now! And while your fingers are clicking away, please find a few pet-friendly hotels in a nearby community and jot down their numbers. (Find links at *dogs4dogs*.) If all your neighbors are affected by the disaster, only early callers will get the rooms.

Because you may have to leave in a hurry, and because someone else may need to rescue your dog, it's important that firefighters and neighbors know that your dogs and other animals need help. Make sure neighbors, know, too—another thing you can do right now. To alert emergency workers that you have a dog inside, your house, post a sign near exits. Find a great form at *www.2ndchance4pets.org*; click Emergency ID Cards.

You also need to have emergency supplies handy, as well as written instructions for caring for your dog until you can rejoin him. Assemble a kit and mark it with a catchy name like Dog Emergency Kit. Detailed instructions await you at *www.hsus.org* (search for Disaster). In the meantime, here's the minimum you need:

- Enough good canned dog food or sealed packets of dry food to last for several days. Include instructions for feeding your dog.
- If your dog is on medication, include instructions detailing what your dog needs and when she needs it. If the medication isn't rapidly perishable, include at least a few pills, plus a copy of your prescription or an empty bottle in case the prescription has to be filled in your absence. Your veterinarian might be overwhelmed with casualties and be unable to get to prescriptions right away.
- A current picture of your dog on which you write 1) your dog's name, breed, and sex, 2) relevant mobile and emergency contact phone numbers for you, your family,

your veterinarian and your dogsitters in case you can't be reached, and, 3) instructions for feeding and medicating.
- A pet first-aid kit.
- An extra collar and leash with a current ID tag.
- A pet carrier your dog likes.

We dogs are domesticated animals who are *no longer capable of fending for ourselves,* and an emergency situation is the worst possible time to throw us to the wolves. If you plan ahead, an emergency might end up being little more than a bump in the road on our journey through life together. If you don't, well, it was nice knowing you. (A little more guilt.)

And remember when I told you that you don't have to be a knight in shining armor? I'll let you in on a dog secret: you *are* our knights in shining armor to rescue us during an emergency, so please do a little polishing for us right now.

Chiclet's Trivia Treat: *Emergency rescue is not a one-way street. For several hundred years, the St. Bernard dog has bailed out Human victims of avalanches and storms in the Alps.*

The breed was named after Bernard of Montjoux, a missionary who founded two 11th century hospices to help lost alpine travelers. St. Bernards did not, despite popular myth, carry little casks of brandy around their necks. They did, however, save many lives.

Alas, helicopters and heat sensors are supplanting the dogs today. (But can they offer the wonderful warm, sloppy kisses the dogs did? I think not.) In 2005, the Augustinian monks of St. Bernard's hospice decided to "rehome" the remaining 18 dogs. The myth about the brandy notwithstanding, I think you Humans should raise a glass and salute those dogs for their centuries of fine rescue work. It's the end of an era.

HOME ALONE

I know a journalist is just supposed to report the facts, but I can't help thinking there's a moral to most of my stories. (Here's the subtext if you've been skimming: our Humans sometimes love us to death.) So instead of being just a reporter in this chapter, I think I'll also be a teller of tales with morals, a fabulist if you will. Aesop, of course, is the most famous fabulist of all. Dozens of his fables feature dogs (which explains his popularity for almost three thousand years).

Aesop wrote about a Maltese in my favorite fable, "The Donkey and the Lapdog." In this tale, a jealous donkey tries to imitate the behavior of a Maltese who was favored by their master. The donkey cavorted around the house, smashing tables and dishes, and even tried to sit in his master's lap and lick his face. Instead of being praised, the donkey was booted back to his stable. Aesop's moral was that the donkey should have been content to be what he was, rather than trying to be something he wasn't. Of course, the moral is a little flawed. Who wouldn't want to be a Maltese?

Another of Aesop's fables, I fear, is very telling of our relationship with you. In "The Dog and the Hare," a Hound is chasing a Hare through a meadow. At one point, the dog bites hard at the Hare as if to kill him; at another point, the Hound playfully curries his favor at the Hare. Finally, the Hare has enough and says to the Hound, "If you are a friend, why do you bite me so hard? If an enemy, why do you fawn on me?"

Aesop's moral was that to be a true friend one must be trustworthy. I hate to say it, but sometimes we wonder whether or not we can trust our Humans. I mean, how can you trust someone who abandons an animal for hours on end when that animal is one who literally lives for companionship? I know you feel bad when you leave us, and that you have to work to support us, but if you'll forgive me for saying so, your guilt doesn't help either of us.

Happily Home Alone The majority of our most annoying habits springs from the lack of a strong leader or too much time alone. We bark too much. We redesign furniture and accessories. We fail Potty Training 101. Unfortunately, when we displease you, we risk losing our home. You know it, and so do we.

Mom and Dad have made it easy on Jiggy and me to be home alone. We have each other for company so we don't get bored and find destructive ways to amuse ourselves. We also have a safe potty area that can be accessed through our very own tiny door so we don't have to squeeze our knees together to keep from peeing on the floor.

If you're a Human who works all day, comes home briefly (to the hero's welcome we give you, I might point out), and then rushes off again, it's time to find a way to make your dog's home alone situation easier on him, and on you.

Perhaps you should get your dog a dog. Even a cat would be someone to talk to. (Yes, the situation is that desperate.) Or maybe you could hire a neighborhood child to stop by and play ball, or could leave the TV tuned to Animal Planet, or could enlist the help of the lonely widower next door. Someone you know loves dogs but for any number of reasons doesn't have one right now. Maybe that person would like to spend time with yours.

In addition to companionship, your dog needs safety. Home might be where the heart is, but it's also where an unsupervised dog finds every danger you can imagine. That's just one reason why dogs left alone need a room of our own. Think of this as our "safe room," and make it that way. I'm not talking about a maximum security prison; I'm talking about a room without electrical wires for us to chew, or containers with poisons for us to drink, or dangerous plants for us to eat. Unless you want your shoes chewed, they shouldn't be there either. Some Humans like to say they "dog-proofed" a room, but that's not a term I like. It sounds like you're protecting the room from *us*. Still, it does give you an idea of what needs doing.

Another reason for a safe room is that your dog will feel far more secure in an enclosed area than he will with an entire house to patrol. Keeping us confined means good things for you, too. No newspaper confetti when you come home, no bedroom papered with Charmin, no squishy brown surprises under the dining room chair. And on those little signs you have for fire fighters—the ones I'm going to insist you have on your major exit doors—you can tell them where to instantly find us during a fire. Some people give us the run of the house, thinking it's cruel to confine us, but we'll mostly sleep or make trouble while you're gone. How much space do we need?

Dog walkers

Humans who work for long hours often rely on dog walkers to keep our bodies slim and our minds active. We love this idea, though not just anyone will do.

If you use a service, find out who'll actually be walking your dog, and whether it'll always be the same person. Ask about experience, their knowledge of first aid and doggy CPR, their discipline standards (and tactics) and what plan they have to stop dog fights.

Learn what route or routes they plan to take, and whether other dogs are will be coming along (and if so, what kind and how many).

Protect your interests, and your dog's. Is your walker bonded and insured? Are you covered if your dog bites either Human or dog, or gets bitten herself? Once you've thoroughly scrutinized your potential walker, go along on a walk. Try to also watch her someday when she doesn't know you're there. As we dogs like to say: better sneaky than sorry.

Finally, ask for at least three references, and actually check them! Yes, they'll probably give you the names of people who like them, but they don't know what great tricky questions you're going to ask.

If your dog walker is a non-professional, go on a few walks together and talk about all the topics we just discussed. Know that Humans with small dogs don't always understand the power and proclivities of big dogs. Conversely, Humans with big dogs don't always understand the needs of little dogs (like our constant need for fawning, tickling and adoration). Don't be afraid to educate them.

Day care

If your dog spends her days staring at the ceiling or eating holes in the floor, doggy day care might be a good option a couple of days a week. Some dogs seem to thrive in this canine version of romper room. Other dogs, especially small fry like me, can be over-whelmed and even endangered by the group environment. Whether or not this is a good option for your dog depends on how well the day care center is run, how safely they transport dogs (if they pick up and deliver), how many people watch over the dogs, and how they separate participants for playtime. It also depends on how well your dog plays with others. The best time to learn about all this is before your dog gets hurt.

Playthings

Our room doesn't have to be solitary confinement. Leave us some toys, will you? But make sure those toys are safe: no eyeballs we can chew off and swallow, no destructible soft rubber toys that might get stuck in our throats, no dangerous materials of any sort (like anything stringy or too plush). Toys need to be small enough for us to get our mouths around them, but not so small we choke or swallow them.

Toys that exercise the mind are especially important if your dog spends long periods of time alone. Unfortunately, what captivates one animal will often bore another, so you'll have to try various toys (and maybe donate the rejects to a shelter). When you find something your dog really loves, take it away from him. Yes, take it away. Save it for those times when your dog has a long stretch alone. The freshness will make the toy all the more exciting. And rotate favorites from week to week. We get tired of the same ol' same ol'. You might also want to wash that same ol' from time to time. If they're sturdy enough for your dog, they're sturdy enough for your washer.

Fighting fire with information

Since fires kill more Humans than all other disasters *combined*, I suspect dogs don't fare too well in fires either.

Post a small sign (see *www. 2ndchance4pets.org*; click Emergency ID Cards) near your main entrances telling fire fighters how many animals live in your house and where they might be hiding, and date those stickers within a year so fire fighters know they're current. Give a trusted neighbor (or two) a key to your house and dog care instructions—just in case.

If you have an alarm, set it when you leave the house. Most systems aren't just for burglars; they call the fire department if sensors detect smoke. They could keep your dog from becoming a crispy critter.

Speaking of fire, do you know why Dalmatians ride on fire trucks? Is it for luck? For color? For crowd control? No, silly. It's to find the fire hydrant!

Potty Areas

Now I know housebreaking doesn't seem like a safety issue, let alone a matter of life and death, and yet one of the common reasons for a dog ending up in a shelter is unbridled piddling and pooping.

Dogs who use the canine equivalent of an outhouse (that is, a yard) can and should be taught to defecate in a specific area. Poop left all over the place attracts flies and provides a growth medium for worms. A product called Simple Solution Pee Post Pheromone-Treated Yard Stake purports to attract dogs to a certain spot. If poop is overtaking your yard, it's worth a try.

If urine spots are a problem, "Dogonit" advertises that it uses enzymes to break down pet urine in your yard (not in your dog). We're not fans of those consumable products that purport to make our urine less problematic. What that goes into our mouths should build doggy health, not lawn beauty.

Newspapers are probably the cheapest *indoor* potty "appliance," but they're also the messiest and dirtiest. "Pee pads" are a better bet,  and work great with puppies and small housedogs. These pads come in both disposable and washable versions. We use Pooch Pads Reusable Housebreaking Pads, which have a permanent anti-bacterial agent that helps keep odor away. Ours have lasted for years and still work great. Find them in stores and on-line.

Doggy doors come in different sizes, and can be put in doors or through walls, and some even work with sliding glass doors. If you have a big dog and a big bank account, you might want a door that opens with a radio or infra-red device attached to your dog's collar to help keep burglars from wiggling through. (Find products and installation tips at *dogs4dogs*).

Most dogs can easily be taught to use a door. Some will pop through the first time you say "come." Others need coaxing. Jiggy *pretended* to need enticement in the form of treats. He was a quarter pound heavier when Mom finally got wise.

Because I weighed less than two pounds when I first encountered a doggy door, I found the flap problematic. Mom taped it up for a while and got me used to going through the open hole. Next, she taped a zip-lock bag in place. When I got used to that, down came the flap.

Wherever you put the doors, just make sure they lead into a secure locked area so neither dognappers nor varmints can get us. (Attention Mr. Dognapper: Our potty area has video surveillance and armed guards patrol our neighborhood. I'm hoping to add a retired CIA agent and a cranky Doberman. Also know that I have teeth and knowhow to use them.)

Barking

Think of unwanted barking as complaining: "You're not earning my respect . . . I'm bored and have too much energy . . . I hate the dog next door . . . you leave me alone too often." That's not to say that barking isn't obnoxious. It is. It's also hazardous to a dog's well-being and to his continued residence at his current address. Barking drives otherwise-kind people to convince themselves that cruel measures aren't really cruel. Desperate people take desperate measures.

One desperate measure they take is an anti-bark shock collar. Trainer Maureen Hall hates them. She says, "Shock collars should be illegal. Period. Many shocked dogs have jumped right through a glass window; another ran under a bush and became so terrified that the humane society had to be called to capture him and remove the collar."

When I think of electro-shock therapy the picture that comes to mind is Nurse Ratched from *One Flew Over the Cuckoo's Nest*. Maureen must think so too, because she added, "We have a lot of cruel gadgets on the market that bring in tons of money for the seller but should never be allowed. In training I ask the person to consider if the method they are using creates a closer loving bond with their animal. If it does, it can't be bad. If the method causes a wall between you, and you become the one on the other side of the fence so to speak, then it is ALL BAD. None of us (man or beast) can learn anything when the flight or fight mode kicks in. The brain as is used for intellectual learning is not accepting anything at that time."

Some people report success with citronella spray collars, but while artificial methods may stop the noise, remember, the sadness or aggression behind the barking remains.

What about *debarking?* A laryngectomy—the medical term for the procedure also called "debarking"—doesn't end barking but rather mutates it into something pitiful. Many vets describe it as dangerous, unnecessary and fraught with complications. Learn more at *www.cliniciansbrief.com*, click Polling Place, and search for Debarking.

Barking is tough to stop for the same reason overeating is: sometimes it serves a good purpose. A behaviorist who specializes in humane methods to cure the underlying cause is your best bet. In the meantime, try to find ways to occupy your dog be it toys, frequent visits, or a canine friend. And give your dog lots of exercise.

Escape artistry

If your dog is a frequent runaway, it's time to ask yourself why he isn't happy. Is he lonely? Bored? Looking for love? (*Neutered* male dogs are generally less prone to roam than their "intact" counterparts.)

Please don't resort to chaining your dog or using shock collars. They're just too dangerous. If your yard and gate cannot be properly secured, keep your dog inside when you're not home. This is a good idea in any event. You'll protect him from outside dangers and his bad impulses.

The Humane Society has a great article about "hairy Houdinis." Read it at *www.hsus.org*; search for Escape.

Separation anxiety

Some dogs go berserk when their Humans leave. They bark and howl and cry for hours. They eat the floor and shred the upholstery. They pee small lakes or squeeze out brown "messages" everywhere. Neighbors complain of the noise. The vicious cycle gets worse. It's up to you to break that cycle.

These dogs are telling you in every way they can that they're lonely and suffering and afraid that they've been abandoned. They are not bad but merely unhappy and insecure. Separation anxiety is a complex problem you won't solve overnight, and is best addressed by a behaviorist if one is available and affordable. In the meantime, read all you can. Go to *www.hsus.org* (search for Separation Anxiety) or *www.kibblesnbits.com/dogcare/article.aspx?i=20*. Also try Dr. Patricia B. McConnell's book, *I'll Be Home Soon.*

There's a medication available for separation anxiety—some call it Prozac for dogs—but do not expect a miracle or to be able cure the problem without behavior modification. Also remember: most medications have side effects. Before giving any drug to your dog, check out possible adverse reactions. (See my index for how to do it.)

When You Go Away Frankly, dogs don't understand why you wouldn't want to spend all your time with us. Who could possibly be as much fun as we are? What we *particularly* can't understand is why you would abandon us at a group home or leave us for days and even weeks with a breeze-by kibble-dumper just to go on some dumb trip.

Jiggy and I are lucky. When Mom and Dad have to leave town, one of our favorite dogsitters sleeps over. In fact, when Mom and Dad are out of town, we party, party, party!

Staying in our own home not only gives us the feeling that Mom and Dad will come back, it also keeps us safe from the kennel cough, parasites and skin diseases that come with groups of dogs. We also avoid those needless vaccinations required for compliance to some arbitrary and unscientific standard. Surprisingly, dogsitters are often no more expensive than a kennel and are even *less* expensive if you count potential savings on veterinary bills. You also get a housesitter thrown in for free!

Of course, not just any dogsitter will do. Ask responsible friends if they'd be interested, particularly fun friends who already know and love your dog. Also inquire at your vet's office, grooming establishment, or local shelter. They often have lists of people who'd love to stay with your four-legged waif.

If you still can't find a sitter, try the National Association of Professional Pet Sitters (at 800-296-PETS or *www.petsitters.org*) and Pet Sitters International (at 336-983-9222 or *www.petsit.com*). They'll help you find an insured and bonded professional and their sites are full of helpful tips.

Before entering into any arrangement, make sure the dogsitter understands your expectations. Our *numero uno* question is always: how much time can you spend with us? If they work all day and party all night, keep looking. The next question is: are you willing to prepare our meals and give us our meds and rub our tummies endlessly? The answer must be a resounding *yes*!

A home away from home

There are kennels, and then there arc kennels. Some of the swankiest (and surprisingly, not always the most expensive) have cable TV with the Animal Planet channel playing all day, spa services, no cages, a webcam to ease parental worries, lots of organized play time, and tapes of Mom and Dad saying they love us and will be home soon.

The worst places are dirty jails, rampant with disease and neglect.

How do you find a good kennel? The best way is to make an unannounced visit. Check out the premises and ask to talk to repeat clients. Also, find a place certified by the American Boarding Kennels Association. Go to *www.ABKA.com* to find operators that are in voluntary compliance with ABKA standards and whose premises have been inspected by professionals. Look for a current certificate on premises, along with a CKO plaque, given to Certified Kennel Operators.

When checking out a place, make sure it looks and smells clean. Ask about decontamination procedures: when, where and with what? Find out about ventilation, and how the temperature is regulated (or isn't). Check out the sleeping areas. Do they look comfy and safe? If yours is an "indoor" dog, can they handle his special needs?

Look for security between dogs, and from outsiders. Make sure your dog, pining for his family, can't scale fences or dig his way back home. One German Shepherd we know escaped from the same kennel three times in a week!

Inquire about areas for public areas, and ask how often dogs are exercised. Use your eyes and nose to make sure the runs and play areas are free of feces. Ask, do they have people who'll play with your dog? Can you buy *extra* playtime if you want it?

Good kennels tend to book up early during the holidays, so make your reservations early. Expect to be asked for your dog's vaccination records and perhaps a health certificate. If they let your dog in without them, they'll let others in without them, and that's not good. On the other hand, you know how I feel about over-vaccination, so find out if the kennel owner will accept titer testing in lieu of shots. Be forewarned: this may require a vet's letter of exemption and a pushy personality.

If you do have to leave us, bring along our favorite foods and bottled water (if we use it) to save us from tummy upset). Make

sure we have our meds; if the medication schedule is complicated, provide a chart showing times and doses. In your absence, comfort is hard to come by so bring along our bed, favorite toys, and safe things to chew. And be casual about the separation. We don't want to think something bad is happening and get freaked out by your leaving.

I know you probably think I'm a little paranoid when it comes to kennels, but I'm really not a yellow journalist. I'm just concerned. Not too long ago a fellow writer, *New York Post* columnist Cindy Adams, left her dog in a kennel selected by her dog's trainer. That should have been safe, huh? It wasn't. Her beloved Jazzy didn't make it out alive. Since that terrible occurrence, Ms. Adams has become an advocate for kennel safety.

Was Jazzy's death an anomaly? Unfortunately, not. A friend of Mom's lost her 14-year-old dog to bronchitis contracted in a kennel. (Sleepovers away from home are especially hard on the old and the weak.) Mom's niece Stacey also lost a dog to a kennel-related illness. Still another dog we know developed a lifelong case of separation anxiety. Promise me you'll remember these stories when you're next confronted with the dogsitter- or-kennel decision. Promise? Good.

I wish Aesop had written a fable about kennels, but he didn't. He did write one called "The Dog's House." It's a story of a dog who, one winter, began contemplating building himself a house. He knew that a *wintertime* dog needed a small space where he could curl up and stay cozy and warm. A *summertime* dog, however, needed a big place where he could stretch out and be cool. This was indeed quite a problem.

There is no handy moral to this particular fable, except perhaps, that dogs don't make good architects. Morals aren't what dogs need anyway. We just need a secure room that's warm in winter and cool in summer, complete with a suitable potty area, and maybe a radio playing. We need water and toys and comfort food—and lots of time with you when you come. Wait. I just thought of a moral to this chapter: take care of your dog even in your absence and you'll both live happily ever after.

Don't you just love happy endings? Speaking of endings . . .

Chiclet's Trivia Treat: *As I wrote about potty areas, I began pondering poop. Did you know that the word, when used as a euphemism for excrement, probably came from the Middle English poupen, which meant to toot or "break wind?" Stop that giggling! I don't make this stuff up.*

Poop contains water, fiber, bacteria, mucus, dead cells, and protein. If it's black or streaked with bright red, it may contain blood; save a sample and call your vet. Runny poop can be caused by infections, parasites, food intolerances, reactions to meds, and intestinal or bowel diseases. Short-term diarrhea is seldom anything to worry about, but long-term diarrhea is.

Some dogs eat poop (theirs and others') and it seems to bother their Humans. Experts differ on what causes this charming practice (called coprophagia). Some vets think dogs do it to get protein or other nutrients missing in their diets. Others believe that coprophagia grows out of boredom or is a lingering puppyhood habit. How do you stop it? Join the poop patrol. What isn't there can't be eaten.

Disappearing Dogs

Whenever my Mom goes hunting for something our house has swallowed, she mumbles an adage under her breath. The first few times I heard her, I didn't quite understand what she was saying. Still, I listened with my usual interest, cocking my head in a really cute way. Even when it's not clear what Humans are saying, their weird sounds fascinate me endlessly. Anyway, Mom's adage now makes sense to me, and even pertains to the subject at hand. I think it's called a proverb:

SCARED POOPLESS

For want of a nail the shoe was lost;
For want of a shoe the horse was lost;
For want of a horse the rider was lost;
For want of a rider the battle was lost;
For want of a battle the kingdom was lost;
And all for the want of a horseshoe nail.

No, I'm not writing about nails or lost kingdoms. I'm writing about dogs and the ways in which they disappear. Every year *millions* of dogs are lost or stolen. Yes, that's the figure with six zeroes after it, and that's what this chapter is all about. And lest you think all of those animals were lost, there are a number of animal advocacy groups (In Defense of Animals, Stolen Pets and Last Chance for Animals) that believe between one and two million dogs are *stolen* every year. Even if you think that figure is way off, that's still an enormous number of my fellow dogs who are purloined every year. Mom has her favorite adage about nails, but it makes more sense to me this way: *the dog was lost; and all for the want of Human intervention.* About a hundred sentences precede it.

Since you're reading this book, I know you're a good Human. Like Mom, you must really hate the sight of a confused dog trying to navigate a busy street all on his own. Maybe you're one of those Humans who've stopped to help a woebegone stray. Too often, though, the dog is not wearing a collar (for want of a collar . . .) or ID (for want of a dog tag . . .). You might want to help, but are rightfully afraid of the risks a stray dog might bring.

The Humane Society of the United States estimates that only 30% of dogs who made it to surveyed shelters were ever reunited with their Moms and Dads. Want some more bad news? Only about half the dogs making it to shelters are even wearing collars, let alone tags.

Think your beloved friend will never be separated from you? As dogs say, poop happens. Is your dog wearing a collar at this moment? With ID tags containing current information? If she slips the collar (which happens all the time), do you have a Plan B?

With an ounce or two of prevention (say it with me, "The dog was *not* lost") you can prevent this from happening. Start by helping your dog want to stay at home. Dogs who get exercise and have plenty of Human or canine company seldom roam to find fun and excitement. Neutered or spayed dogs, like Jiggy and me, don't leave home looking for love.

If we see a rabbit hopping along outside a screened window, or if little Jimmy leaves the back door ajar, fenced and locked yards will keep us safe. If your dog slips out the open door (because no one taught him to wait for an invitation to leave), knowing to obey the word *come* may save his life. *Come* must be the first commandment in your dog's vocabulary. It must be The Law, enforced every day and everywhere. If you don't enforce it, bad things could happen. (For want of a Human teaching the word *come*, the dog was lost.)

And please, don't make me tell you again about pet carriers and doggy seat belts. Mom's friend Patti told us that her two unsecured Scotties escaped during an accident. Bonnie, who was older and wiser, came back right away. Casey endured 16 days in the wild (and two snowstorms) before they found her skinny and shaking and laden with ticks. Most dogs aren't so lucky. There are few happy endings to the canine version of the Great Escape, especially when dogs escape far away from home. Even if they make it to a shelter, unidentified and unclaimed dogs are too often euthanized after only a few days.

Identifying Your Dog

Tags

For want of a dog tag . . . well, you know. When it comes to tags:

- Information is useless if it's not current and complete. (Does it list all your phone numbers?)
- Have duplicates handy (because they always break off);
- Dogs with special medical needs should have a doggy Medic-Alert tag to alert Good Samaritans as well as veterinarians.

SCARED POOPLESS

I hear Humans are always trying to improve mousetraps (though, so far, the mice don't seem too scared). Fortunately they've done a better job on dog tag and collar innovations. The Dog-E-Tag, for example, scrolls up to 40 lines of digital data and can be updated at a moment's notice. Collars can be embroidered with your phone number (which is great for big, scary dogs that people might be afraid to approach). Find links at *dogs4dogs* for collars and IDs mentioned here.

Microchips

Many Humans have already gone high-tech with dog identification. We did years ago. When we were pups, Mom had Jigs and me fitted with microchips. I know that might sound a little Orwellian, but it's the latest thing for beloved dogs. And it sure beats being adopted by strangers or ending up being euthanized at a shelter because nobody knows we have parents who love us and want us back. As a bonus, if someone ever steals us, Mom and Dad can prove we belong to them.

Getting chipped is no big deal. (Don't make me say *for want of* again.) The vet implants this thing that's about the size of a grain of rice between our shoulder blades. I got mine when I was spayed, but you can get it anytime. Mom says she can feel it, but I don't even know it's there.

Chips are a great innovation, but aren't perfect. I don't think you should say Good-bye, Mr. Chips, but you need to consider the following:

- Not all scanners can read chips, and no one chip is readable by all scanners. In fact, *the scanner your local shelter uses may be incapable of reading, let alone detecting, your dog's chip.* And if the chip isn't read, and you don't rescue her in time, your dog may be killed. In fact, this has already happened. Lawsuits rage and the controversy over scanners continues. (Search for "ISO" at *www.AVMA.org* for current information.)

- If your dog is already chipped, check with your local shelters (not just the closest one) and see if they have the scanner your dog needs. If not, call the microchip company and ask them to send one—free of charge. If they won't do it, ask your vet to take action. A chip that can't be read gives you a false sense of security and your dog a potential death sentence.

- As a backup, make sure your dog wears a tag, as Jiggy and I do, identifying the microchip company and giving ID numbers. Then, even if they can't read our chips, they'll know to call the company so we can get back home really fast.

- If you haven't already "chipped" your dog, call local shelters to see what scanners they have, and then ask for the names of vets who install that chip. Find local shelters at *www.pets911.com* or 1-999-PETS911.

- World travelers should know that other countries use a different scanner than the most common ones here. If your dog is traveling to the European Union, you'll need a chip or tattoo matching the number on your dog's rabies certificate. Might as well get it now, before your dog starts hinting about that vacation.

Tattoos

On Humans, tattoos are too scary. I know one man with a giant, growling lion on his bicep that looks like it's attacking when the man flexes his muscle. Yikes! On dogs, however, tattoos are much more becoming and also serve a good purpose. Aside from providing an identification number, they offer an important added bonus if a dog is ever stolen: research laboratories are forbidden to do testing on dogs with tattoos. How good is that?

Most people put the tattoo on the inside of a dog's rear thigh. Don't use the ear; some sociopath might cut it off. Your vet (not your local tattoo parlor) can numb the area so it doesn't hurt, although some dogs might still find the whole process unnerving.

SCARED POOPLESS

Try a little Rescue Remedy first. Jiggy wants a tattoo that says MOM. (Why not *CHICLET*, I'd like to know?) Mom says he can have it if he pays for it himself, but something tells me she doesn't mean it.

So should you get a tat rather than a chip? Not if your dog has long hair that'll hide it. And maybe not if your dog isn't one who'd take kindly to being flipped over while rescuers hunt for it. I know a few dogs with both a microchip and a tattoo. So far it's not a doggy status thing (you know, my Human loves me more than your Human loves you), but dogs sporting both tat and chip do seem to be acting awfully smug.

Whether you get chipped or tattooed or both, you'll need to join a national registry. Otherwise, it's useless, like having a license plate that isn't linked to a car. Use the registry connected with the chip or tat, or the American Kennel Club's registry (*www. AKCCAR.org*).

Gadgets

Not *Brave New World* enough for you yet? There are lot of high-tech dog gadgets poking their heads over the horizon. You can locate your prodigal dog with global positioning satellite (GPS) technology as fast as your sophisticated dog can proclaim himself, "Beagle, James Beagle." Or you can get the collar that E.T. the Extra-Terrestial would have really enjoyed wearing. Just push a button and it calls home. Find the latest gadgets by searching on-line for "dogs and GPS" or "dogs and cell."

ID photos

Of course, sometimes low-tech solutions can be the most effective of all. Don't underestimate the value of current color photographs of your dog. I'm not not talking glamour shots, either. You're not trying to get your dog a guest shot in Benji's latest movie; this shot is for identification. It needs to actually look like your dog, show-ing size, color, breed and important stuff like that. And while you're at it, take a couple of close-up photos of any identifying marks (beauty marks or freckles or notched ears) that your dog might have. (I have a secret beauty mark. *Shhhhhhhh.*) If your dog isn't tattooed or microchipped, you may someday need identification to prove you're the guardian of your rover. You know how police withhold certain evidence from the public? You need to do the same thing. Keep these photos safe and don't ever use them on a "Lost Dog" poster. They are your proof positive that you are our Mom or Dad.

Lost Dogs If despite your best efforts your dog gets lost, don't panic or despair. That wastes a lot of time and energy. Instead:

- Contact nearby vets and animal shelters. Start with those nearest you and work your way out. Someone may have thought they were helping your dog by picking her up, but then deposited her in a shelter a town or two away. (Why *do* people do this?)

- Tack up flyers everywhere. Identify your dog with a name, a photo, description (breed or mix), color, and size and weight. Include a telephone number (preferably a cell phone number that can't be linked to your home address). List your *first name only*. DO NOT list your address. An opportunistic thief might lift your TIVO knowing you're out looking for your dog.
- Make your flyer impossible to miss; big and bright with easy-to-read lettering works best. An 8 1/2 x 11

black-and-white photocopy is easily overlooked. Your dog deserves better. Emphasize the words *Reward* and *Lost Dog* (or better yet, say something like *Lost Black Lab*). Laminate the poster to make it rainproof. A poster with bleeding letters and a damaged photo won't get your dog back.

- Place ads in newspapers.
- Extend your search online. Find sites with important information at *dogs4dogs*; many post "lost dog" notices.
- Go to the National Pet Recovery (find a link at *dogs4dogs*) and download their free Pet Detective's Guide. This investigative reporter was impressed at the 32 pages full of valuable information and instructions for finding your pet. For a fee, they'll even help you.

Unfortunately, there are Humans who might try to benefit from this stressful situation. Some experts insist it's best to offer a big reward on the posters you circulate; others suggest just adding the word REWARD, fearing that you might be tempting scam artists. Whatever you do, proceed with caution. I know you're desperate to be reunited with your best friend, but be careful about meeting the "rescuer." If you're offering a reward, pick a safe public place. Your bank might work. Or you could meet at your vet's office or an animal shelter. Do not, in your grief, forget to protect your own safety. You'll do your dog no good lying unconscious in some ditch. Remember: most dogs can be trusted not to rob you, but some Humans can't.

Finding a Stray

So what do you do when the paw is on the other leg and you find a lost dog? Ask your local shelter or vet to check the dog for a microchip or tattoo. If they find one, call the registry. If not, call, email or fax all the local shelters and provide them a photo, particulars of the dog you have found, and your telephone numbers.

Should you leave the found dog at a "kill" shelter, and you don't want the worst to happen, Best Friend's Animal Society suggests you request "first and last rights." First rights give you a chance to adopt a dog not claimed by his owners; last rights give you a chance to adopt him before he's euthanized. Keep calling the shelter, too. Think of how terrible it would be if they forget to call you.

For more information on how to deal with a found dog, go to *dogs4dogs* and read our S.O.S. (Save Orphaned Strays) tip sheet. We also provide a link to several wonderful organizations that offer pertinent advice on how to deal with found dogs.

Stolen Dogs With so many poor dogs looking for homes, you wouldn't think that you'd have to worry about your dog being stolen, but that's not the case. Small (very portable) purebreds like me are at the most risk of being snatched, but even big dogs are vulnerable. (Remember Buck from *The Call of the Wild*?)

I hate to say this, but you need to think of your dog as a bag of cash. The more money in the bag, the more tempting it is to strangers.

You may want to think that some sweet old Granny stole your dog to take her to live in her mansion, but that's seldom what happens. Thieves sell the dogs through ads usually with some sob story about an imminent move or a new allergy. (They don't call them lying thieves for nothing.) Some turn "intact" dogs into breeding machines in "puppy mills" (Their pups grow up in crampled wire cages).

Lucky dogs are stolen for ransom and returned; *unlucky* dogs turn up dead (although death may be a better alternative than being sold to a research lab or a trainer of fighting dogs). If you're not convinced about the need to keep your dog safe, go to *www.pet-abuse.com;* but be forewarned—what you'll find there is truly shocking.

The Animal Welfare Act, passed in 1966, was pushed through Congress because of the disappearance of so many dogs and cats. Currently, the U.S. Department of Agriculture (USDA) is responsible for enforcing the act, although detractors say enforcement is sketchy at best. Although the theft of animals is theoretically illegal, they may be "collected" (I say, sacrificed) for biomedical research. (The USDA says 68,253 dogs were officially registered for research in 2002, although these figures are probably low.) Help support legislation to close loopholes at *www.stolenpets.com*.

I don't like it when dogs pick fights with each other, but I really hate it when Humans make dogs fight for profit. This practice involves not only the fighters, but also "practice" dogs that are stolen to teach the fighters to maul and kill. I'm telling you all this to show you why you must keep your dogs safe from the monsters who traffic in blood money.

And as unsavory as all of this is, it only gets worse. An article in the *Honolulu Star-Bulletin* (August 20, 2004) said dogs might be in danger of being stolen and slaughtered for their meat. I can't believe it, but in some cultures dog meat is considered a delicacy. Some years ago, one of Mom's friends says she had a puppy who was stolen for food by her next-door neighbor; they retrieved her just in time. It's not just a dog-eat-dog world, it's also a Human-eat-dog-world.

Unfortunately, dog thieves don't necessarily look (or act) like monsters. Mom's friend Anne had her gorgeous Springer Spaniel

stolen from her yard. Earlier that day, a sweet-looking woman had fawned over the dog at a local pet store. Anne thinks the woman must have followed her home. She hasn't seen her dog since. (Do you keep your dog inside when you're gone? You should. Or at least make sure the poor dear is not visible from the street.)

Pretending your dog isn't at risk only puts him more at risk. There will always be strangers who want your dog and will be brazen about snatching him. Last month a woman gave us a flyer for a Miniature Pinscher who'd been snatched in broad daylight from her locked S.U.V. The woman said she'd always left him in the car and nothing bad had ever happened. I wonder, would that woman have left a pocketbook full of money in her vehicle? (Remember, your dog is a bag of cash.) Little dogs can easily and quickly disappear into knapsacks, purses and boxes. Big dogs have been known to vanish into an accomplice's waiting car. Your dog is an especially easy target if she's tied up outside a store or left alone in your car.

If you know your dog was stolen, rather than lost, take immediate action. To my thinking, dog thieves are like cattle rustlers and the laws of the Old West should apply. I suspect Mom feels the same way, although she says now that public hangings are frowned upon, you should do the following instead:

- Post *Stolen Dog* flyers around your community. Maybe a snitch will speak up if you offer a reward.
- If your dog was stolen from a shopping center, post signs and talk to merchants. Maybe this has happened before and someone has information.
- Ask the local police if dogs have been disappearing a lot. Insist they file a report in case your dog is the first theft of a new dog-theft ring.
- Check the newspapers in your county, and surrounding areas, to see if a dog matching your dog's description is offered for sale. Your dog may have been taken by professional thieves so proceed with cleverness and caution. Don't go alone to "buy" the dog back.
- The free 32-page *Pet Detective's Guide* at *www.petrecovery. com* could be your best chance to get your dog back. If your dog is gone, download it now.

Recently CNN reported the theft of an 80-year-old man's beloved terrier. After paying over ten thousand dollars in ransom, the terrier was returned. Only then did the man call the police. I wonder, what will keep the thieves from taking the same dog again? I also worry that this is the start of a trend. Soon after, Paris Hilton's Chihuahua Tinkerbell went missing. She reportedly gave five thousand dollars for Tink's return.

Whether or not your dog lives out her life with you is largely within your control. Let's make this our new adage: *Because a Human intervened, a dog lived happily ever after.* Won't you please help your dog stay with you forever and ever? We don't want to disappear. If you help us, you'll get a treat.

Chiclet's Trivia Treat: *Mom remembers as a child singing a little ditty, never knowing it was called "Der Deitcher's Dog," and not knowing all the awful final lyrics. Written during the Civil War in 1864 by Septimus Winner, it was a big hit with Humans (but not dogs or horses), and tells of the loss of a German's dog. It begins and ends with these lyrics:*

Oh where, Oh where ish mine little dog gone;
Oh where, Oh where can he be . . . .
His ears cut short und his tail cut long:
Oh where, Oh where ish he.

Un sasage ish goot, bolonie of course
Oh where, Oh where can he be
Dey makes em mit dog und dey makes em mit horse
I guess dey makes em mit he . . . .

The Not-So-Great Outdoors

Sometimes a "Lost Dog" poster means a gator or coyote is no longer hungry. Theoretically, I empathize. If a juicy Gecko ever dares cross my path, it's history! But when I think of me or Jigs on someone else's menu, well, that's another matter entirely. I'm glad we have an overprotective Mom who will make sure that doesn't happen. Other dogs aren't so lucky. If you'll pardon me saying so, Humanity stinks at keeping us safe.

All sorts of canine serial murderers are lurking out there. Especially if you're new to an area (move just a few blocks and everything can change), won't you please call the nearest emergency vet clinic and ask what predators stalk local dogs? Do it now. I'll chew on my worry beads until you return.

SCARED POOPLESS

Welcome back. Those of you who made the call were probably surprised at how long your predator list was. Depending on where you live, you could have been warned about coyotes, alligators, wolves, bears, moose, elk, bobcats, mountain lions, large raptors, raccoons, skunks, or poisonous snakes. Even in mostly residential areas, potential dangers lay in wait as you Humans encroach on predators' territories. And don't forget about roaming dogs; our brothers and sisters can be the biggest threat of all. Humans say: "know thine enemy." Hey, you need to know our enemies, too. That means learning if predators are aggressive (like coyotes that snatch dogs off leashes and doorsteps) or whether they're just a problem on nature walks.

When walking or playing where predators or loose dogs can be a problem, Mom carries a cell phone in case she needs to summon emergency help (or make emergency dinner reservations). She also carries DirectStop Animal Deterrent Spray, a citronella spray intended to deter "aggressive animals." I can't guarantee that it works against lions or tigers or bears, but we feel safer with it than without it. And if coyotes patrol your property line, also check out *www.coyoteroller.com*, a product claiming to keep predators from scaling fences.

Coyotes

This is a safe coyote.

At first glance, coyotes look way too scrawny to be dangerous, but underestimating them can prove fatal. They can scale a six foot fence with a Dachshund in their mouth. They stalk their prey. They wait. They dig. They offer to play, then pounce. Coyotes have even been known to lure dogs away during crowded lawn parties. They know nothing of party etiquette.

Because coyotes are such avid hunters, Humans with small or medium-sized dogs should avoid early morning or late after-noon/evening constitutionals in areas where these predators are known to roam. If coyotes watch your house, allow no unsupervised outdoor play, and never tether your dog in the yard. Keep him tethered on walks, however. A leash is a lifeline to pull your pup back to safety, and has saved the lives of more than a few of our friends. Even big dogs need to be wary. A pack of coyotes killed a German Shepherd in a canyon near us. Another pack besieged a woman in her driveway and snatched her Labrador pup; hikers found his collar, piled with others, in a canyon not far away.

Coyotes live throughout the U.S., but are particularly danger-ous in the Southwest from Texas to California. If their eating dogs and cats isn't enough danger for you, know that they also can carry a form of rabies dangerous to Humans.

Other wild predators

Alligators, I hear, are as sneaky as coyotes. They come slithering out of nowhere to gobble you up. Watch for these eating machines if you live or play near any fresh water throughout the southeastern United States.

Moose and elk have been known to charge and kill dogs. Bears can be dangerous, too, especially for dogs defending their homes. And don't even get me started about large raptors. When you're a baby-bunny sized dog as I am, you're vulnerable to attack from air, ground and water. (Think I'd better stay out of the military.)

Danger from our own

Our friend, Kitchie the Beagle, was minding her own business in her own yard when a roving white German Shepherd dug his way in and attacked her as she dove under the house for safety. It was touch and go for three days, but Kitchie pulled through. Unfortu-nately, the attack left her body deformed and her nerves shattered.

Your vet will tell you that one of the greatest dangers we face is from unrestrained dogs. Whether you have the little guy who's torn to pieces, or the big guy who does the tearing, the experience will surely haunt you. And cost you. The Shepherd's family had to pay Kitchie's substantial vet bills. Had Kitchie died, the Shepherd's folks might have been liable for her reasonable market value along with legal fees and maybe a kicker for emotional distress. Look for laws to become even more punitive as lawmakers start seeing us more as family than property.

I know your dog keeps telling you he wants to run free, and if you have a safe place to let him run *while you watch*, and he's well socialized and obedient, you may want to indulge him. But know that what seems like harmless fun can turn into danger in a heartbeat. A loose dog is *a potential victim* (from cars, snakes and other animals, not to mention Animal Control), *a potential weapon* (if he attacks another dog or a Human), and *a potential defendant* (so we hope you like lawyers and court fees).

Not long ago seventeen dogs running loose were poisoned in a Portland, Oregon park that was at the center of an ongoing controversy over unleashed dogs. All but three of the dogs died.

Socialization Dogs are social creatures. In fact, we're the ultimate party animals. We'll readily make friends with people or with other animals, although we have to learn how to behave with both. Jiggy and I were home schooled for the most part. In hindsight, Mom wishes we had gone to classes with other dogs. The best way to socialize your dog is in a puppy group class. If it's too late for that, talk with trainers, be candid about your dog's shortcomings, and enroll in an appropriate class as soon as you can.

I don't want to sound like Miss Maltese Manners, but if you want your dog to be part of your social life, you'll have to teach him to play well with others. Properly socialized dogs go to dog beaches, dog parks, and dog charity events. Unsocialized dogs stay home and too often end their lives in shelters.

When dogs *don't* play well together, and biting and growling are involved, fights happen. If you don't want to get bitten yourself, never step between fighters. Instead, try stopping aggression with a good dousing of water. You can also try throwing a blanket, towel or jacket on the warriors' heads. If you have DirectStop, this might be a good time to use it.

Walkin' the Dog When we venture out into the great outdoors, Mom always insists that we "heel." At first I resented this, thinking she was cramping my free-roving style, but then I realized she was just trying to keep us safe. No one will trip on us if we stay close to Mom's side. No predator can grab us without bringing her wrath into play. And we can't wander into danger without Mom seeing it first and pulling us away. And you know what? Being six feet ahead of her isn't really the fun it's cracked up to be.

Walks are a great time to enforce your position as your dog's leader. And don't forget that if you don't have two hands on our leash, you're risking that a jerk on the leash (no pun intended) will set us free. When you let the handle end of our leash trail behind us, it could get tangled or stepped on. Good way to break a neck. (See *dogs4dogs* for more about leadership.)

Collars to die for

Jiggy and I wear harnesses. Some vets suggest that small dogs who strain against leashes are better off wearing harnesses rather than collars so as to distribute the stress onto our whole bodies rather than on our fragile throats and necks. Harnesses also allow you to airlift your dog to safety in an emergency with less risk of injury.

They're great if your dog, like me, suffers from "reverse sneezing," a condition where you go around honking like a wounded goose. If you saw me during one of my attacks you'd probably start wondering how to do a doggy Heimlich maneuver (instructions for which you can link to from *dogs4dogs*). Rubbing my throat helps alleviate this condition, as do efforts to relax me. (This should be distinguished from a collapsed trachea, which is more like a chronic cough and requires medical attention. Learn more at *www.maltesonly.com/trachea.html*.)

Collar selection

There are three things to think about when buying a collar and a leash: you want to be able to slip two fingers between collar and neck so your dog doesn't choke or wiggle out, you want security and strength and buckles that don't slip, and you want a weight appropriate for your dog. Wait! You also want it to look cool.

If your dog spends a lot of unsupervised time outdoors (or in a crate), consider a breakaway collar. Hands-free leashes are available for joggers and chronic cell-phone users and others who'd prefer holding something other than a leash. Night owls who take their dogs on nocturnal strolls should check out all the choices for reflective, flashing, and glowing doggy vests. There are even special flashlights we dogs can wear around our necks. (Ever see a four-legged lighthouse?) You'll find links to some of these neat collars, harnesses, leashes, and items at *dogs4dogs*.

By the way, nothing looks dorkier than a four-pound-dog dragging a 300-pound linebacker down the street. If you're an obedience class dropout, re-enlist. In the meantime, you might try a Gentle Leader on your dog. It looks like a muzzle, acts like horse's halter, and is recommended by many trainers and veterinarians.

You might also consider the routine that Mom uses on us. When we start pulling, without saying a word she stops to smell the roses. When we settle down, she starts walking again. If we pull again, she stops again. Periodically, to keep us alert, she changes directions and routes. It doesn't take us long to realize we're getting nowhere fast, so we settle down. Until we get anxious again. Then once more she stops to smell those roses, which isn't such a bad thing for either dogs or Humans when you think about it.

Runaways

You call, but Fifi runs away. You get anxious and yell. She runs faster. You chase her. Bye bye, Fifi.

If your dog gets away from you, many trainers suggest you stay calm, call the dog in your *let's have fun voice,* and then run *away* from her. Yes! Run in the opposite direction. She's more likely to chase you than let herself to be caught.

Choke collars

Dogs behave properly for people we respect. No amount of pain will make us respect someone we've deemed unworthy. We are no fans of training gimmicks that are coercive or cause pain.

If you decide to use a choke collar remember that they're strictly for training and never for use on an unattended dog. Learn to use it properly. There's a right way to attach it, and a wrong way. And never tether a dog wearing a choke. You could return home to find him hung.

The Straight Scoop on Poop I'm mortified that, in the 21st Century, I still find myself with no better alternative than pooping in the street. I mean, would doggy toilets be so much to ask?

I know you'd clean up after me as a courtesy to your fellow Humans who otherwise might find the remains of my last meal adhering to their Manolo Blahniks. But there's another reason to tidy up after me and my friends: *disease.* If you leave Bruno's poop where I sniff, and Bruno (unbeknownst to you) is sick or wormy, I, too, might end up sick or wormy. Ever think about that?

Columnist Dave Barry once said, "The ground is a giant dog newspaper, containing all kinds of late-breaking dog news . . ." He couldn't have been more right. He failed to mention that much of that news is bad. Your dog may be sniffing up bacteria and other bad things. Two of the worst things your dog can pick up sniffing around other dog's feces and urine are distemper and parvovirus. You vaccinated adult dog is probably safe from the two diseases, but watch out for your puppy.

SCARED POOPLESS

Mom taught us to pee and poop on command when we were pups. Every time we'd start to squat, she'd say "go potty." Upon completion of our task, a treat would magically appear. Hey, we were going to go anyway. The treat just made it worth our while to go when she wanted. We don't get treats anymore, but still do as Mom asks. Guess we're creatures of habit.

Weathering the Outdoors I don't sweat the small stuff. In fact, I don't sweat at all except through minimal glands in my feet and the tip of my nose. Because of that, I'm in danger of dying during hot weather. We canines have only one cooling mechanism: panting. And it's woefully inadequate. (You did read my warning in AUTO ANXIETY, didn't you?)

If you see our tongues hanging out, and our breathing is noisy or labored, please give us water or an ice cube to lick, and find us some shade. (Note: Flat-faced dogs get distressed especially fast.)

If it's really hot, we might even need a cool (not cold) sponge

bath or a dip in a pond or pool. If distress continues, get us to a vet fast.

Where hot weather activities are the norm, get your pooch a cooling vest. Dogs die of heat-stroke. We can tell you when we're in danger, but you have to listen.

My dawgs are barking

It's probably appropriate that some Humans refer to their feet as barking dawgs when they're hurting. Our paws bark, too. Most dogs spend more time frolicking on plush carpets and sliding on cool travertine tiles than they do pounding asphalt, so when you take us for walks on a hot day, remember our tender tootsies. If you wouldn't walk barefoot on hot asphalt, don't ask us to do it either.

And just as heat can hurt our tootsies, so can extreme cold. So if I'm an inside dog walking in the snow, please get me some booties. Rubber-sole booties might even save your dog's life. Snow and salt can become deadly conductors of "hot spots" on city streets. Live wires can electrically charge gratings, manhole covers and metal service boxes which can then electrocute dogs (and Humans, too). CNN just reported the death of a Boxer, and the near death of three other dogs, in three northeastern cities.

Oh, one more request: after a walk in dirty snow or on salted roads, if I'm not wearing booties, please wash my feet with tepid (not hot) water. Otherwise, we'll have to remove any poisonous chemicals with our tongues. Yuk!

Freezin', freezin', for no good reason

Dogs have been domesticated too long to sleep outdoors. Maybe you can cuddle up under a hundred blankets, but we dogs sleep *au naturel* and need mild temperatures. Heating pads are great for must-be-outdoor dogs, sick dogs, arthritic dogs, and the like. If you go electric, just make sure it has a chew-proof cord.

And if we spend all day in the snow helping you make snowdogs (so much cooler than the average snowman), give us more calories and a special supplement to keep our skin from getting dry and flaky. Unless we have long, thick hair, we're also going to need winter clothes. Just remember, our bodies warm up with sunshine and exertion just as yours do.

Dangerous Places

Camping

Mom won't let us go camping. We're too likely to get bitten or eaten. Bigger, sturdier, dogs, well, that's another story. Just be sure to get your four-legged camper his own camping accessories. Check out the links at our website.

SCARED POOPLESS

On the water

Our friend Anna once saw some jerk on a waverunner with a puppy strapped to his chest. Another idiot taunted a dog with a hunk of beef on a fishing line until the dog caught the beef and impaled a hook in his mouth. We can only hope these sadists were freaks of Nature and that they're not allowed to spawn.

Safety on and in the water is as important for dogs as it is for infants. Yes, we can swim, but not for long unless we've been in training. Responsible parents make us wear a life preserver on boats. And they monitor our movements. A dog overboard, too often, is a dog dead unless he's wearing a life vest or float. Some of the best life vests have a handle on the back to help you lift your dog out of the water. We're not that good with ladders.

Going swimmingly

A Yorkie in our neighborhood drowned in her family's pool while her Mom gardened nearby. When *our* Mom heard about that, she set about teaching us to swim to the steps from any place in the pool. She also showed us how to get in and out of the spa. When your legs are four inches long, even a fountain can be a deathtrap.

Cycling

Okay, you're cruisin' the park with your dog in your bicycle's basket. You're checking out all the cool guys, who are checking you out in return, when you crash into a barrier and send your dog soaring through the air. Your dog cracks his skull. The guys no longer think you're cool.

Or maybe your dog is running along beside you. She sees a friend and dashes in front of you, breaking her leg, and yours. Never forget what I told you: poop happens!

Bike riders and dogs can hurt each other if they're not very careful. We've seen enclosed handlebar-mounted baskets that solve some problems, but not others. Dogs running along loose can be a danger to bikers, cars and themselves. On leashes . . . well, we've seen a product called "Springer" at *www.springerusa.com.* We've never used it, so decide yourself.

As for dogs and motorcycles, we don't mix. I don't care if your dog looks cool on your Harley. When you crash, so does he. You've made that decision; he didn't. Now you might have to make the decision about what to do with his remains.

Stranger Danger Strangers terrify me, especially strangers who want to hug. Who's to say they won't steal me or squish me or hold me so loosely that I wiggle and fall? You wouldn't let just anyone hold your Human baby. Don't let just anyone hold your dog.

Kids might not scare Humans, but look at them from our perspective. They race up to us, screaming bloody murder, flailing their hands and arms as though they're practicing Kung fu. More than once I've been grabbed and squeezed like a rag doll. One toddler grabbed Jiggy's whiskers and pulled so hard that he squealed. The smaller the kid, the scarier they are. Were I not possessed of the disposition of a saint, I might snap a warning that I don't appreciate their behavior. Some of my friends do.

To protect us from kids, step between us, or airlift us to safety. Explain that your dog is fragile and breaks easily. Don't let toddlers pet us and don't let kids pick us up.

It's very important to show kids how to safely pet us. First, ask permission from the dog's Human. If they give their permission, then approach the dog from the front with your hand low and the palm up, not high and palm down (which looks like a hit ready to happen). Tell them to move slowly, and to always be gentle. And tell them they must never hit us, even in play, or hug us too tight. It's for *their* safety as well as ours.

Speaking of hugs, I'd like to give you one. And a treat!

Chiclet's Trivia Treat: *In the early 1940s, Swiss inventor George de Mestral took his dog for a walk in the field. (I wonder if the dog was leashed.) Upon returning home, he found his dog's coat full of cockleburs. Curious, de Mestral examined the burrs under his microscope. Their shape intrigued him. One side of the burr had hooks; the other, loops. Almost as fast as you could say, "Voila!" the result was Velcro, named for the French words "velour" and "crochet."*

Did de Mestral ever think to name his discovery after his dog? Fat chance of that! So the next time you use a Velcro product, you should at least thank your own dog for her species' unending service.

Car Trouble

When it comes to other drivers, all of us have pet peeves. (I'm not sure if I like that phrase.) Dad hates people yakking away on their cell phones (overlooking the fact that he's one of them). Mom is most annoyed by women applying makeup while speeding down the highway (though apparently her application of lipstick doesn't count.) Then there are the drivers who use their car as a library, and those who think it's a Karaoke bar. Yes, there are a lot of distracted drivers out there. But you want to know *my* pet peeve? It's just that: a pet peeve. Many of you are driving the highways and byways with unrestrained dogs.

Whether you know it or not, every time you do this you're playing Russian roulette. Unrestrained dogs in a car are a danger to Humans, and at risk of serious injury themselves. Did you know that a 30-pound dog in a car traveling at just 30 miles an hour becomes 600 pounds of force that can smack into your head and break your neck? (It won't improve your dog, either.)

Humans buckle up themselves and their loved ones, but leave us to fly around the car like some sack of groceries. I take that back. They even secure their groceries. Heaven forbid some orange should get bruised during a sudden stop. Why aren't dogs as important as citrus?

I know what you're thinking: my dog loves hanging his head out the window, or standing on her tiptoes peeking out. Nothing bad has ever happened. I'm not listening to some killjoy. If that's the case, I hope you continue to experience only the joy and not the kill.

Last year, Jiggy and I were at our vet's office waiting for Jiggy to get a blood test when a man rushed in with a black Lab in his arms. The poor dog's tongue was hanging out, and she was as still as a sack of sand. I heard the Human say his Lab was riding in the back seat, hanging out the window, when he slammed on the brakes to avoid hitting the car ahead of him. Later, I heard the tech say the Lab died. Her neck was broken. That wasn't the only thing broken, the tech told Mom. So was her Human's heart.

I don't want that to ever happen again to a dog or a Human, and it doesn't have to. If you want to protect *all* the occupants in your vehicle, secure your small dog in a carrying case and strap it in with a seat belt. Secure your medium-to-large dog using a harness with a seat belt attachment. Help us travel with you in safety. You can even crack the window to give us a sniff of some of those wonderful outdoor aromas (like car exhaust). But, please, restrain us. We don't want to become unguided missiles any more than you do. (Find links to products at *dogs4dogs*.)

Need some more convincing? I'd be willing to bet that if you haven't had an accident recently, you almost have. According to The Federal Highway Administration, more than 6,000,000 accidents are reported to police every year. The NHTSA (National Highway Traffic Safety Administration) says almost half the accidents result in injuries, and more than 40,000 people are killed.

About 10,000 people don't die simply because they were wearing seatbelts. In fact, in a highway crash, *you cut your risk of death in half just by wearing a seatbelt.* What makes Humans think these same laws of physics don't apply to dogs?

A dog roaming around your car, or hanging over your arm with his head out the driver's side window, is a distraction to your driving. This intrepid reporter researched some alarming statistics. The NHTSA says distractions cause *more than a quarter* of the accidents that occur each year, and every safety authority lists unrestrained dogs as one of the worst possible distractions. We don't want to get hurt, and we don't want you to get hurt; we prefer being an *attraction* to a *distraction.*

Even though many states have laws requiring dogs to be restrained in a vehicle, most people ignore them. Of course, that doesn't make it right. Forty years ago most cars didn't even *have* seat belts, and no one was using infant car seats. I wonder how many adults and children died before buckling up became law and actually *using* seat belts became common practice? How many dogs will have to die before our Humans start protecting us?

You're probably thinking I'm a big 'fraidy cat (pardon my cursing). I'm not. I'm a concerned dog. There's a big difference.

Did you know that the California DMV says that merely using a cell phone while driving increases your chance of having a traffic accident by 400 percent? Now we all know that dogs are a lot more interesting and diverting than some ol' phone conversation between Humans. What does that tell you about increasing your chances of having an accident with an unrestrained dog?

There's also the possibility that you and your dog can be innocent victims. Maybe you're the greatest driver in the world. You've never had an accident. Still, when you get on the road, you're at the mercy of other drivers. If a huge SUV suddenly swerves into your lane, a crash might be unavoidable no matter how good a driver you are. Even if you swerve out of the way, your dog likely won't escape injury. She'll be thrown into a door or window, or into you or your child.

Law enforcement officials say the danger doesn't stop there. Sometimes Good Samaritans and paramedics can't get to an injured driver after an accident because of "dog problems." Dogs have even been shot for interfering. Excuse me? We're just doing our jobs. We might be hurt and confused and scared, but we still have to guard our injured Human. Don't make us the fall guy. And don't make us a victim.

There are plenty of other scenarios that go from bad to worst case. I think death is worst case, but some Humans are more impressed by dollars and cents. Let's say your dog suffers broken ribs and a broken leg because of being unrestrained in the car during an accident. Being a good guardian, you'll probably spend the next 3 or 4 months nursing him back to health while, thanks to you, your veterinarian gets richer and your therapist adds a new wing on her house. Restraining your dog isn't a matter of dollars and cents, but dollars and sense.

I wish I could tell you how many dogs are killed and injured every year in automobile accidents, but I can't. The government doesn't think we merit statistics. The Human picture is bad enough, though. The National Transportation Safety Board (NTSB) says that on a typical driving day, 4 Human children die and 622 are injured riding in cars. That's *every* day. Half of those hurt or killed are unrestrained. Those figures would be *much* worse if children under the age of 12 weren't riding in the back seat of the car, as required by most state laws.

Most dogs aren't restrained at all, and few (except really big dogs) are in the back seat. Usually we're in the front seat, head way out the window, innocently unaware that we're in danger. Again, I have to rely on Human data (since dogs don't rate statistics), but The National Center for Injury Prevention and Control found that merely *seating children in the rear seat of a car reduces risk of fatal injury by 36%*. Think of it: 36 out of 100 children would have survived if they'd only been in the back seat! Just like kids, we're safer away from the windshield and dashboard, especially in an accident when an airbag inflates. But unlike kids, many of us sit with our noses practically *on* the dashboard. Yes, I know, you can't tickle our tummies when we're in the back seat, but you endure having your kids there because their safety is more important than your own need for touching. Anyway, how well could you be driving if tickling tummies is your priority?

I might not be able to tell you exactly how many dogs are injured or killed every year in car accidents (or even from just braking hard or hitting a bad pothole), but there are a lot. If you don't believe me, just go to the waiting room at a vet's office offering critical care. This is an everyday occurrence. And what makes this so bad is that it's entirely preventable.

But . . . but . . . but . . . my dog enjoys the drive . . . my dog looks so cute . . . my dog doesn't like to be restrained . . . my dog just loves sticking her head out the window . . . my dog and I only go on short drives together.

Come on, Humans. Your dog will still enjoy the drive inside his carrier or wearing a restraint, and will also live to bark about it. While the breeze-in-face thing and the hey-look-at-me thing are enjoyable, they're probably not worth death or injury. As for what your dog likes or doesn't like, remember that you're the general and we're the privates. Make the right decision and lead. Sure, we love the breeze in our faces and our noses pressed to the window, but children love to race their bicycles down perilous obstacle courses without helmets. Do you let them? As for the "short drive" excuse, what it doesn't excuse is your responsibility to restrain your dog. Statistically, we're more likely to die a block from home than we are five hundred miles from home because we do it more often. If you don't restrain us, we're an accident just waiting to happen.

Want another good reason to restrain your dog? Power windows. Some cars' power window controls are situated in such a way that your dog can step on them and send the window guillotining up on her tender neck. Your dog is in danger of being strangled unless she's restrained from doing so. Some windows auto-reverse when they encounter resistance, while others don't. See if you can cut a banana in half with yours to find out if children and dogs are safe. The website *www.kidsandcars.org* states that at least 91 U.S. children were killed by power windows in 2003, and many more were injured. Did you know windows exert an upward force of 30–80 pounds? Humans at the control of power windows sometimes don't even realize where their dog's head is until too late.

Carriers and Restraints I hope I've convinced you to contain and restrain. If so, it's time to take a closer look at that ounce of prevention. The American Society for the Prevention of Cruelty to Animals recommends that small dogs ride in crates, and larger dogs use harnesses and restraints that attach to the seat belt system.

For restraints, visit your local pet store or see our website. Look for a harness that's comfy and strong and really easy to attach. Never secure your dog by her collar; that's a broken neck waiting to happen.

For carriers, look for something that encloses your dog completely. If she can jump out, or get thrown out, you don't have a safe carrier. You have an injury waiting to happen. Your container should be large enough for your dog to stand up and turn around in, but not so large that being thrown from one side to the other during an accident would cause injury.

When Jiggy and I are cruisin' with Mom and Dad, we're enclosed in sturdy soft-sided carriers safely buckled in place in the back seat. Our carriers are made of leather and nylon mesh, with steel spines, so we can see everything around us yet be safe and cozy inside. If we're ever slammed against the sides of the carrier, it will give a little but hold. Yes, the view's not so great, but to tell the truth, we never knew sightseeing was an option. You see, we view our car carriers as portable sleepers. You drive; we get our 40 winks. After my beauty sleep, I arrive at the destination alert and ready to receive compliments and adoration from friends and strangers alike.

A few more things about car safety. Ask yourself:

- If your vehicle screeches to a halt or rolls over, is your dog likely to survive? Some restraints and carriers look like they're made more for doggy fun than for doggy safety.

- Are airbags a potential problem? If small Human children can't withstand the 200 mph force of impact of a bag deploying, what chance does your dog have? (The NHTSA says that whether or not an airbag deploys depends on whether the seat belt is engaged, and in some cases, how much the passenger weighs. Some auto makers now have switches to turn off bags; others have indicator lights showing whether or not the bag is engaged. Check with your dealer. Better yet, keep your dog in the back seat away from airbags.)

What about securing us in the cargo area of an SUV with a mesh or barred barrier? Well, that'll help protect *you*, and lessen your chance of an accident, but may not do enough for your dog. Would you feel right about your two-year child or grandchild roaming around the cargo area while you're driving? Jiggy (an unimpeachable source) collected statistics that say that dogs riding in soft-sided crates anchored in the cargo area (crates that collapse for easy storage) work harder at keeping their toys picked up than dogs who don't. They say they owe it to their loving parents. Your results may vary, but it's certainly worth trying, don't you think?

If riding unrestrained in the back of an S.U.V. is bad, riding in the bed of a truck is horrible. Dogs tied to the truck by a leash can get strangled. Unrestrained dogs can easily be stolen, or may jump or be thrown from the truck. Even if they land safely, it's often a case of jumping from the frying pan into the fire. Cars can smush us. We can panic and cause accidents (for which you'll probably get sued). We can run away and end up forever lost.

If that weren't enough, we can get skin cancer from constant exposure to the sun, and the pads of our feet can get burned on hot metal surfaces. We need shade, water, and a carrier or restraint. If you don't give us those things, you are not doing your job. Bad Human. Bad!

Easy Tips For Non-Believers I sense that a few of you are still resisting my pearls of wisdom. If so, won't you at least try to mitigate potential damage to your dog by doing a few easy things? (I offer these tips reluctantly, you understand, as one might suggest it's better to play with firecrackers than with dynamite.)

If you let your dog hang out the window, get a window edge cover. Find a link to one at our website. You might save her neck from being cut or broken during a quick stop or crash. Also know that wind buffets ears and eyes and throws dust and dirt or small projectiles at them. This can cause infections or even loss of an eye. (Don't believe me? Ask your vet.) A Human with his head stuck out the window (not something you see a lot) would wear protective eye gear. Your dog can, too.

Doggles makes all sorts of cool looking goggles. Take your guy

to your local pet store and make a big fuss over how "with it" he looks in his new shades. (That's what we did with Jiggy.) If he knows they please you, he'll grow to like them, especially if you reward him for wearing them and build up wearing time gradually.

Get your dog some sunscreen, too, especially if he has pale skin or a pink nose. And get a window shade to keep the sun from baking down, especially on long trips. Find links to these products, and eye wear, at *dogs4dogs*. Also find tips for vacationing with your dog.

Dangers in a Parked Car Sometimes the greatest danger to dogs occurs when the car is stopped. Really. Your Human sets out with good intentions. He doesn't mean to leave you in the car, but suddenly there's an emergency (like an urgent need for beer). Because dogs are seldom allowed inside stores selling food (retailers thus missing a major opportunity for impulse buying), you leave Poopsie in the car. Thoughtful Human that you are, you crack the windows, telling your Poopsie you'll be right back and not to worry.

Not to worry? Are you crazy???? Even dogs used to being left in cars don't like it. How could they? As far as they know, you're never coming back. Dogs not used to waiting in cars may suffer separation anxiety and claustrophobia. Barking and whining often ensue, quickly followed by Houdini-like attempts to escape. If they don't succeed, they look at other alternatives. You, in turn, might be looking at new upholstery.

Heatstroke

In 2003, John Van Zante of the highly-acclaimed Helen Woodward Animal Center, performed an experiment for the media. It was a pleasant 79°F outside. He locked himself in a parked van, with windows cracked, holding a large thermometer for the reporters to see. Almost immediately, he started sweating. Within a few minutes the thermometer read 108°; John says this is the temperature at which a dog's heart, brain, liver, kidneys and intestines start to shut down. Several minutes later, the thermometer read 110°, the temperature at which both dogs and Humans become vulnerable to heatstroke. At this point, John bolted from the car soaked with sweat and gasping. (The temperature inside the van rose to 120° within ten minutes.)

John explained to the reporters what a dog locked in a hot car might experience. First, he would pant and drool and become dizzy. (Ever try panting? It's not that useful. And unlike you, we dogs can't cool ourselves by sweating.)

As the dog's internal body temperature rose, his heart would begin to race, he'd start crying and would likely experience seizures. Next would come collapse, vomiting, coma and, finally, the relief of death. One former paramedic and vet tech, having witnessed a dog dying of heatstroke, said it was the worst way she could imagine for an animal to die.

According to *www.kidsandcars.org*, at least 165 Human children died in hot cars between 1999 and 2003. The dog stats have to be worse because so many of us are left in cars. I'm sort of glad, though, that dog statistics aren't available. It would only depress me knowing all the suffering going on every day.

All dogs are at risk, but especially dogs who are large, overweight, older, flat-faced, or are on certain medications. Symptoms of passive heatstoke (as opposed to heatstroke brought on by exertion) may develop over two to three days, so a dog's not out of the woods just because the immediate crisis has passed. And don't fool yourself into thinking that parking in the shade will keep any of this from happening. Shade can shift to sun in a heartbeat. Did you know the dog word for *car* is *oven*?

Other Disasters Nothing good can come from taking your dog on a drive if you know you'll have to leave him alone. Contrary to what our whining might have you believe, we won't die of loneliness if you leave us at home alone for a few hours. And if you think tying your dog outside a store is the answer, then I ask you to think again. Dogs of all sizes and breeds are stolen every day. Dogs get loose and run into traffic. And curious kids can leap upon us with pinching fingers quicker than you can say Personal Injury Lawyer.

Backover Deaths In 2003, at least 72 Human children were backed over and killed by cars and trucks (so says *kidsandcars*). Many more were hurt. As with power windows, if they kept statistics for dogs, the numbers would surely be worse.

Harlee, a Springer Spaniel friend of ours, was backed over by her Mom's father. After seeing what he'd done, he tried to get Harlee into the car, but moving hurt and she bit him. When he finally got her to the vet, the vet said her back end was paralyzed and she had internal damage. They operated and waited. In the meantime, the man's bite got infected with some unknown bacteria and he ended up in the hospital in Intensive Care. In the end, the Human lived. Our friend didn't.

I hope you'll remember this story the next time you back out of your driveway.

Chasing Cars Dogs who chase cars get hit by cars. Some of them die. Others spend the rest of their lives hobbling around on three legs. Their Humans have lots of vet bills. Sometimes, their Humans even get sued because their dog damaged a car or caused an accident.

The best way to stop your dog from chasing cars is to keep your dog from running free. There is no second best way.

Poop Happens Sometimes, you have to prepare for bad things and just hope they never happen. Because Mom is a worrier (have you noticed?), she's given some thought about how to protect us from car-related disasters. If you follow her tips (most won't take more than a few minutes), you and your dog will be much better prepared to hit the road. Why not start right now? I'll nap for a while.

Mom's Auto Dog Insurance Plan

- Make sure your dog has a microchip or tattoo. And never let her leave home without ID tags.
- Attach business cards from any vets who know your dog; secure them in or on your dog's carrier or restraint. Mark the card with your dog's name, your name, and your phone numbers.
- Inside the glove box of each of your vehicles put a note giving potential Good Samaritans emergency information. Attach vet's business cards and a short medical history (better yet, fill out the MY DOG'S LIFE form at *dogs4dogs*). Also attach a letter giving permission to treat your dog and authorizing any charges. Sign it.
- For those rare occasions when you're out without your dog, make sure you have a card in your wallet saying you have a dog(s) at home that will need care if your emergency contact numbers don't answer. Otherwise, you could lie unconscious in a hospital while you dog starves to death at home.

- Keep a photo of your dog in the car to make up an emergency Lost Dog flyer. Mom says it's not just about being proud, it's more a matter of being safe than sorry.

Remember: many of the dogs killed in shelters are unidentified escaped family members. The more information you can provide, the better. If you're traveling out of town, put a tape on your dog's collar or harness with a local phone number (unless your current mobile phone number is already on his tag). Or try The Pet Protector™ System (see a link at our site). If someone finds your dog, they can call the 24-hour toll-free number; they say they'll track you down at your various phone numbers, pager, email addresses, and so on. They say they'll even recommend a nearby vet and authorize treatment if your dog is injured.

Rescuing Hot Dogs That takes care of *your* dog. What about other people's dogs? What if you see one overheating in a car? Mom has gone so far as to have owners paged inside of stores to alert them of the condition of their animals. (So far, every person has thanked her that she showed such concern and I'm pretty sure none of them will ever leave their dogs in such straits again.) Sometimes, Mom determines that the conditions of the cooped-up dog are not life-threatening, but just darned uncomfortable. She has an answer for that as well. She created a *Dog Safety Information* sheet (available at *dogs4dogs*) that she keeps in her car. All you have to do is print out a few and distribute them when needed. By educating others, you might be saving a dog's life! (Okay, by now you know that both Mom and I are safety fanatics. But it feels really good to be saving all those lives.)

When a paper warning is not enough because a dog is already suffering, be it panting hard, severely panicked, or near collapse, you must take immediate action. Call Animal Control or the police (or if at a mall or store, shopping center security). If it's likely the owner is in a particular store, have him paged and warned that his animal is in distress. Seconds sometimes count. Listen, how often do you get a chance to be a hero?

SCARED POOPLESS

Have you made your dog road ready? Good. It's time for your trivia treat.

Chiclet's Trivia Treat: *The people at BMW must think the Japanese love dogs more than any other people in the world. (Obviously, they don't know you or my Mom.) As I write, they've offered their Japanese customers the first "dog safety belt" produced by an auto maker. For a mere 21,000 yen (less than $200 U.S.), Japanese doggy Moms and Dads can buy one of three different sizes designed for dogs between 7 and 40 kilos (15 to 88 pounds). We hope BMW will decide that dogs in all countries deserve a safety belt. In fact, we hope ALL auto manufacturers will. While they're at it, a TV playing the Animal Channel in the back seat would also be great.*

Flying Without Dying

Excuse me if I'm not very enthusiastic about the idea of dogs venturing into the wild blue yonder. Let's face it: Humans have a pretty bad record when it comes to dogs and flight.

Take the example of Laika, the dog the American press nicknamed "Muttnik." Laika (which means Barker in Russian) went into space on Sputnik 2 in 1957, giving her dubious distinction of being the first dog in earth orbit. Scientists failed to tell Laika that she was going to boldly go where no dog had gone before—and she wasn't coming back.

Lots of Humans were upset at Laika's mission, not that their sympathy did her any good. As the batteries operating her life-support system failed and Sputnik 2 ran out of air, people around the planet mourned. Although monitors showed that Laika died several days into her journey, it wasn't until more than five months later that Sputnik 2 fell back into earth's atmosphere and burned. Russian scientists called Sputnik 2 "a great success." I seriously doubt that Laika agreed.

Fortunately, few dogs are doomed to die in space as poor Laika did. Still, flying—especially in "the belly" of a plane—can be a dangerous ordeal. If we're little and you can carry us onboard, that's one thing; our Humans will be there to protect us. If we're traveling as baggage or cargo, forget about it.

The situation isn't that easy for Humans either. If you don't take lots of precautions, and follow airline and immigration rules to the letter, travel can be a nightmare—maybe even the last nightmare your dog ever has. And even if you Humans get the rules down pat, consider the effects of flight on us dogs. Flying, especially in the belly, is a major stress.

Your vet may give the okay for travel, but only you can decide if flying is in your dog's best interest. If your best friend is old or sick or a nervous Nellie, or doesn't seem to be feeling up to snuff, she'd be safer at home with a friend or dogsitter.

You're probably thinking: why not just use a tranquilizer to take the edge off? Inside the cabin, with your vet's okay, that might be fine. In the belly, it's probably not. Even though we'd love to zone out for the whole flight, you shouldn't consider any kind of medication for a dog flying as baggage unless your vet specifically okays it. If the poor thing should suffer a bad reaction, no one will be there to help her.

Good To Go Let's say your dog passed the health and psychological hurdles and is all decked out in her Snoopy flying suit, ready to go. Now the real hassles begin. You need to:

- Confirm that your airline accepts pets and reserve space well in advance for your dog and yourself. Reconfirm 24–48 hours before travel.
- Get a health certificate from your vet. This certificate has to be current within a week to 10 days of each leg of the trip, with proof of rabies vaccination. Some airlines require vaccination within the year (the very thought of which raises my hackles). Fortunately, most will accept a vet's letter of exemption in lieu of the shot.

- Calculate how your dog's weight and size affect travel methods. Check with your airline to see if your dog can go inside the cabin, or has to fly as accompanied baggage, or as cargo. (Note: cargo doesn't have to travel on any particular flight.)
- Make sure your pet carrier conforms to your particular airline's regulations. Visit the website of every airline on your itinerary, or call them for information. Select the wrong pet carrier and they'll send us back home.
- If you're flying outside the U.S. (or are going to aloha-land), you'll need to follow agricultural and immigration rules exactly. Contact every carrier on your itinerary (boats and trains, too). Also check The International Air Travel Association (*www.IATA.org*) and *www.pettravel.com*. Double check everything; policies change. If you mess up, your dog may be quarantined for months—at your expense and your dog's physical and emotional peril. If your itinerary is complicated, and especially if your dog is traveling as cargo, consider a pet travel agency like *www.puppytravel.com* or *www.airanimal.com*.

IATA suggests that you feed your dog lightly the day before your flight. Gayle Martz, CEO and Founder of Sherpa's Pet Trading Company, the woman responsible for getting dogs comfortable in-cabin carriers, says you should feed your dog six hours before flight time and offer water two hours before. (One exception: dogs traveling as baggage or cargo must get both food and water within *four* hours of flight time.)

Let your dog pee and poop before leaving for the airport, and again just before entering the airport, picking an inconspicuous spot where people who don't like dogs (I call them mutants) won't see her and make trouble. Mom also carries a disposable pee pad—most pet stores have them—so we can discretely pee in a stall in a Human restroom in case of a delay. Unfortunately, dogs checked as baggage or cargo don't have this option and may have to wallow in pee the entire flight.

Sharing Space with Your Feet Lucky little canines like Jigs and me can ride inside the cabin with our folks. To qualify for this privilege, dogs must be smaller than 18" long, 11" high, and weigh less than 22 pounds. For some dogs out there, this could be the incentive to diet.

To keep us from freaking out and being subjected to x-rays, politely inform the agent at the security checkpoint that you have your best friend in your carrier and she should be checked by a hand-held detector, not passed through that claustrophobic tunnel x-ray machine.

We have to stay in our carriers through the airport and for the whole darn flight! That means no playing ring around the gate agent, no chatting with the other passengers, no running up and down the aisle to stretch our legs.

Some people sneak their dogs out of their crates and attach them to their bodies with a belly pack of some sort, or hide them under a blanket (that they keep talking to). They don't realize that we're more comfortable in our carriers (where we can turn around and stretch out to sleep) than *they* are in their seats. Okay, we can't see the in-flight movie, but that could be the *good* news. Besides, Ms. Martz warned us that taking us out is against airline rules and can lead to a loss of privileges for everyone. Hey, I don't know about you but I don't relish the idea of being off-loaded in Timbuktu.

In flight, dehydration can be a problem. You know how thirsty you get on airplanes? Well, we do too. Like you, we'll fare better if we stay hydrated. Slurping up water causes a gotta-pee problem, so just syringe a little water into our mouths from time to time (with a needle-less syringe).

Because some of us can't hold our pee no matter how hard we try, airlines require our carriers to have absorbent liners. We think it's a great idea to use a PoochPad crate pad, or to wrap your carrier's pad with one of their pee pads. PoochPants are great, too, if Fifi suffers from incontinence. These products absorb liquids and keep tootsies and bottoms dry while also reducing odor and bacterial growth. (Find a link at *dogs4dogs*.)

More and more companies are making carriers for your dog. Select something well-ventilated, durable and soft-sided so you can use a generous size and squeeze it into place. Our carriers have wheels which Mom says is a life-saver in big airports. An eight-pounder like Jiggy can feel like a twenty-pounder by the time you reach the plane. (Find links to carriers at *dogs4dogs*.)

By the way, don't assume that the carrier you used last year, or one you used on another airline, will be acceptable this year on this flight. Check it out. Airline executives like to keep us guessing.

One more thing: don't forget to book ahead. Canines per pet carrier, per cabin and per plane are limited. Jiggy and I can't even ride together in one carrier, says the mean ol' USDA Animal Welfare Act. They think we'll go berserk and eat each other or something. I can't even bring Jiggy along unless both Mom and Dad fly, or at least buy two tickets. They also have to make advance reservations for us and pay a special fee. But at least we're in the cabin with our Humans, not stuck in the belly with a bunch of no-nothing suitcases, a nonstop barker of a Beagle and a hungry-looking Akita trying to break out of his crate.

In the If you're thinking of transporting your dog in the airplane's belly,
Belly please be aware that the Air Transport Association reports that
of the approximately 1% of all pets flown on commercial aircraft (that's
Beast about 5,000 animals yearly) are lost, injured or killed. That's *lost,*
injured or killed! What Human would fly with odds like that?
(Starting in July of 2005, the Department of Transportation began
reporting on pet safety by airline. You'll find a link at *dogs4dogs*.)
Think of animal transport as baggage transport, because that's
what it is. Bags don't need temperature control, ventilation or
pleasant flying conditions. They don't care if they're thrown

around, or if they're stranded in cargo holding areas or on unsheltered carts. Bags don't get panicky or lonely. They don't need to poop or pee. Bags don't even care if you lose them.

Dogs are *not* bags. Don't subject us to this torture if there's any way you can avoid it. If you have absolutely no alternative, please take as many precautions as you can, starting with your vet's absolute approval (not just a quick signature on the health certificate). Take special measures during hot or cold weather. Airlines have rules about flying at such times, but delays may put your dog in deplorable conditions on the plane and in holding areas. Also, if you have a snub-nosed breed, like a Pug or Pekinese, he shouldn't fly in the belly at all as he may have difficulty breathing. The same goes for the aged or health-compromised.

If you're considering shipping (or receiving) a puppy via air cargo, don't. Many behaviorists believe that stressing an infant during the Fear Imprint Period (between roughly 8 and 11 weeks of age) can have long-lasting consequences. The psychological trauma a pup might experience while trapped in an unfamiliar situation for a long period of time might do irreversible damage, and result in her being neurotic. If your puppy must fly, please go get her and fly with her on board where you can comfort her and keep her from harm.

If we haven't talked you out of shipping your dog, and you really have to do it, please go to *dogs4dogs*. You'll find a number of very important tips and suggestions regarding taking your dog into the sky.

Bon voyage? Here's your treat.

Chiclet's Trivia Treat: *Before there was glasnost and perestroika, before there was any détente between the United States and Russia, a dog helped bridge peace between the world's two superpowers. Yes, the Cold War was threatening to put an end to Humanity, but a dog saved the day. I love it when that happens!*

Strelka (Little Arrow in Russian) and Belka (Squirrel) were the first animals to orbit the earth (aboard Sputnik 5) and actually live to bark about it. Later, Strelka had a litter of six puppies, one of which was given to President John F. Kennedy's daughter Caroline. The gift of a puppy made it that much harder for Humans to go to war. Countries might disagree, but Humans love their dogs.

And now a moment of silence for the five space dogs who gave their all for space exploration: Laika, Bars, Lisichka, Pchelka, and Mushka. The Russian government remembered Laika's sacrifice in their monument to fallen cosmonauts in Star City just outside Moscow. Behind the cosmonauts' statues, just peeking out, is Laika.

DIVORCING YOUR DOG

According to *Divorce Magazine,* only a third of married Humans celebrate their 25th wedding anniversary together. Almost half your marriages end in divorce—more than a million a year in this country alone. But when Humans separate from one another, typically neither one of the parties ends up on death row. Alas, with us dogs, it's a different story.

The idea of ending up homeless and alone is our worst nightmare. Most of you, I know, would never give up your canine friend unless you had to. Unfortunately, poop happens. Things change. Soldiers get shipped abroad. The kids develop allergies. New landlords are unenlightened. Small behavior problems become seemingly insurmountable.

If you to have to separate from your dog, or know someone who does, perhaps you'll permit me to show you how to find a good home for your special friend.

Evaluating Your Product Mom says people who are successful placing dogs pretend they're selling a "product." Though I personally object to being objectified, if a marketing strategy can save a fellow dog's life then I'm all for it. So let's start out by evaluating your product. I can make it less painful. Really I can.

Well-behaved, young and healthy dogs

These have a great chance of finding a home, so you can skip this section and jump ahead to the PREPARING THE PACKAGE section.

Old or sick dogs

The ailing and the aging are considered unadoptable by many people, and their Humans may think their only option is permanent sleep. If the poor soul is in constant pain, with no hope of better days, well, sleep could be a blessing. Otherwise, these dogs deserve a chance to find people who will love him bunches. Your best bet will probably be a breed rescue group or a private rescuer, although your vet may also have some ideas. More about this later.

Overly-devoted dogs

Afraid your dog will pine for you forever, and that he might be better off dead? Well, I'm sorry to burst your bubble, but your dog will adapt. He'll probably mourn your absence for a time, but in the end he'll move on—if you give him a chance. It's Nature's way.

The fixer-upper

If your dog has a major discipline problem, and you think no sane Human would want him, won't you please consult a professional before giving up? It's conceivable that the problem is partly you. Well, it does happen.

One of the best ways to help your "fixer-upper" is to find a behavior expert. Though understanding is a lot more complicated than jerking on a leash, it's a lot more rewarding, too. Dr. Myrna Milani, vet, consultant, teacher, and author of nine books, spends 95% of her time working with problem dogs and their families. Her website (*www.mmilani.com*) is a fabulous place to spend hours at a time. Dr. Milani does phone consultations, as does animal trainer Maureen Hall (*www.animalcoaching.com*). Find more information on behaviorists at Purdue University's School of Veterinary Medicine (*www.vet.purdue.edu/chab/links.htm*).

If your dog is not a total disaster, you might try to find a good shelter, rescue group or private "rescuer" willing to rehab him. You might consider kicking in a donation for training and food. We're talking survival.

The Menace to Society

If your dog has sharp teeth and a rotten attitude, and you've worked with a trainer or behaviorist to no avail, it may not be possible or wise to place him in another home. In fact, beware of people who want to adopt him. They might not be acting in your dog's best interest.

If you live near Los Angeles or are close to one of his traveling shows, you might check out Cesar Millan (*www.dogpsychologycenter. com*). He hosts *The Dog Whisperer* show on National Geographic television and is famous for rehabilitating "incorrigibles." If all your efforts fail, and your dog is a danger to himself and others, is it time to talk with your vet about other, sadder options.

Preparing The Package Okay, let's say your dog is no menace. He's a pretty good citizen, in fact. How's his packaging? Is he clean and presentable? If not, it's Extreme Doggy Makeover time. He needs a bath, a nail trim and, maybe, a new 'do.

Next, if you haven't done so already, it's time for spaying or neutering. Sterilization is a positive selling point and, of course, helps the overpopulation problem on Planet Dog.

Targeting The Public Once your dog's all spiffed up grab your camera and take dozens of color shots. Put something in the shot that shows the dog's size, maybe a basketball or a person. Also remember that a white Westy in the snow won't get anyone's attention. Keep backgrounds contrasting and not too busy.

Get the message of your available dog out there to everyone you know. Use e-mail and photo postcards to distribute your dog's image and resume far and wide. Someone out there may be looking for a dog just like yours. If they're thrilled about the match, and you're thrilled with them, yippee! If you have qualms, keep looking. You want the *right* home, not just *any* home.

Ads and flyers

When you advertise your dog, try something quirky and inviting. Try "Handsome hunk looking for love," in lieu of "used dog, for sale cheap."

Never offer a dog "free to a good home." You want someone who can afford to offer good care and pay for vet expenses, not someone hunting bargains or getting a dog on a whim. Last Chance for Animals says "free dog" also invites vultures seeking bait for fighting dogs or "subjects" for research labs. The people at Best Friends Animal Society call these vultures "bunchers" and say that putting "no bunchers" in your ad tells them you're on to their deadly business.

The shotgun approach

Wild-colored posters with adorable, offbeat photos often get the best results. Would your dog look best in a beret? A cute sweater? A Santa's hat during the holidays? Jumping to catch a Frisbee? If you do use an action shot, add a facial close-up.

Tack up flyers at vets' offices, grooming and doggy day care establishments, kennels, spas, pet stores, grocery stores, car washes and dog parks. Any place with a window or bulletin board is a potential home for a poster. And try this *TV Guide* trick: make several posters, using different colors and photos. It's said that half of all advertising works, it's just that nobody knows *which* half that is.

Tell a story with your poster. Brag about your dog being neutered or spayed. Say what a sweet dog he is and why you can't keep him.

If he likes kids, hates cats, loves jogging, and enjoys watching *Frasier* reruns, say so. (That Eddie is *so* handsome.) Tug at heart-strings, but stay truthful.

Don't forget to include contact numbers, and maybe an e-mail address, printed on a fringe of pull-tabs along the flyer's bottom edge. A friend of ours posted photos on the web and marked flyers with the web address. His Golden Retriever found a new home in only two days!

The target approach

Often you need to think out of the box in order to reach the right people. Because "horse people" go nuts for Jack Russell terriers, post flyers at stables, farm stores and tack shops, or place a Want Ad under "Horses for Sale."

The perfect family for your Lab may be picking up kids outside a school or dance academy right now; rush over with flyers. Snap photos of your bashful Pekinese snoozing away in your granny's lap and tack them up at "senior" centers. Got a little jock like Jiggy? Target an agility-training school, or maybe high school athletes, with a flyer of your jock doing something amazing or decked out in school colors. For even more ideas on how to place

your dog, go to *www.bestfriends.org/theanimals/petcare;* search for *How to Find Homes for Homeless Pets.* Their article is terrific.

Screening potential parents

After finding promising prospects, you still need to check out the new parents before handing off your ward.

Start by asking why they want a dog. Have they had a dog before? What happened to it? Are they aware of all the potential expenses? Ask about their work schedule, and whether they'll have the time and inclination to exercise the dog. Find out if they have a nice yard with a suitable fence. Go to *dogs4dogs* for some good links to some more good questions.

Let your instincts guide you during your interview. If something seems wrong, it probably is. If you suggest checking out their home and they balk at the idea, you should balk at the idea of giving them your dog. Please, look out for your dog's interests. Even if he's currently driving you crazy, remember, he still loves you so much. If he disappointed you, he's really sorry. Please, don't disappoint him.

Finalizing the adoption

If the parents check out, get something in writing about the terms of the adoption. Find a form at *www.petrescue.com* or make up your own. And, please, if you haven't already filled out the MY DOG'S LIFE form at *dogs4dogs*, please do one now for your dog's new parents. They'll need to know about food and veterinarians and vaccinations and things like that. And won't you please give them your copy of this book? I'll try to start them out on the right foot.

Other Options
Re-homing purebreds

If your dog is a purebred, call your breeder. The best of them will take their dogs back, and may already have prospects waiting. If that doesn't work, contact your breed's rescue organizations (go to *www.AKC.org*, click Breeds, and scroll to Breed Rescue Groups).

SCARED POOPLESS

Private rescues

Veterinarians, humane societies and shelters can connect you with kind souls who rescue dogs they think they can place later. These people generally have lots of mouths to feed and may take special interest in a dog with a trust fund. Even $100 goes a long way. Our friend Mary is a dog-rescue angel. Her dozen or so foster dogs have so much fun they never want to leave!

One cautionary note: some people, not as skilled as Mary, take in more pets than they can possibly handle, so check out their facilities and plans for your dog. And ask what happens if they can't find your baby a home. There are some deranged Humans out there called "animal hoarders" whose sense of charity has mutated into obsession. A check (and sniff) of their facilities can tell you if you've found one. Dogs suffer and die in their custody, so please don't just run away from this tragedy. Call your Humane society or SPCA and report them.

No-kill shelters

A "no-kill" shelter, if you can find one, will sterilize your dog, get him a cool microchip, and maybe even put him through obedience school to help him find a great new home. In our area, the wonderful Helen Woodward Animal Center is just such a place. To find one in your town, try *www.pets911.com* or your local Humane Society. Also search online for "no-kill shelters" and your city's name. Puppies are generally welcome at these shelters, and sometimes they'll even spay the pups' mom for free, or almost free, to make her stop littering. Talk about a great woofer twofer!

Always visit any shelter before handing over your dog, making sure it's clean and that they have room for your dog. Also check their criteria for placement and be sure you like their terms. This is your dog's adoption agency. Make sure it's a good one.

Last ditch stand

If all other efforts fail, and you have absolutely no other alternative, and the only shelter that will accept your dog will put him to sleep if they can't place him, find out how many days your dog has and try to find a better place in the meantime. Ask for "last rights" so they'll offer him back to you before they put him to sleep, and call every few days to see how things are going. While you're waiting, call that private rescuer who turned down your dog last month; maybe he or she has room now. Explain your problem, but don't try to guilt them into helping. They've heard it all before.

One option for your dog could be an animal sanctuary. Find one at *www.petguardian.com*, click PetGuardian Community, then Alternatives to Pet Trusts. Just be sure to consider carefully whether or not your dog would be happy in the facilities the sanctuary offers.

The kind Humans at Best Friends Animal Society invite you to e-mail them at *bfnetwork@bestfriends.org*. The Best Friend's Network is made up of people and organizations working together to help homeless animals in their own communities. First visit their site (*www.bestfriends.org*) and learn about their sanctuary and other services and programs. While you're there, consider making a donation and subscribing to their terrific magazine. Places like this save lives that would otherwise be lost.

Thanks for your extra efforts at re-homing your dog. You deserve a special treat—my friend Benji.

SCARED POOPLESS

Chiclet's Trivia Treat: *The American Humane Association attributes the adoption of a million shelter dogs to the publicity surrounding the finding of the first Benji, doggy star extraordinaire, in a Burbank, California shelter. Benji's rags to riches story helped so many dogs find homes that Joe Camp, Benji's producer, director and favorite Human, spent months searching America's shelters for the star of his latest movie:* Benji: Off the Leash.

He finally found his star in Gulfport, Mississippi. Don't be shocked, but the latest Benji is a female. (Hollywood, you know.) Can you think of any Human roles that have been played so successfully by both sexes?

Looking for Love in All the Wrong Places

ADORABLE BASSET HOUND, 7, SEEKING SENIOR COUPLE FOR LOVE AND COMPANIONSHIP. LARGE COUCH A PLUS. KIDS AND PETS DISCOURAGED. ASK FOR SAD SAM AT YOUR LOCAL SHELTER. PLEASE ACT FAST.

SCARED POOPLESS

Matchmaker, matchmaker, make me a match, find me a find, catch me a catch. Those are the lyrics from a musical originally entitled *Fido on the Roof* (before some Human had the dumb idea of giving the Fido role to a Fiddler). Anyway . . . .

Are you looking for another dog? Fantastic! So many of us are desperate for homes. Just remember: for a dog, the difference between a good match to a Human and a bad match can literally be life and death. If our "marriages" don't work out, our lives may end in some lonely shelter.

So what's the best way to make a great match? Plan ahead. Don't "wed" some stranger you met briefly at a pet shop. As Humans say: marry in haste, repent at leisure.

Before buying or adopting a dog because of her winning ways or dreamy eyes, consider the immortal words of President John F. Kennedy's dog: ask not what your dog can do for you, ask what *you* can do for your dog. That is, forget about what that Great Dane will do for your image. Will he be happy in your tiny apartment? Will that Border Collie enjoy life locked indoors while you spend 80-hour weeks at the office? Will Sad Sam, the aging Basset, be happy with a couple who hikes and jogs all weekend long? Remember: if we're happy with your lifestyle, you'll be happy with our behavior. If we're not happy, we all lose.

Self Analysis Before you fall in love with the wrong dog, take a look at your personality, physical condition and availability. If you're a nervous type, get a calm dog (and vice versa). If you're meek, you'll fit better with a submissive dog rather than a hair-trigger attack dog who's always cocked and loaded. If you believe cleanliness is next to godliness, don't adopt a shedding machine who'll make you pull *your own* hair out.

And don't just think about today. Maybe your nest is empty now, but will it be filled with kids tomorrow? Some of us like kids; some don't. Others, like me, adore kids but are too fragile to even think about a life with a toddler. If your "kids" happen to be four-legged, don't forget to test for compatibility.

Is security your priority? Don't fall for a dog who thinks the whole world is a playpen. Like peace and quiet? Don't match up with a barker. And remember: some dogs like it hot; some like it

cold. Don't expect that Husky to take to desert hiking or that Chihuahua to take to the snow.

One more thing. I hear arranged marriages went out of style in most countries years ago. Loved ones need to find each other by mutual attraction. Unless you're absolutely sure you know *exactly* what someone would want in a dog, please don't give a dog as a gift. Instead, give a leash and the promise to pay for the dog to go with it. That way, you get to be the hero, the recipient gets the dog he or she wants, and the dog ultimately chosen gets to live happily ever after.

High maintenance versus low maintenance

While there is no predicting what your dog might eventually cost in terms of medical and other expenses (expect double or triple what you think), some breeds are particularly high maintenance. Can you afford weekly grooming (or are you willing to do it yourself)? Are you willing to pop for surgery for genetic defects? Traditional Human marriage vows include a line about committing through sickness and in health. Remember: that same commitment goes for dogs.

Purebred vs Mutt

Once you've assessed yourself as a future guardian, consider what kind of dog complements your profile. Whether you want a purebred or a mixed breed, you need to be an educated future parent. *Paws to Consider: Choosing the Right Dog for You and Your Family* by Brian Kilcommons and Sarah Wilson is a good place to start. On-line, try *www.animal.discovery.com* (click Pet Guides & Tools then Dog Breed Selector). Then search for breeds you like at *www.petplace.com*; they show the pros and cons of a breed, and even point out common genetic defects to watch out for.

Looking for Mr. Gooddog *Where* you search for your soul mate is of more importance than you could ever imagine. Whatever you do, please don't buy a dog from a pet store or on-line puppy farm. You could be perpetuating more cruelty than you could ever imagine. I'll tell you more about this in a minute.

Finding Purebreds Have your heart set on a purebred? Did you know that 25% of the dogs in shelters are purebreds looking for new homes? Think of them not as rejects, but as exiled aristocrats. Click on to *www.petfinder.com* to find aristocrats in your area.

Breed rescue groups are also great places to find purebreds available for adoption. (Search for say, "Maltese Rescue" on-line—a little commercial for my orphaned cousins—or go to *www.AKC.org* (click Future Dog Owners, then Breed Rescue Groups), or call The Humane Society at 202-452-1100, and ask for the Companion Animals section. Vets and local shelters may also have leads on local rescuers.

Do you reject shelter dogs because you want to show your dog in dog shows and fear these dogs will have no papers? Go to *www.AKC.org* and search for Indefinite Listing Privilege. You may be surprised at all the opportunities available.

Breeders we shun

Finding a reputable dealer is a tough task—but a vitally important one. Know this: Responsible breeders don't sell puppies in pet stores or to strangers from Internet puppy emporiums. Period.

There's an old song: *How much is that doggy in the window?* It's a song you might keep singing, and singing, and singing, accompanied by the ring of a cash register, if you buy a puppy from a seller whose only goal is making money off dogs.

Have you ever thought about how horrible it is to be a pup in a pet store? You were probably taken away from your Mom too soon and over-vaccinated. You spend days begging for attention and suffer long nights alone. You're jammed into cramped quarters with no love, no play, no socialization, and no potty training.

So how much is that doggy in the window? Too much! If your local pet store sells puppies, stop shopping there and tell them why. Pet stores that sell puppies keep puppy mills in business. So do Internet puppy stores. (Superstores like PetsSmart and PETCO sponsor adoptions from area shelters. This, we applaud.)

So what are puppy mills? They're mass breeding operations. In the worst cases (and there are many), puppy moms are often jailed in wire cages, and are never exercised or played with. They're bred every time they come in season, and when they get old or sick they're abandoned or killed. Their pups are raised like chickens, growing up in cramped, filthy cages with no loving Human contact, and sometimes never even seeing daylight. They're bred indiscriminately, not socialized, fed poorly, over-vaccinated, and are prone to genetic diseases. These poor puppies come into the world as damaged souls who too often become behavioral and medical nightmares. Think of them as thousands of dollars in vet bills and training fees dressed up in cute fur.

I know you might be tempted to rescue one of these poor pups, but consider what happens if you do. Whenever one pup is sold, another will be bred to take his place. His poor mom stays in servitude and his new brother or sister is born into the same cruel conditions. Not until Humans stop buying these abused and defective babies, and not until they stop patronizing shops and websites supporting the puppy mills, will the cruelty end.

How do you spot a puppy mill? Ask to see the breeding facility and the pup's parents, and to speak to other patrons. Look for happy dogs raised indoors with their Human families. And visit *www.stoppuppymills.org* and click Take Action. They have a fabulous checklist for finding good breeders and can show you how to spot mass breeders. If you're not computer savvy, ask someone to download their booklets for you. This is really, really important.

Responsible breeders

So now that you've ruled out puppy mills, where do you get your pup? You might start your search for a private breeders is at *www.AKC.org*; click Future Dog Owners and study their referral lists.

Be wary of backyard amateurs. Their pups are undoubtedly cute (ever see one that wasn't?), but unless breeders are experts on the breed and on breeding, their pups may be long on looks but short on mental and physi-cal soundness. This is espe-cially true for purebred dogs who often suffer from in-breeding.

One good way to judge a breeder is to see what they want from you. Responsi-ble breeders screen potential Moms and Dads, not just their credit cards. How else can they ensure their pups a loving environment with suitable parents and a com-patible lifestyle? If they're willing to send their pup into the great unknown, what kind of people must they be?

The best breeders usually have pups available only several times a year because they keep only as many dogs as they can properly care for. Because their pups have sound temperaments and constitutions, these breeders have waiting lists for their dogs. They also:

- Refuse to ship pups in the belly of a plane. (Early trauma can cause permanent neuroses.) They insist that you pick up the dog and accompany it home, if at all possible, in a car or inside the cabin of the plane.
- Let no dog leave home before she's ready. (Find specifics at Breed Standards, *www.thedogsbestfriend.com*.)
- Breed only one or two breeds and welcome you to their facility.
- Offer money-back guarantees while you get the pup vet checked.

Important! AKC registration is no guarantee of responsible breeding. Papers tell you only that the breeder says this puppy came from a particular set of registered dogs. It *says* nothing about temperament or freedom from genetic defects. USDA inspection guarantees only that minimum care standards are followed. A statement that pups don't come from puppy mills or puppy auctions means nothing at all.

What about dogs advertised in newspapers? Things have changed little since Roman times. It was *caveat emptor* then, and it is still buyer beware now. That Dog For Sale may be the misguided experiment of an inexperienced backyard breeder. It could even be stolen. If you're tempted by an ad, take a big, burly friend and go to the dog; don't let them bring the dog to you. If they won't let you come over, maybe that should tell you something.

"Purse" dog alert: we know plenty of people who'd need a steamer trunk to haul around a pup guaranteed to mature at "four pounds tops." If portability is a priority, say so at your vet check (which you must get). And be sure to check for genetic defects. The smaller we are, the more problems we're likely to have.

Mixed Breeds That bad villain Hitler called America a "nation of mongrels." Mom says he didn't mean it as a compliment, but maybe we should have taken it that way. Mixed breed dogs sometimes get the best of all the breeds that went into them, and don't suffer from typical genetic defects of the breeds they came from. (It's called hybrid vigor.) Of course, some get the worst genetics of both parents. As Vegas dogs say, it's a crap shoot. *Mutts* by Michael Capuzzo and Brian Kilcommons will tell you more.

Finding your mutt is easy. Just go to *www.petfinder.com* and see what fabulous dogs are waiting in the shelters near you. Another cool thing to do is to volunteer at your local shelter. Not only will you help the "inmates," you'll also have first pick when that perfect dog comes along. Shelters also need foster parents for dogs with special needs. They couldn't function without their wonderful volunteers.

My editor (the infamous Gator) found his mixed breed dog Nux at a shelter. (Gator gave him a Latin name—how that man assumes airs.) Nux was a "third chance" dog, meaning that two different Humans had adopted him, then *un*adopted him. Gator is sure that the problem had to be with the Humans, not Nux. (Isn't that usually the way?) The Gator doesn't have a clue as to what breeds went into Nux, and doesn't care. He claims his dog is "perfect" (an adjective *I* had always thought was reserved for Maltese).

Vet Checks Few breeds trot through life problem free. Small dogs like me and Jiggy often have luxating patellas (translation: bad knees). Large breeds may have bad knees, too, and also hip dysplasia. Deep-chested large dogs are prone to bloating (GVD). Glaucoma and cataracts strike some breeds and not others. The same goes for all sorts of other ailments including deafness, shoulder dislocation, misaligned teeth, and gum disease. Be an educated parent. Research your breed in bookstores or on-line.

Consider joining a breed group or two at *www.groups.yahoo.com* and pick members' minds about breed problems, good books and helpful websites. Then, before your new furry friend comes to live with you, have a vet alert you to what problems she might have, and how expensive and time-consuming those problems might be.

My vet check revealed that my knees would probably require surgery someday. The vet *failed* to mention how expensive the surgeries would be, or how long it would take to recuperate, or how painful it would be. At the time Mom was already in love with me (luckily), so she shrugged off the warning. Years later, Mom's memory of the warning prompted her take action when she saw me skipping instead of running. Thankfully, I didn't have to grow old in pain, with knees too far gone to repair.

Be forewarned, however, that some ailments can't be fixed by any amount of love or money. I've heard enough horror stories about inbred dogs, troubled offspring of puppy mills, and misbegotten puppies sold by inexperienced breeders, that I feel compelled to play town crier wherever I can to expose those travesties. (Read the Horror Stories at *www.stoppuppymills.org*.)

If major potential health problems are found during a pre-adoption check, don't feel guilty about returning the dog. I know that this sounds heartless, and it's probably not the kind of advice you'd expect from a dog, but look at it this way: every year three to four million dogs and cats will die for lack of a loving home. (I wonder, if that many homeless Humans died every year, do you think things might change?) Why not find a dog who has a chance for a good, long life rather than give your heart to a dog with no chance?

Of course, the last thing I want to do is scare you from getting a dog. I love dogs. They're fabulous! My boyfriend Jiggy is a dog. But you owe it to yourself and your potential dog-mate to make a union with a good chance of success. Jigs and I were lucky. We found a match made in heaven. Mom even calls us, "her little angels."

Chiclet's Trivia Treat: *The new trend in dog breeding is "designer" mixed breeds. It apparently started when Aussies bred a Labrador retriever to a Standard Poodle resulting in smart, good-tempered, non-shedding dog that made an excellent service dog. Humans, loving profits, quickly started selling poodles bred with Maltese (Maltipoos), with Pekinese (Pekepoos), with Schnauzers (Schnoodles), and with Yorkies (Yorkipoos). There are also mixes with Shih Tzus, Bichon Frises, Golden Retrievers…if they will buy it, they will build it.*

SCARED POOPLESS

So, is this a good thing? The "pro" is that when two unrelated breeds mate, their pups may benefit from "hybrid vigor." And some of these dogs are really cute (even compared to me).

The "con" is that amateurs and puppy mills are getting into the act. We've seen websites with a dozen different hybrids lined up like flavors of ice cream. These dogs are getting very expensive, approaching and even surpassing prices for purebreds. I beg you to be careful where, and with whom, you find love.

The Big Sleep:
Yours and Ours

We've all heard one version or another of the story of the wise old woman who dies and leaves every cent of her vast wealth to her poodle. I consider this a happy ending; it's when the entire fortune goes to cats that I get seriously depressed. What depresses me even more is that everyone knows these "happy ending" stories, but hardly anyone knows that more than 500,000 dogs and cats are euthanized every year because their Humans died, or became incapacitated, without making any plans for their welfare.

Nonprofit groups like 2nd Chance 4 Pets (*www.2ndchance4pets. org*) are trying to whittle down the zeros in that terrible statistic. Can you imagine suddenly going from a comfortable, loving home to a noisy, loveless prison where your chance of "parole" stinks? Young and healthy orphan dogs have a chance at a happy life, but older and infirmed dogs all too often end up having to be "put down"—and I don't mean *criticized*. I know this isn't what you'd want for your dog, but have you done anything to prevent it?

Selecting a Caregiver Do you know who's going to take care of your dog(s) when you're not around? Do you think Mary Puppy Poppins will suddenly materialize when you need her? Don't count on it.

Ideally, you want someone who loves your dog, and is well-suited to take care of her, keeping in mind that no one on earth is as wonderful as you. Do you have someone in mind? Good. Now think of a second person, and a third. Check with each of them to see if they'll act as guardians.

Don't sugarcoat the job. Explain exactly what it entails (fresh steamed green bean treats, organic meals, non-stop playtime). If your prospective caregivers don't know your dog, please introduce them and make sure they "click." If something terrible happens and you disappear, you don't want your Bruno to be traumatized by a stranger entering his home and whisking him away. This is especially important if Bruno is big and scary and might give your caregiver reason to reconsider the commitment.

Money, money, money

If your potential alter egos can't afford to support your dog in the manner to which he is accustomed, or aren't prepared for the increased costs an aging dog may bring, they'll need help from you. You can leave money directly to the caregiver (risking financing their next trip to Acapulco) or you can leave funds safely in trust. The law won't let you leave anything directly to your dog (all those wealthy widow stories notwithstanding). I can't imagine why. Do the courts think dogs will blow their inheritance on toys and cute outfits? And two-leggers won't?

Although laws are starting to change, your state probably considers your dog property. That's so dumb. Even cats aren't property. Even gerbils aren't property. We're all beings just like you, only some of us are furrier. Maybe dogs shouldn't be surprised given some of the crazy laws on the books. In Alabama it's against state law to wear a fake mustache that causes laughter in church. In New Mexico, "idiots" may not vote (although nothing says they can't run for office). The four-legged shouldn't completely despair, however. Oklahoma has a state law stating that Humans who make "ugly faces" at dogs may be fined and/or jailed. There *is* hope.

You can provide funds for your dog through your estate or from life insurance proceeds, or arrange to have them come from a bank account or savings if you become incapacitated. Unfortunately, your wishes must be in writing. No one will take your dog's word for it.

Legalities count

Money left *in trust* for your dog is available immediately if you're disabled or dead. Money left *in your will* can be stuck in probate while your dog sells old bones on the street to raise money for bargain kibble. That's something to think about.

There's a wonderful nonprofit website (*www.estateplanningforpets. org*) offering sample documents and information on various kinds of trusts (which differ from state to state). They even help you calculate how much money your dog will need over her lifetime. (Find other useful sites at *dogs4dogs*.)

If you have a large estate and want to leave a lot of it for your dog's care, you may need a brilliant estate attorney to set up a trust. Diverting inheritances to a dog can bring out the worst in your heirs. Make sure you don't overfund the trust or it may be invalidated. (Ask you lawyer about adding an *in terrorem* clause which says that if heirs contest the will, they'll lose their entire inheritance. This is especially important if you want to leave a large sum to a four-legger. Dog-hating judges or heirs may question your sanity. Well, we question *their* sanity right back!)

One new trend we love is leaving your house in trust to your caregiver for the life of your dog. Talk about enlightened thinking! The trauma of losing a Mom or Dad is bad enough without having to lose our home and TIVO, too. Consult your attorney if this option appeals to you. One caveat: to keep the gravy train coming, Humans have been known to "milk" funds left for animals, even substituting a look-alike long after the designated doggy "heir" has died. Circumvent potential shenanigans by having your dog's DNA tested. Also inform your trustor that ten-year-old dogs won't generally live another 35 years.

If your good intentions are bigger than your fund for legal expenses, you might contact PetGuardian (*www.petguardian.com* or

888-843-4040). For a fee much smaller than most estate attorneys charge, they'll provide a comprehensive Pet Trust Program. They'll allow you to go on-line and make as many changes as you like at no additional cost, will do a cost analysis to help you to understand how much to leave, and will document care instructions for your potential caregivers. They even offer a Backup Caregiver Program provided by Best Friends Animal Society (*www.bestfriends.org*) in case your designated caregivers back out or die before your dog does.

Want to read more? Check out attorney Peggy Hoyt's *All My Children Wear Fur Coats: How to Leave a Legacy for Your Pet*; or try *When Your Pet Outlives You,* by David Congalton and Charlotte Alexander; or Lisa Rogak's *PerPETual Care: Who Will Look After Your Pets If You're Not Around?*

Wait! I have more ideas. If you have a close relationship with your vet, he or she may be willing to help find your baby a new home should something happen to you. Or you might leave money to your local shelter with the *written* promise that they'll put your dog in foster care until they find her an appropriate home. Contact the head of the nicest shelter in your area and see if they'll accommodate your wishes. And don't forget sources closer to home like pet sitters, groomers, and friends active in animal rescue organizations. Chances are they'll not only *be able* to help, but will also actually *want* to help. Finally, check out Alternatives to Pet Trusts at *PetGuardian* to locate a facility in your area offering lifetime care. Just make sure the facility can offer the same kind of care your pets are accustomed to. Housedogs like Jiggy and me wouldn't adapt well to an outdoor sanctuary, but bigger, tougher dogs probably would.

Your Dog's Biography Chances are you don't fit in a cookie-cutter mold, and your dog doesn't either. We all have quirks and weird habits. Even if you have someone who loves your dog and wants to care for her, if she doesn't know all about your dog your baby will suffer.

If you write a short biography of your friend now, it could be helpful not only to the ultimate caregiver, but also to dogsitters and other temporary caregivers. Most of us have a particular comfort food we can't live without (like broccoli) or a favorite toy (don't you dare throw away my purple, squeaky frog even if you think it looks like a purple slug). Maybe we're not good around tots (I'm too small) or other dogs (Jiggy's too macho). You also need to spell out your philosophies about food and vaccinations and such so no one pollutes us with chemicals. Pretend you're Kitty Kelley, telling all. (Have you ever wondered why there are so many women named Kitty and so few named Puppy? What's up with that?) Mom's "short biography" of us now runs seven pages long, and she revises her *magnum opus* as needed.

If you have two or more dogs who love each other, make sure you tell everyone that they absolutely positively have to stay together no matter what! Jigs and I have never been apart for more

than a few hours. Losing Mom and Dad would be tragic; losing each other would be fatal.

Making a bio of your dog is easy. Just fill out the MY DOG'S LIFE form at *dogs4dogs*. Of course, what's a filled out form if it doesn't get into the right hands? Leave a copy near where you keep your leashes and your doggy emergency kit. And make sure your good intentions are circulated to anyone that might be called upon to care for your dog in your absence (like neighbors, vets, dogsitters, butchers, bakers, and candlestick makers).

What You Can Do Now I know it's a lot more fun to play with your dog in the here and now than to plan for the future with you gone, but please don't procrastinate. Poop happens when you least expect it. Do the following right now. I'm not busy. I'll wait.

- Fill out the MY DOG's LIFE form at *dogs4dogs*.
- Go to *www.2ndchance4pets.org,* click on Emergency ID Cards, fill them out; put a card in every family member's wallet and glove box and post one or more at your home.

- Call those people who say they'd love to have your dog and see if they'd *really* love to have your dog.
- Print and fill out the simple document from the Humane Society (*www.hsus.org*: Planning for Your Pet's Future Without You) or make a handwritten and signed codicil to your will.
- Write something referring friends or heirs to this book to help them care for your dog or to "re-home" her if that becomes necessary.
- Write a check to your designated caregiver if you have one.
- Put all the above in an easy to find place in an envelope marked: TO BE OPENED UPON MY DEATH OR DISABLEMENT. Give it to your kennel or dogsitter if you go out of town without us.
- Tell everyone concerned where your dog likes to hide when she's scared.

Other Things To Consider If you followed our suggestions above, you've made a good start. You still need to formalize arrangements. (Mom says laws make even the most logical things illegal, especially things like codicils to wills.) Remember, friends and relatives (who otherwise appear sane) may not share your love for your dog or even for animals in general. If you don't want us dumped in a shelter, exiled to a garage, or shuffled off to some evil stranger, then make arrangements now to keep that from happening. Update arrangements every six months or whenever circumstances change. You don't want to leave this world with a guilty conscience? That's bad karma (and you don't want your karma to run over your dogma).

Mom has this saying that I borrowed to use on Jiggy when he's being obnoxious. You can use it on yourself: LOVE IS A VERB. It's not enough to *feel* love; you have to actually *show* love. And nothing shows love more than providing for our welfare in the absence of you.

SCARED POOPLESS

The Big Sleep: Ours Matchless, the beautiful dog to the right, has gone off to the Big Dog Park in the sky. She was loved. She is missed. Don't you just hate stories that begin with sad endings?

This is probably a section you'd rather skip, because this is a subject no one likes to think about. Maybe it's a beautiful day outside and your four-legged companion is resting comfortably at your feet (warming them, no doubt). Put off reading it if you must (but don't miss my "Tale" at the end). But if your dog, or any dog you know, is nearing the valley of the shadow of death, come with me now. I'm a little scared and would love your company.

Planning a peaceful exit

Most Humans and dogs hope to die in their sleep at home in their own beds. Lots of us aren't so lucky, but we *are* lucky enough to have our Moms and Dads plan a painless exit for when we have no quality of life . . . or our suffering is endless and unfixable . . . or our mind goes . . . or we become a danger to ourselves and others.

There are bad reasons for euthanasia, too. Millions of my fellow dogs are euthanized after being deemed "unadoptable" at a shelter. Do you hear my howls, Humans? Maybe sadder still is when a person finds an older dog inconvenient, or thinks her dog can't live without her when she goes. Mom says there was a time not so long ago when Human widows used to throw themselves (or be thrown) on their husband's funeral pyre, because their lives were theoretically over. Called *suttee*, it was practiced by Germans, Slavs, Greeks, Egyptians, Chinese, and Vikings (whatever they are) and wasn't outlawed in India until 1829. Humans realized this kind of sacrifice (or murder) was just plain wrong. Don't you think it's time to eliminate this canine form of suttee?

Most veterinarians refuse requests to euthanize a healthy animal, preferring to give the dog to a rescue organization, but some have been known to acquiesce lest the Human do something brutal. Believe me, this would not be our choice. We're co-dependent, not suicidal. If you ever hear a friend contemplating euthanasia of a dog, determine if this is really a mercy killing or just convenience in disguise. If it's just convenience, HELP!

When is it time?

Jiggy and I know you wouldn't be reading this unless euthanasia would be a kindness for your dog. In fact, you're doing everything you can think of to avoid it, right?

We asked our friend, Michael Paul, veterinarian and past president of the American Animal Hospital Association, how to know when a dog's time has come. He said, ". . . there comes a point when the bad days or hours or moments far outnumber the better ones, and when you will know in your heart that you are no longer extending your pet's life but rather prolonging its death. At that point, you are not doing your pet any kindness by allowing further suffering. At that point, it is time."

Special Needs Pets (*www.specialneedspets.org/euthanasia.htm*) has a wealth of information on this sad subject. Also search the index for Pet Loss at The American Veterinary Medical Association site (*www.AVMA.org*). If you have children, check out their *Animated Journeys*. It might make the loss of a four-legged playmate a little easier.

SCARED POOPLESS

The sleep

Euthanasia comes from a Greek word meaning "good death," which is what we want. The Humane Society of the United States, the American Humane Society, People for the Ethical Treatment of Animals and the American Veterinary Medical Association all recommend a shot of sodium pentobarbital for a quick, humane end. Your dog will fall to sleep immediately and painlessly. Other drugs and methods may cause pain or fear, and a slow death, so we don't like them.

Don't presume your vet uses sodium pentobarbital. Ask. A vet in Utah not long ago reportedly killed a dog with truck exhaust. Others have employed violence. Though only a tiny number of veterinarians would consider doing such things, do us this last favor and make sure.

When the sad time comes, if your dog is the nervous type (or your hysteria has made him nuts), ask your vet for a tranquilizer (for your dog, not you). Unless you're a really good actor, we're going to know something bad is happening. We'll be especially traumatized if you just drop us off at the vet's. If you can bear it, stay with your buddy throughout the process, holding him and loving him to the end, as he would do for you.

To make death as stress-free as possible for you and your dog, some vets will even come to your home. Our vet provides a "peaceful transition" for her clients, a ceremony followed by a gentle exit. Jiggy and I have decided that's what we want. If your vet doesn't offer this service, she may know someone who does. Or ask owners of pet cemeteries for a recommendation.

The whole family, including children, may want to be present to say good-bye. This will be kinder and less stressful for your dog, will serve as closure for the family, and will end your dog's suffering in the kindest possible way. I know it will be painful, but you've watched your dog fall off to sleep countless times before. Help him do it this one last time—if you can. If you can't, well, don't worry. We've always forgiven you everything.

By the way, when I say "the whole family," I mean just that. If your dog has canine companions, they need closure, too. We understand death. What we don't understand are mysterious disappearances. Most of us want, and need, that last sniff. I've heard stories of dogs who didn't have this closure and waited by doors and stared out windows hoping for the return of their friend. Remember, this is someone they've lived with 24 hours a day, maybe for years. Surviving dogs have been known to forego food and drink, lose interest in their favorite activities, and become too tired to enjoy almost everything.

It won't help your survivor if you mope around the house and won't cuddle or play or anything. Misery really does love company. By helping your dog adjust to the loss, you can help yourself. Remember, this is a big change in your dog's life. Perhaps he was the "follower" dog and now needs a new leader. (Hint: that means you.) A little Rescue Remedy in our water every day for a while might help, but never forget: the best drug for us is you.

After sleep

Once your dog has passed on, your vet can help you deal with your dog's, uh, remains. Jigs and I both want a private cremation with the ashes returned to Mom in a simple container; more economical group cremations are fine, too. We'll be dead and won't know. If you'd rather, there's the option of burial in a pet cemetery or, in some locales, even in your own backyard. Your vet will know what's legal in your area. ("PetGuardian Community" at *www.petguardian.com* shows the approximate costs of various options.)

If you leave your dog at your vet's to be carried away, ask if he or she knows for certain where the remains go. I wish I didn't have to mention this, but remains sometimes go to meat rendering plants. Asking is the only way to know this won't happen. Recently, a Georgia crematory operator (for Human remains) gave clients cement dust in place of their beloved's ashes. It's shocking what some two-leggers will do for money.

Mourning and Remembering

Our trainer friend, Maureen Hall, once wrote about the passing of one her beloved dogs: "I know that I don't own any of my animals. They are only on loan to me and there always comes a painful time when I must give them back."

When that painful time comes, find resources at the Association for Pet Loss and Bereavement (*www.APLB.org*) or The Delta Society (*www.DeltaSociety.org*). The National Pet Loss Hotline also offers free nationwide consultation to bereaved owners on a 24-hour basis. Call 1-800-946-4646, and punch in 140-7211, then your own phone number. Also, search Grief Counseling at The American Veterinary Medical Association (*www.AVMA.org*) for loads of information. Their link to *Helpful Books* lists books for adults and children. Incidentally, our Dr. Hebbler particularly recommends Rita Reynolds' *Blessing the Bridge: What Animals Teach Us About Dying and Beyond.*

You can spend a lot of money on a fancy funeral for your dog, but Jigs and I really like the idea of having our bodies disposed of humbly and humanely, then having Mom and Dad give a donation to a shelter or pet rescue group in our names. We'd love to know that our deaths helped make some other dogs' lives easier.

In addition to wonderful local groups in many cities, there are groups that help dogs throughout the country. You might also give a donation for research into the disease that took your dog. For links to many wonderful groups, go to *dogs4dogs.* Think how proud your dog would be.

It didn't seem right to have a treat for this chapter, but I do have a terrific story to tell you.

Chiclet's Bittersweet Tale: *Most dogs I know think Mike Arms is a saint. Mike, who's President of Helen Woodward Animal Center in Rancho Santa Fe, California, is believed to be responsible for finding more homes for dogs and cats than anyone else in the world. I'm proud to say he was inspired in his life's work by the kindness of one dying puppy.*

Mike met this puppy after he had already tendered his resignation from his job at a Humane Society in New York; he was worn down by being unable to find homes for all the dogs and cats he so wanted to help. Mike was about to leave work on one of his last days when a call came in about a puppy that had been struck by a car. Since everyone else at the Humane Society had gone home for the day, Mike put on a technician's coat and drove a van to the Bronx in the hopes of rescuing the injured puppy.

He found the poor puppy lying in a gutter; its back was broken. As Mike bent down to pick him up, three men intervened. They demanded he leave the dog, saying they had a bet on how long it was going to take for the puppy to die. Mike responded, "You guys are really sick," and bent over to pick up the puppy. Without warning, the men attacked him from behind, stabbing and beating him and leaving him to die with the puppy.

Bleeding out in the street, Mike went into shock. As he started to lose consciousness, Mike felt a gentle licking on his face. The puppy, whose injuries should have prevented him from being able to move, had somehow dragged his broken body over to Mike. There in the gutter, Mike promised God that if he lived he would devote his life to helping orphaned animals find homes.

More than 30 years later Mike still credits that brave puppy for his rededicating his life to saving animals. I'm sorry to tell you that the puppy didn't survive his injuries, but because he helped save Mike Arm's life,

SCARED POOPLESS

hundreds of thousands of other animals in shelters all over the country have found homes. Like Mike, that puppy is our hero.

I hope that puppy shows you the way as well. Licks to all.

A LAST WAG
OF THE TAIL

Dogs like to greet with a wag of the tail, and we like to bid our farewells the same way. Mom says it's sort of like the way Hawaiians say *aloha*, and Italians say *ciao*, greetings that are used to say both hello and good-bye.

Speaking of Italians, I have one last story to tell you. When Mount Vesuvius erupted in AD 79, raining its ash and debris down on the city of Pompeii, it wasn't just people who perished. Then, as now, dogs were sharing space with our beloved Humans.

Since excavations began in 1748, archeologists have uncovered artwork and murals featuring dogs, showing that the people of that city loved their four-legged friends. (If that's not an indicator of an advanced civilization, I don't know what is.)

More than 2,000 victims of the eruption have been discovered, their skeletons unearthed from hardened ash, mud, and debris. One canine victim was found chained; evidence shows he was biting at the chain in a futile attempt to save his life. The remains of another dog were discovered stretched out over the body of a young boy. Most believe the dog was trying to protect him.

We dogs would give our all for you, and know you'd do the same for us. I hope you've found my advice helpful in your quest to make your dog healthy and safe, and that you've forgiven me my occasional bluntness. It wasn't easy for me to break the dog's code of silence, but some things just had to be said.

I don't want to say good-bye, so I'm just going to wag my tail. Anyway, isn't that the best way to say *The End?*

Index

About the Authors

Jan Rasmusen is a former computer industry executive and a life-long dog lover and equestrian. She has written four books, two of which are hidden in her closet.

Chiclet (right) is a Maltese. Her hobbies are watching TV commercials and barking at bunnies. This is her first book.

Jiggy's illness inspired the research that led to *Scared Poopless*. Pictured left and on the cover, he is well now. His hobby is stalking Jan.

cover photo by Scott Miner